THE BRITISH POLITICAL TRADITION

EDITED BY ALAN BULLOCK AND F. W. DEAKIN

BOOK SIX

THE CONCEPT OF EMPIRE
BURKE TO ATTLEE
1774-1947

THE CONCEPT OF EMPIRE

BURKE TO ATTLEE

1774-1947

EDITED BY

GEORGE BENNETT

SENIOR LECTURER IN COMMONWEALTH HISTORY, OXFORD

SECOND EDITION

ADAM & CHARLES BLACK
LONDON

FIRST PUBLISHED 1953
SECOND EDITION 1962
REPRINTED 1967

© 1962 A. AND C. BLACK LIMITED
4, 5 AND 6 SOHO SQUARE LONDON W.1

PRINTED IN GREAT BRITAIN
BY JOHN DICKENS & CO LTD
NORTHAMPTON

GENERAL PREFACE

ONE of the unique contributions the English people have made to civilisation has been the discussion of political issues which has been going on in Britain continuously since the sixteenth century. It is a discussion which has ranged over the whole field of political thought and experience. It began with the relation of the State to the individual in religious matters; for the last half century it has been increasingly preoccupied with the relation of the State to the individual in economic matters. The strength of tradition, the right of rebellion; the demand for equality, the rights of property; the place of justice and morality in foreign policy, the relations between Britain and her overseas territories; the claims of minorities, the value of civil and religious freedom; the rule of law, the Rule of the Saints; the rights of the individual, the claims of the State—all these have been the subject of passionate and incessant argument among Englishmen since the time of the Reformation.

This debate has never been of an academic character. There are, it is true, masterpieces of political philosophy in the English language: Hobbes' *Leviathan* is an obvious example. But the true character of this debate has been empirical: the discussion of particular and practical issues, in the course of which a clash of principle and attitude is brought out, but in which the element of abstract thought is always kept in relation to an immediate and actual situation. The riches of British

political thought are to be found less in the philosophers'
discussions of terms like " The State ", " freedom " and
"obligation"—important though these are—than in the
writings and speeches on contemporary political issues
of men like Lilburne, Locke, Bolingbroke, Burke, Tom
Paine, Fox, the Mills, Cobden, Disraeli, Gladstone, and
the Fabians. No other literature in the world is so rich
in political pamphlets as English, and the pages of
Hansard are a mine not only for the historian of
political events but also for the historian of political
ideas. It is in the discussions provoked by the major
crises in British history—the Civil War, the Revolt of
the American Colonies, the Reform Bills of the nineteenth century—that our political ideas have been
hammered out.

One unfortunate result of this is that much of the
material which anyone interested in English political
ideas needs to read is inaccessible. Pamphlets and
speeches are often only to be found in contemporary
publications hidden away on the more obscure shelves
of the big libraries. Even when the reader has secured
a volume of seventeenth-century pamphlets or of
Gladstone's speeches, he may well be deterred by the
large amount of now irrelevant detail or polemic
through which he has to make his way before striking
the characteristic ideas and assumptions of the writer
or speaker. It is to meet the need of the reader who is
interested in English political ideas but has neither the
time, the patience, nor perhaps the opportunity, to read
through a library of books to find the material he is
looking for that this present series of books is designed.
Its aim is to present from sources of the most varied
kind, books, pamphlets, speeches, letters, newspapers, a
selection of original material illustrating the different

facets of Englishmen's discussion of politics. Each
volume will include an introductory essay by the editor
together with sufficient explanation of the circumstances to make each extract intelligible. In some cases
it has seemed best to make a particular crisis the focus
of the discussion: this has been done with Professor
Beloff's volume, *The Debate on the American Revolution,*
and with Professor Cobban's *The Debate on the French
Revolution.* In other cases the development of a
particular view has been traced over a long period of
years: this is the case, for instance, with the volumes on
the Conservative, the Liberal, and the Radical Traditions. In a third case, that of the volume on " Britain
and Europe", our idea has been to single out a recurrent
problem in English politics and trace its discussion from
Pitt's day to our own.

To begin with, we have concentrated our attention
on the period between the Revolt of the American
Colonies and the Great War of 1914. When that has
been covered we hope to treat the earlier period in the
same way, notably the political discussions of the
seventeenth century.

We do not believe that any one of these facets can
be singled out and labelled as in some particular way
more characteristic than others of the British Political
Tradition: the rebels have as great a part in our political
tradition as those who have argued the case for the
claims of prescription and established authority. The
wealth of that tradition is that it includes Lilburne,
Tom Paine, Richard Cobden and the Early English
Socialists as well as Locke, Burke and Disraeli.

We have tried to hold the balance even. In no sense
do we wish to act as propagandists or advocates. While
each editor has been given complete freedom to present

his material as he wishes, we have been concerned as general editors to see that equal representation is given to different views in the series as a whole. Only in this way, we believe, is it possible to display the British Political Tradition in its unequalled richness, as built up out of a variety of political opinions and out of the clash between them, as the great and continuous debate of the nation to which, in its very nature, there can be no end.

ALAN BULLOCK
F. W. DEAKIN

Oxford

TABLE OF CONTENTS

THE CONCEPT OF EMPIRE

TABLE OF CONTENTS

TABLE OF CONTENTS

XV

TABLE OF CONTENTS

ACKNOWLEDGEMENTS

I would acknowledge my grateful obligation to the following authors and owners of copyright material for their kind permission to use extracts from these works:

H.M.S.O., The Publishers of *Hansard* (speeches by Wilberforce, Macaulay, Buller, Lord John Russell, Sir Robert Peel, Lord Brougham, Viscount Melbourne, Roebuck, Sir William Molesworth, Gladstone, Lord Derby, Lowe, Lord Carnarvon, Lord Granville, Lord Salisbury, Morley, Mr. Attlee, Mr. Churchill and Mr. Creech Jones).

The Publishers of *The Times* (speeches by W. E. Forster, Lord Rosebery, Joseph Chamberlain, Lord Salisbury, and Lord Curzon).

The Publishers of the *Twentieth Century* (articles by Gladstone, W. E. Forster and Lord Curzon).

The Trades Union Congress (speeches by the Earl of Rosebery and W. B. Hornidge).

Parker and Son, Ltd., Oxford (*The Empire* by Goldwin Smith).

J. F. Wentworth Dilke, Esq. (*Greater Britain* by Sir C. W. Dilke).

The Earl of Rosebery (speeches by the 5th Earl of Rosebery).

The Trustees of Joseph Chamberlain's works (speeches by Joseph Chamberlain).

The Earl St. Aldwyn and Lady Victoria Hicks-Beach (speech by Sir Michael Hicks-Beach).

The Viscountess Milner, Constable and Co., and Cassell and Co. (Lord Milner's speeches and *The Milner Papers*).

Allen and Unwin Ltd. (*Labour and the Empire* by Ramsay MacDonald; *Imperialism* by J. A. Hobson).

J. Keir Hardie Memorial Committee (*India* by Keir Hardie).

ACKNOWLEDGEMENTS

The Earl of Cromer (*Modern Egypt* and *Abbas II* by the 1st Earl of Cromer).

The Public Trustee (*The Man of Destiny* by George Bernard Shaw).

The Union of Democratic Control (*Africa and the Peace of Europe* by E. D. Morel).

L. S. Woolf, Esq. (*Empire and Commerce in Africa*).

J. C. Smuts, Esq., and Hodder and Stoughton Ltd. (speech by Field Marshal Smuts).

Wm. Blackwood and Sons (*The Dual Mandate* by Lord Lugard).

The Lord Balfour and Hodder and Stoughton Ltd. (*Opinions and Arguments* by the 1st Earl of Balfour).

The Rt. Hon. L. S. Amery and The Royal Institute of International Affairs (speech by Mr. L. S. Amery).

The Rt. Hon. Winston Churchill and Cassell and Company (speeches by Mr. Winston Churchill).

The Rt. Hon. C. R. Attlee (*The Labour Party in Perspective*).

The Lord Hailey and The Clarendon Press (Romanes Lecture, 1941).

Brittain Publishing Group (speech by Colonel Oliver Stanley).

Dr. Rita Hinden (*Fabian Colonial Essays*).

In conclusion I would desire to acknowledge my thanks to the University of Toronto where I was a lecturer when I started to prepare this volume. I was there aided by a grant for travel necessitated by this project; while the friendly and stimulating interest of my colleagues in the Department of History will always be recalled with pleasure.

I would also record my thanks for the helpful suggestions of the editors of this series.

Of the libraries I have used I wish to acknowledge in particular the services of the staff of that of the Royal Empire Society.

INSTITUTE OF COLONIAL STUDIES, OXFORD.   G.B.

January, 1953.

INTRODUCTION

I

THE last 450 years have seen the expansion of Europe; a process now almost complete—the ultimate frontiers are being reached in the Canadian north west and in Antarctica. We may look back on a phase of history in which this country has played a leading role such that English has become the most widely-spoken language of the modern world and British political institutions have been taken as a model somewhere in each of the continents. In this period the descendants of the people of these islands have multiplied some twenty times, occupied the majority of those portions of the temperate zone that were formerly slightly inhabited and played a greater part than any other nation in the opening up of the Tropics. In regarding the areas influenced by this development, whether now outside the Commonwealth like the United States, or inside like India and Pakistan, we are clearly facing a process that is of prime importance in the formation of the modern world. Yet when we turn back to the mother country, when we enquire how the political leaders have spoken who have had to deal with this expansion we find often feelings of embarrassment or indifference—only at short periods have politicians been prepared to enthuse over the Empire. It was acquired, said Seeley, " in a fit of absence of mind." Certainly it has sometimes been so governed by Parliament—even if not, as the accusers said, by the Colonial Office. Those few who were interested have found it consistently necessary to form pressure groups and societies to call the British public's attention to the problems of Empire. The word "colonial" became a term of opprobrium worse than that of "country cousin"—he was further removed from the centre of life and had probably gone forth as a convict, a social misfit or a remittance man. The colonies were the haunts of ne'er-do-wells. Hence, in part, visitors from the Empire repeatedly found indifference in Britain to themselves and Imperial affairs.

Yet how could it be otherwise? People will only be interested in their own concerns, will only fight for Empire in relation to a European quarrel. To this rule the Boer War is the one exception, occurring in the one period of great interest in the Empire. Even in this time of the "Scramble for Africa", Imperialism to be tolerated at home—and this was true of the continental European countries as well as of Britain—had to go on furtively, with the promise of easy triumphs, without demanding men or money from the mother country.[1] The expansion of the frontiers was the business of the trader and the missionary, of the pioneer and the prospector. Government only intervened when it had to; hence the weakest governments annexed most—those who could not control the man on the spot.

The attitude in London, whether proclaimed in Pitt's India Act of 1784 or in the report of a Select Committee of the House of Commons in 1865 on West Africa, has generally been against advance and for withdrawal. Advance has come more through quasi-government agencies, the Chartered Companies. The function of government is to govern: Westminster has been more

[1] M. Baumont, *L'Essor Industriel et l'Impérialisme Colonial* (1878–1904), p. 61.

concerned with organisation and management than with acquisition, seeking always to avoid the embarrassments of that first stage. " Africa," Salisbury commented, " is a continent created to be the sore of the Foreign Office."

II

The greatest creation of the expansion of Europe overseas is the United States but it remains, in Goldwin Smith's sense a " colony " of England, in the derivation at least of its language and law. It was the common law "rights of Englishmen " that the emigrants took with them—from the days of the Virginia settlements—that formed the basis of the *Declaration of Independence*, whatever this may have owed to eighteenth century ideas. The same basis remained for the United Empire Loyalists who, while they wished to stay in allegiance to the Crown, were not prepared to come under any " despotic rule " devised for people of another tradition in Quebec. The Canada Act of 1791 separated Upper Canada and gave representative government; Simcoe went out as Lieutenant-Governor to apply the principles of " assimilation " to the Westminster pattern. Already during the war of American Independence the debates in England pointed to the dilemma: somewhere there must be an ultimate authority, "assimilation " would lead to independence.

Burke looked below this recurring constitutional diffi-culty; he saw that the growing estrangement came from the growth of new communities, of societies drawing apart. If the frontiersman thought differently from the polished society of Philadelphia or of the plantations of the South, yet all were out of touch with the ideas of Parliamentary sovereignty evolving in London and made plain in Blackstone. The growing apart was

3

greatest on the frontier. Was it ever to be possible to reconcile its ways of thought with the centre?

Gibbon Wakefield and the Colonial Reformers attempted a solution : the departure of community-units together. They wished to create new Englands overseas, to avoid the dangers of new societies by the transference of portions of the old, retaining their old ties. New Zealand, the country of their greatest success, remains the " most British " and most loyal of the Dominions.

For the most part emigration has been unorganised, a mixed combination of the pushes and pulls of sentiment and economic interests in both the mother country and the new lands. Eighteenth century opinion feared that Britain's population was declining and, following the mercantilists, believed that population was wealth. Only with the counter-revelations of the decennial censuses from 1801 and with the rapid growth of Malthusian fears did the attitude to emigration change. The new outlook dominated the Emigration Committees of 1826 and 1827 over which Wilmot Horton presided, but these led only to the policy that Charles Buller contemptuously dubbed " the shovelling out of paupers." The hard times, first the post-war depression, then the revolt of the new proletariat against conditions in the new towns, then famine—particularly that in Ireland after 1845—drove the workers forth to people the new lands. After 1848 Australia became a haven for Chartists. The new Empire of settlement was the creation of the working classes. Dickens portrayed their hopeful view of new opportunities in the eventual destiny of Micawber.

The Colonies, Durham proclaimed, were " the rightful patrimony of the English people, the ample appanage which God and Nature have set aside in the New World for those whose lot has assigned them but insufficient portions in the Old." [1] The Colonial Reformers attempted to organise the bridge of emigration to the new lands.

Froude, who followed Carlyle in denouncing the new towns, urged escape from their ills and was one of the sponsors of the petition to the Queen of 104,000 working men of London in 1870 against the Gladstone government's allegedly anti-Imperial policy.

Politicians were discovering who were their masters after the Reform Act of 1867. The shrewd Disraeli took up the popular feeling on the Empire in his Crystal Palace speech of 1872, linking it for the working class with a programme of social reform.

Only the excesses of Imperialism at the end of the century separated the Labour movement from Empire. Suspicions were aroused in hearing a mining magnate and company promoter, Cecil Rhodes, utter, as he looked at the uplands of Rhodesia, "Homes, more homes, that is what I want." [2] The attack on the exploitation of Africa, powerfully impelled by Hobson in 1902, coloured the attitude of twentieth century Labour. It hid the natural bonds of relationship between men at home and overseas that formed the real links of the Empire on which Molesworth and Gladstone, Forster and Chamberlain had relied in addressing working class audiences.

But emigration was not an easy path for the worker. Cobbett questioned the value of the destination in the Empire in the 1820's and Aneurin Bevan in the 1930's. It was too easy a sloughing-off of the responsibility to the citizen in this country and might even be worse. Karl Marx rightly denounced the expropriation of the

[1] Durham, *Report on the Affairs of British North America*, 1839 (ed. Lucas), Vol. II, p. 13.
[2] Basil Williams, *Cecil Rhodes* (1938 ed.), p. 181.

tenants in the Highlands driven forth by their lairds. The human and forceful pushes to emigration were often no less compelling than the inhuman and unpleasant life of the towns.

The emigrant and colonial had reason not to look back with favour on the governing class of Britain. From his Radical democracy there emerged Labour governments in Australia and New Zealand which formed new ties for the British Labour movement in the Empire. Ernest Bevin could argue to the T.U.C. in 1930 and again in 1947 for the Joseph Chamberlain policy of treating the British Empire as an economic unit, or for the building up of a customs union within it, while Herbert Morrison could say that he wanted " the British Commonwealth to last not just because it is British, but because it is good." [1]

III

"The trend," said Morrison in the same speech, " is always towards freedom." Herein lies the central problem of the white Empire and now, as the dependent territories come to self-governing stature, of the whole: it is the problem in a Commonwealth of Nations of the interplay of freedom and authority. The overlordship of an Imperial Parliament in which the colonists were not represented was rejected in war in the eighteenth century. Solutions that were offered next varied from representation at Westminster[2] to some form of Imperial Federation. The latter raised the same difficulty of the relation between the Imperial and subordinate legislatures, of the division of powers and functions, as the

[1] Speech at Newcastle-on-Tyne, 10 January, 1943.
[2] This was actually moved by Hume as an amendment to the Reform Bill in 1831.

6

approach of the Colonial Reformers and of the Durham
Report. Responsibility grows by what it feeds upon:
the constitutional history of Canada since 1839 may be
regarded as the whittling away of the limitations suggested by Durham. Canada could not be regarded as a
municipality and compared to Liverpool as Wakefield
attempted.

The main lesson of the history of the Empire's
development into the Commonwealth is that organisation cannot be imposed. Froude, Rosebery and Forster
were right in rejecting the literal interpretation of the
motto of the Imperial Federationists, "federation or
disintegration ", just as the twentieth century equally
rightly ignored the constitutional formulations of Lionel
Curtis. The cohesion of the Commonwealth comes from
intangibles. Now that there is not even a common
citizenship and a common allegiance to the Crown it may
well be asked what are the bonds of Empire. Burke saw
in 1775 that " close affection " growing " from common
names, from kindred blood, from similar privileges, and
equal protection " formed ties " light as air " but " strong
as links of iron." [1]

Can the Commonwealth of Nations hold together
where some of these links are missing? The importance
of the constitutional struggles in the history of the
Empire consists in the demonstration of the growth of
national feeling. This central problem was not understood in the eighteenth century: the American colonies
were lost. By 1839, after Canning's and Palmerston's
work in support of national movements, it might have
been thought that the toughness of this spirit would have
been fully recognised. Yet Durham considered that by a
union of the Canadas the French identity could be

[1] 22 March, 1775 (No. 2).

7

destroyed. The greatness of the Durham Report, however, is that he saw that the way of holding Canada was to allow her to develop her identity to the full, for her thus to prove her difference from the United States and to reach the maximum of her development inside the British Empire. This was an experiment in freedom indeed, which challenged the logic of the political theorist who declared two years later: "A self-governing dependency (supposing the dependency not to be virtually independent) is a contradiction in terms." [1] But the British tradition is pragmatic, not logical, as Lord John Russell pointed out in advising Poulett Thomson in Canada in 1839 on the method of dealing with the demands for responsible government: "Every political constitution in which different bodies share the supreme power, is only enabled to exist by the forbearance of those among whom this power is distributed." [2] The difficulty of the advice was that the distribution of power might imperceptibly shift without total self-government ever being formally conceded at any given moment. It is by such changes of convention that the challenge of nationalism has been contained. Convention moulds the British constitution by the withering away of powers from the Sovereign's veto downwards. Hence long before the Imperial Conferences of 1926 and 1930 and the consequent Statute of Westminster the Dominions were in fact self-governing and the Imperial Parliament had no power over them except with their consent. It was only the pressure of those unaware or mistrustful of this power of convention that demanded the statement of the fact in a Statute.

[1] Cornewall Lewis, *An Essay on the Government of Dependencies* (1841), (ed. Lucas, 1891), p. 289.
[2] Printed in Berriedale Keith, *Selected Speeches and Documents on British Colonial Policy,* 1763–1917, I, p. 178.

The preservation of a common foreign policy was long an objective. It disappeared as by successive stages the Dominions, led by Canada, obtained representation in treaty negotiations and diplomatic missions and then asserted their independent international status in separate signatures of the Treaty of Versailles and in separate membership of the League of Nations. Subsequently votes of members of the Commonwealth have cancelled each other out in the League and now in the United Nations. We are left with the hope and not the surety—for Eire set an example of neutrality in the last war before leaving the " club "—that in the ultimate tests of war the Commonwealth will stand or fall together.

Not even in preparation for such tests has organisation been evolved: instead there have often been unseemly wrangles about the proportions each unit was contributing in a haphazard way to Imperial defence. When the Colonies obtained responsible government after 1846 they did not at once assume responsibility for their own defence. These remaining costs convinced home opinion that the Colonies were a useless burden: there were constant Maori wars and there was the indefensible border of Canada, pricked by Fenian raiders and under threats from a United States confident in its "manifest destiny". As part of Cardwell's army reforms the garrisons were withdrawn; Gladstone and Granville called on the " self-reliance of Englishmen " to take up their duty. Despite the gloomy forecasts that this would lead to the break-up of the Empire the policy received its justification in Colonial offers of help, for the Sudan campaign in 1885, and in the Boer war; while the self-governing Dominions entered each of the World Wars on their own decision, in 1939 formally expressed in their Parliaments.

Common interest alone can hold the Commonwealth

together, as the declarations of 1949 showed at India's choosing to remain inside when she became a Republic. That there can be community of interest has frequently been challenged: distance at least would seem to be against it. The interests of the parts may even conflict: this was said in discussing transportation, it has constantly prevented the formation of a customs union, and of an Imperial economic policy. A yet more fertile source of difference between the mother country and settlers has developed repeatedly over the treatment of aboriginal populations, while in the twentieth century the status of Indians in the Dominions has been a disturbing issue. In the end the right of each autonomous unit to determine the composition of its own population has been conceded as a necessary concomitant of self-government. In thus carrying the trend towards freedom to its logical conclusion is not the very expression " Commonwealth " meaningless, unless there are some moral standards that receive general acknowledgment?

IV

Chamberlain's attempt to force a commercial form of organisation upon the Empire had this in its favour: it was part of a strong tradition of Empire. His expression "The Empire is commerce" recalls Burke's definition of the Old Colonial System: "purely commercial." The main reason for the weakness of Imperial feeling in the mid-nineteenth century was that a succession of writers from Adam Smith to Cobden had attacked the bases of the old system. When their arguments appeared to be borne out by the continually increasing trade with the now independent United States, when South America in the 1820's became part of the economic, but not of the political, Empire without any demonstrably harmful effects upon trade the optimism of the economists seemed justified. The increase of trade was often asserted as a reason for the encouragement of emigration: overseas there would be new customers with new purchasing power, as well as new suppliers of raw materials.

It was this last that made for the strength of attachment to tropical Colonies in the old Empire. In 1760 there had been argument: was it preferable to retain in the peace settlement Guadeloupe or Canada? In the revolutionary wars the younger Pitt continued to mop up West Indian islands. This mercantilist view of Empire persisted on both sides in the struggle until 1815.

The triumph of the Manchester School was not complete even though the repeal of the Corn Laws was followed three years later by that of the last provisions of the Navigation Acts. Corn Law repeal led to discontent in a Canada which lost thereby a preferential position in the British market. In 1859 Canada disappointed the facile optimism of Cobdenites and Colonial Reformers alike by imposing a tariff on British goods. They had failed to see that protection is necessary to the building of new industrial countries. By such they were now to be faced in North America and in Europe.

In expanding, these countries sought new mercantilist areas of raw materials and customers in relation to those industries. The victory of free trade was hollow and temporary. This was marked in England by the resurgence of Chartered Companies which the economists had condemned — ironically the first two of the new ones received authorisation from Liberal governments. In them, as in the old East India Company, trade and expansion went together, but more normally did " trade follow the flag ", as had been so frequently asserted and as was the renewed cry from 1869?

The period is full of assertion and counter-assertion, which continue to the present, that it is possession of Empire that has enabled trade to build up a higher standard of life for all in these islands than they would otherwise enjoy. Considerable research is required and even then comparisons with other European countries introduce elements of dubiety. The clearest advantage would appear to lie in the relation of the products of colonial territories to metropolitan markets which form focuses for world prices: the Liverpool cotton exchange or the tea-mart of London.

The desire for raw materials as much as that for trade can carry the frontiers forward. The chaos of the prospectors' frontier in Malaya compelled an unwilling government to step in to provide order—an abrupt change of policy for the Gladstone government in 1873. In this particular case the prospectors for tin were primarily Chinese and protection was given to the Malay Sultans against the disorder of their faction fights. Africa held out prospects of vast mining operations: diamonds at Kimberley in 1869 and a rush for the gold of the Rand in 1886. Beyond were hopes of other riches and the certainty of ancient copper workings in what are now the Rhodesias. In all this, Government would have to adjudicate between the conflicting claims of Bantu, Boer and Briton. It might temporise by using Rhodes's British South Africa Company but that only led to trouble in the explosion of ambition in the Jameson raid of 1895.

V

The frontiers of the Empire have gone forward under varying drives with equally various pressures upon opinion and the home government. We have noted the settler, the trader and the prospector. No less important in the nineteenth century were the missionaries and the philanthropists. The Evangelicals combined interests in the ending of the slave-trade and in the formation of the missionary societies at the end of the eighteenth century. They brought about the settlement of the freed slaves in Sierra Leone and the beginning of a struggle for influence in West African policy with the traders of Liverpool, who changed from slaving after 1807, and with the palm-oil ruffians. The missionary drive was in competition with settlers in South Africa—its influence produced the retrocession of Kaffir territory in 1835, a factor in persuading the Boers to trek from British rule—and in New Zealand in 1837, where, as in the islands of the Pacific, some even thought in terms of the establishment of a theocracy.

Their influence has perhaps been strongest in Africa where the journeys of Livingstone—in particular the story of his end in 1873—were factors in rousing the new Imperial ardour after 1870. Nyasaland is Livingstone's country, while Uganda became a protectorate in 1894 partly under pressure from the Church Missionary Society. Livingstone, following Buxton and Wilberforce, had a solution for the woes of Africa which fitted the prevailing attitude to Empire: " Christianity and Commerce." The Evangelicals would replace by legitimate trade the sole and devastating one in human beings that they saw Africa to possess. Their most signal failure was the Niger expedition of 1841, but on the coasts they were able to hold the navy to first West, then East, Africa, obtaining in this, so powerful was their influence, the constant support of the cynic Palmerston at the Foreign Office.

By their attacks on slavery in the 1820's and by the passage of an Imperial Act to end it in 1833 they raised again the old question of the American war, the respective authority of the central and local Parliaments. Now it was a question not of taxation but of ethics. The Evangelicals provided a standard for the judgment of action in native policy throughout the Empire: under Buxton's chairmanship this was stated by the House of Commons Select Committee on Aborigines in 1837, while Buxton's inspiration lay behind the powerful body established in the same year to maintain that standard: the Aborigines Protection Society.

VI

The Evangelicals made a no less powerful contribution to the discussion of the other main problem of Empire: the rule of dependent peoples. The loss of America left the Empire predominantly one of conquest, no longer of settlement. This coincided with the rise of the eighteenth century Evangelical conscience.

Already in 1774 the problem had been broached in the discussion on the Quebec Act (No. 1). But the French were of the same European Christian tradition; the issue was deeper, the problems graver in ruling India. Hence the importance of Burke's insistence from the beginning that all rule partakes of the nature of a trust. But a trustee holds a duty of more than merely allowing the growth of the child, of providing peaceful conditions for it; he must often provide the means of education.

14

Whatever the virtues of the *pax Britannica* it was but negative; the finer Imperial rulers aspired to more. Thus Bentinck in abolishing suttee for "the benefit of the Hindus" sought to persuade and carry Indian opinion with him. The tradition of British rule in India was with the Lawrences: to preserve the peasant from oppression—an aim Cromer carried over into Egypt—then to improve his lot by irrigation and famine control.

The two means attempted in the rule and education of dependent peoples have been entitled "direct" and "indirect"; the former by British modes and institutions, the second by working through those found native to the soil. In the period of the development of British rule in India there were some who sought the latter: Warren Hastings investigated Hindu and Muslim law, Munro as Governor of Madras maintained the *ryotwari* land-tenure system of South India, and supported the *panchayat*, the organisation of government at the village level.

Such an approach was not to continue. The Evangelicals opposed the presence of East India Company officers at Hindu temple-ceremonies, the Company being "the dry nurse of Vishnu." Indirect rule demands sympathy: this could not be in a ruler whose moral sentiments were outraged by suttee, thuggee, female infanticide, and the abuses of the caste system, all tolerated—as he saw it—under the cloak of religion. Moreover, the nineteenth century Englishman was convinced of his own righteousness and ability. Imperialism and self-confidence go together. In India the tone was set by Macaulay who served as law member on Bentinck's council: himself the personification of the coming Victorian optimism, he declared in his Minute on Education in 1835 the belief that " a single shelf of a good European library was worth the whole native literature of India and Arabia." The result of education in the English manner was necessarily that government, if Indians were to participate, could only be in the English forms—their education cut them off from their own traditions. A generation at least was necessary before they could take part; in the meanwhile British rulers and observers understood that the period of British rule was lengthened—"we are wedged in the oak that we have rent," commented Goldwin Smith.

The father of the Indian National Congress was a retired member of the Indian Civil Service. Its formation was welcomed by the Viceroy, Dufferin, as providing another means of ascertaining Indian opinion, a safety-valve comparable to the local councils that had been set up. The Indian demand for Dominion status could not be checked by the English reservation, common alike to both Liberals and Conservatives at the time of the Morley-Minto reforms, that British institutions were the product of British conditions and were not for general application. Only in 1929 was Dominion status proclaimed as the goal.[1] From the Round Table Conference Indians increasingly shared in the making of their constitution until they completely followed the development of the white Dominions in this as in all else.

"The Westminster model" of constitutional development was in the main taken as the pattern. Such an outcome of equality in the Commonwealth had emerged from direct rule. Was it then surprising that Africans who had received the other treatment should ask whether this was not designed to hold them back?

Indirect rule is the common procedure of an Imperial ruler, Roman or Briton, wherever his resources in

[1] Declaration of the Viceroy, Lord Irwin, 31 October, 1929.

16

administration are slight. Thus it was with Lugard in Northern Nigeria. The strange thing in British experience is that a doctrine—a "theology" it has been called —has been developed to justify the procedure; it is the more strange in the case of the British who are commonly pragmatic and opposed to theory. The text-book was Lugard's *Dual Mandate*, further developed by Sir Donald Cameron in official papers in his governorships, first of Tanganyika and then of Nigeria. Here is a complete change of attitude to the people ruled: from Cromer's contempt for the Islam and the men he found in Egypt to Lugard's supporting the Fulani—however much their methods of rule might stand open to condemnation—and seeking to graft his political education on to their native stock. The nineteenth century despised "the lesser breeds without the law"; the twentieth, through the insights of the anthropologist, has sought to understand and build upon the foundations of society such as they are found to be. It has almost approached *Tout comprendre, c'est tout employer* and is far from the righteous indignation of a Wilberforce regarding India. The policy has been accused of screening native rulers from the condemnation of the modern world, of perpetuating not of transforming—for it is in terms of adapting the African that both the greatest advocates and the strongest opponents of indirect rule would judge it. Africa, it is certain, cannot be preserved as the zoological gardens of the anthropologist.

The irony of the British response to Africa is that she has sought to apply indirect methods in a situation where the forces of change are far greater and the powers of resistance of the African are less than in India where the method of direct rule was used. The result however is the same: the African, like the Indian, demands political fulfilment on the Westminster model. The national movements of West Africa followed at the remove of one world war in the steps of that of India: in 1939 the leaders had the objectives of Indians in 1914. However since 1945 there has been a speedier reply from the British side than there was in India after 1918.

VII

"Italy," said Metternich, "is a geographical expression." He might have said the same of India, while the very word "Nigeria" was not devised until 1897. Dufferin, reporting on Egypt in 1883 spoke of implanting there "those instincts of patriotism and freedom which it has been our boast to foster in every country where we have set our foot."[1] If this remark has a certain irony in the Frankenstein of Asian and African nationalism which has answered Imperialism, it must be remembered that first India and Ceylon and then Ghana and Nigeria have but followed in the steps of the United States, Canada and Australia. The first basis for colonial nationalism was found in opposition to the Imperial ruler, from the consciousness of "the unity of common subjection," as Nehru once phrased it in India. Dilke and Seeley, writing on India, sensed the beginnings of this process.

The growth of nationalism has been difficult for the rulers to face. Cromer rejected its Egyptian form as an artificial plant nurtured in Paris, while Curzon considered the Indian nationalist movement so little that he partitioned Bengal in the face of it and expressed the belief in 1900 that the Congress was tottering to its fall, saying that one of his greatest ambitions was to assist it to a peaceful demise.[2] Their attitudes arose

[1] Quoted C. E, Carrington, *The British Overseas*, p. 732.
[2] Ronaldshay, *Life of Lord Curzon*, Vol. II, p. 151.

largely from their directing their attention to the peasant and his lot; neither understood nor sympathised with the outlook of the educated minority, the lawyers, journalists and doctors, the middle-class spear-head of the young nationalist movements. Lugard, as well, condemned the "over-educated" of India, the products of the Western style of education, and hoped that he would be spared their like in West Africa.

Such thinking overlooked the inherent contradiction of British Imperialism. The Mills condemned British rule in India, the elder by his history, the younger by the ferment of his political ideas. We have taught our critics: Lenin's attack on Imperialism is derived from Hobson. We have provided for the subject peoples both the objectives which limit the period of Empire and the standards by which that rule shall be judged. We have taught our language and our history which we are prone to call " the growth of freedom," and have sometimes forgotten that:

> " We must be free or die, who speak the tongue
> That Shakespeare spake."

The best of British rulers have seen with Macaulay that " the proudest day in English history " would be when the peoples had become desirous and capable of governing themselves. To this they have bent their efforts without always seeing the paradox. With the white Empire the view was held that the colonials needed tutelage—still more then with those who were not of the British tradition; so Lord North in 1774 would be cautious about the French-Canadians and Balfour in the twentieth century about India. The danger lay during the period of tutelage. Munro sought to avoid this " emasculation " as Gandhi was later to call it, by employing Indians in the public service (No. 11); only by practice can government be learned.[1] The problem remained whether Indians could learn from a people conscious of race superiority, whether a bridge could be built across the divide of superiority and consequent inferiority complexes.

In the end the remarkable development was that, despite such divisions, India chose to remain within the Commonwealth after her independence. Then Gandhi's desire, expressed at the Round Table Conference in 1931, that India should "become a partner with Great Britain"[2] was fulfilled. Indian nationalism has proved a creative force in shaping the new Commonwealth. It may be argued that as Smuts's ideas (e.g. No. 115) largely shaped the first Commonwealth, that of the Statute of Westminster, so Nehru has in practice shaped the second.

VIII

Questions of Empire have produced a strife in British minds between economic and moral considerations. The search in the Tropics for raw materials produced vast fortunes in the eighteenth century for East and West Indiamen, but Adam Smith and the classical economists could reassure stricken consciences: trade benefited both parties, it was an exchange of wealth. Marx declared that this was not necessarily so and the new towns demonstrated to the Victorian exploitation in England. Was it certain that the natives to whom the traders went were any " freer " in their contracts than were the wage-slaves of the industrial towns?

[1] On this point the Soulbury Commission on Ceylon quoted the " wise observation attributed to Aristotle, ' The only way of learning to play the flute is to play the flute.' " (Cmd. 6677 of 1945, p. 110.)

[2] N. Mansergh: *Documents and Speeches on British Commonwealth Affairs, 1931-1952* (1953) vol. I, p. 228.

"Exploitation" of the raw materials of the earth and of the natives became the cry of the humanitarians: from the 1890's they struck at Leopold II's administration of the Congo and at those of the various British Chartered Companies. Yet they knew Africa must be opened up—it was "the task of the twentieth century." The best that could be hoped was that it should be in the hands of responsible agents, of governments rather than of traders, prospectors and adventurers, and preferably under international supervision. They remained hopeful despite the ineffectiveness of the Berlin Conference of 1884-5 and that of Brussels in 1889-90. Theirs was the germ of the Mandate system, though few seriously regarded the idea of the extreme Left that the British colonial territories should be put under the supervision of the League of Nations.

As these ideas were arising "Development" was on foot: the prophet was Joseph Chamberlain. He stood appalled at the "neglected estates" of the British Empire, in particular the West Indies, to which he sent the important Royal Commission of 1897. Of a new territory he said in 1894: "What is wanted for Uganda is what Birmingham has got—an improvement scheme."[1] These were the days when Roman roads were to be equalled by a burst of railway activity: Salisbury pushing on with that to Uganda, and Chamberlain supporting those in three West African territories. Africa was a Continent of "routes": Rhodes and the Cape to Cairo, Goldie with visions of a trans-Sudanic Empire. Chamberlain's lieutenant and pupil later offered the apologia of development in the *Dual Mandate*: the peoples both of Africa and of Europe should be the beneficiaries. This necessitated the "open door" to

[1] *Foreign and Colonial Speeches*, p. 136.

colonies which Chamberlain proclaimed in 1896, though earlier in the same year he had advocated a *zollverein* (No. 87), to which he was to revert in 1902.

The fulfilment of the *Dual Mandate* comes in the coupling of Development and Welfare in the title of the Acts of 1940 and 1945. It meant a change in economic thinking, but the change was based on an old tradition. The peasant farmer was now to be protected not only from the oppression of his own ruling classes but also from the exploitation of the European. Plantations were barred from British West Africa. As a result Lord Leverhulme told his shareholders in 1923 that the Colonial Office system of administration was no longer, as before the war, based on the encouragement of trade and commerce and the development of the Colonies as the first consideration.[1] In the Colonial Development Act of 1929 the interests of the mother country still predominated: it was passed in the economic depression by a Labour government, with the limitation that all schemes under it should be for " promoting commerce with and industry in the United Kingdom."[2] The change came in the thirties and was marked by the comment of the West India Royal Commission of 1938-9: " We do not think that the interests of the maintenance of British export trade, or employment in Great Britain, should be allowed to stand in the way " of certain suggested industrial developments in Jamaica.[3] The reward of the British taxpayer for his expenditure under the Acts of 1940 and 1945 will often be indirect; both Acts implied an utter reversal of the Gladstonian Treasury traditions that Salisbury and Chamberlain had to fight in setting development on foot.

[1] M. Perham, *Native Administration in Nigeria*, p. 319.
[2] Cmd. 3357 of 1929.
[3] *West India Royal Commission Report* (Cmd. 6607 of 1945), p. 249.

This new attitude was the completion of the idea of trust. It raised, however, large problems in the political sphere: how could the dependent peoples be convinced of the economic *bona fides* of the ruler? When the government purchased the cocoa crop of West Africa who could adjudicate the just price between the producer and the British housewife? Always economic questions return to political ones.

IX

The expression "trusteeship" became in the twentieth century increasingly irritating to the emerging colonial leaders. In speeches during the Second World War Colonel Stanley, as Secretary of State for the Colonies, recognised this, preferring, he said, "to combine with the status of trustee the position also of partner."[1] The idea was current that the colonies would enter, as Gandhi had claimed, into partnership with Britain.

The words " trust " and " partnership " have also proved catchwords of political discussion in the British territories of East and Central Africa. There minority European groups looked to obtain political power, to follow in the path of South Africa whence so many of them had come. In 1923 the Southern Rhodesians obtained internal self-government but the Kenya settlers were answered by a famous declaration. The British Government announced that "the interests of the African natives must be paramount, and that if, and when, these interests and the interests of the immigrant races should conflict, the former should prevail."[2] The Kenya Europeans fought back; they

[1] *Hansard*, H. C. vol. 391, c. 48, 13 July 1943, see also No. 123 *infra*.

[2] Cmd. 1922, p. 9. A similar declaration had been made in the case of India by a Parliamentary Committee in 1833: " It is recognised as an indisputable principle, that the interests of the Native Subjects are to be consulted in preference to those of Europeans, whenever the two come in competition." (R. Muir, *The Making of British India, 1756-1858*. p. 305.)

claimed a share in the trust, although the British Government had denied this in 1923. The Hilton Young Commission saw through the claim; reporting in 1929 on the situation in East and Central Africa they replied: " What the immigrant communities may justly claim is partnership, not control.[1] In 1930 the settlers were further rebuffed when a Labour Government extended the paramountcy declaration to the whole area. In later years, starting with the Report of the Parliamentary Joint Select Committee in 1931, the defence of the native position through the doctrine of paramountcy was, it was felt, being slowly whittled away.

After the Second World War " partnership " became the key word for policy in multi-racial territories. This idea may have helped in the progress of Malaya towards independence in 1957 but its application was more problematic in Central Africa. There the preamble to the constitution of the Federation of Rhodesia and Nyasaland in 1953 set one of its objectives as to " foster partnership and co-operation " between its inhabitants. Since then Africans have challenged whether " partnership " had any effective meaning.

This story has only continued that of South Africa. There the liberal was repeatedly faced with the dilemma of choice between his two ideals: trusteeship for the native races and self-government for settlers. The Conservatives' answer was to trust the man on the spot, to argue that Europeans were responsible people and that through the responsibilities of government they would evince responsibility to the native peoples.

The story of the Rhodesian federation, and that of

[1] Cmd. 3234 (1929) p. 239.

Ceylon since 1958, cause doubts whether partnership can be more than a pious aspiration in multi-racial countries with wide differences of culture and economic power. " Partnership " may be applicable only to the relationship between independent nations in the Commonwealth.

x

Empire as part of external affairs has necessarily shaped foreign policy. With the loss of America, India was, in Dundas's phrase, "the brightest jewel that now remained in his Majesty's crown."[1] The route to India was vital: it led to a series of Near Eastern crises to guard the land routes and to the seizure of posts on the sea route: Mauritius and the Seychelles and above all the Cape as fruits of the Napoleonic wars. At the peace the relevance of annexation to the safeguarding of India was made clear: Ceylon was retained but Java was returned to the Dutch.

Palmerston proclaimed that he sought to keep the eventual meeting of Cossack and Sikh as far away from India as possible. The supreme problem for the foreign minister in Imperialism thus is one of frontiers. In the case of India the mountains and sea round it off. Africa has few natural frontiers; it is a continent of routes. That of the Nile illustrates well how the needs of protecting previous acquisitions could lure men forward. Britain entered Egypt in 1882 partly to protect the route to India. Soon it was necessary to ensure the water supply of Egypt, to maintain the unity of the Nile valley —hence to ascend to Khartoum—here also was the strategic motive in the control of Uganda.

Dispersal of force, the danger of Empire, was well

[1] *Parliamentary History*, XXII, c. 1285.

illustrated in the weak response to the German challenge of 1884-5. The seizures of territory in Africa and New Guinea alarmed South Africans and Australians, while Derby and Gladstone could only congratulate themselves that such rivalry would bind the colonies in closer dependence on the mother country. No adequate answer was made because of Gordon's involvement in the Sudan and " Merv-ousness " over the Russian threat to India.

In the scramble for Africa the function of the Foreign Office came to be the balancing of one Imperial interest against another. The British East Africa Company felt they were constantly being sacrificed by Salisbury to some other Imperial interest.[1] He had to consider the general picture in the series of negotiations of 1889-91 with Germany, France and Portugal on African disputes. It was this that led Rosebery to comment in 1892, " our foreign policy has become a Colonial policy, and it is in reality dictated much more from the extremities of the Empire than from London itself." [2] Yet on these issues negotiations and adjustments could always take place: Imperial interests might form the bases for an Entente in 1904 but not for a war in 1914—that was related predominantly to European considerations.

XI

It has been argued that British participation in a European federation is prevented by Britain's special relations with the United States and with the Commonwealth. Many have felt that the Empire was incomplete without the other portion of the English-speaking world. Chamberlain, addressing a Toronto audience, refused " to think or to speak of the United State of America as

[1] P. L. McDermott, *British East Africa or I.B.E.A.* (1893), passim.
[2] Crewe, *Life of Lord Rosebery*, p. 315.

a foreign nation."[1] In his Imperialism of the "Teutonic"
race, he was following the racial Imperialism which
became increasingly strong after 1870. Dilke in the introduction to his *Greater Britain* (1868), declared that in
his world tour of 1866–7, which had started in the United
States, he had " followed England round the world." In
his parable of the flies (*infra* pp. 233–4) he illustrates
the "Darwinian" ideas that were then becoming current.
Natural selection was challenging God as the justification for Britain's Imperial position. With the competition of the new Imperialisms the racial doctrines
become flamboyant—earlier in the century the Englishman's supremacy was taken for granted as part of the
established order. Chamberlain again expresses the new
view: " I believe that the British race is the greatest of
governing races that the world has ever seen." (No. 86).
The full assertiveness is found in the *fin de siècle* atmosphere: in Kipling at home, in Rhodes in Africa and
Curzon in India—they typify the age in which the *Daily
Mail* raised the motto " Empire first and parish afterwards."

Even in the high flood of Imperialism the questioning
that had been constant continued. The most powerful
criticism ever to appear, J. A. Hobson's *Imperialism: a
Study* was published in 1902. He consciously went back
to many of the old arguments, quoting James Mill's
definition of the Empire, "a vast system of outdoor
relief for the upper classes." He developed Burke's,
Bentham's[2] and Cobden's belief that despotism in the
Empire was incompatible with democracy at home;
that the influence of the retired rulers was as corrosive
as was Oriental luxury upon the Roman republic. He

[1] 30 December, 1887 (*Foreign and Colonial Speeches*, p. 7).
[2] cf. *Panopticon versus New South Wales: Letter to Lord Pelham* (1802).

27

deals with the connection between business and Empire
which was so apparent in the methods of the opening-up
of Africa and which had found such powerful support
in a screw-manufacturer turned Colonial Secretary.
Above all he answers the " *cui bono?* " of Empire with
" the investor." The English then are like other men—
they only assume a mask of "duty" before their actions,
Bernard Shaw told them. (No. 110).

<h1 style="text-align:center">XII</h1>

The problems of Empire and the answers that were
given followed regular patterns. Those who sought to
take the Empire out of the party strife had this in their
favour: the main division, that between " separatists "
and " Imperialists " cut across the party lines. Among
Conservatives Peel and Disraeli have uttered separatist
sentiments; the Liberals have been divided into
Little Englanders and Liberal Imperialists; in the
Labour party the Fabians have taken a positive view
while the critics were usually those further to the left.
The Empire illustrates well how close the parties were
together: modern thought on the subject takes its rise
with Burke who, while a Whig, has been adjudged part
of the Conservative tradition; the Colonial Reformers
influenced Gladstone and John Stuart Mill on the one
hand, Carlyle and Conservative thought on the other;
in the nineties it is difficult to tell who is the greater
Imperialist, the Liberal Rosebery or the Unionist
Chamberlain; more recently the House of Commons
gave a unanimous passage to the Colonial Development
and Welfare Act of 1945. On the main lines there is a
great body of agreement: with all the differences shown
in this volume the concept of Empire illustrates the
essential unity of the British political tradition.

Part I

THE FOUNDATION OF THE SECOND EMPIRE

1 : DEBATES ON THE PASSAGE OF THE QUEBEC ACT

House of Commons, 1774

The retention of Quebec in the peace-settlement of 1763 presented the first large problem of the administration of conquered territory. A proclamation of the same year promised representative institutions on the pattern of the colonies of settlement but no assembly was called by the first two governors; the unanimous opinion of the authorities at Quebec was against such an institution. The Act of 1774 recognised French-Canadian desires by confirming the feudal landholding system, accepting the "Laws of Canada" for civil suits, and giving the church statutory authority to collect the tithes. While the Act played a part in alienating opinion in the Thirteen Colonies—especially with its concession of the lands beyond the Ohio to Quebec—the debates and the problem of the rule of a non-British people foreshadow much in the future. Barré, like Burke, often voiced American opinion in the House of Commons.

26 May 1774

THE ATTORNEY-GENERAL (afterwards LORD THURLOW): My notion is, that it is a change of sovereignty. You acquired a new country; you acquired a new people; but you do not state the right of conquest, as giving you a right to goods and chattels. That would be slavery and extreme misery. In order to make the acquisition either available or secure, this seems to be the line that ought to be followed—you ought to change those laws only which relate to the French sovereignty, and in their place substitute laws which should relate to the new sovereign; but with respect to all other laws, all other

33

customs and institutions whatever, which are indifferent
to the state of subjects and sovereign, humanity, justice,
and wisdom equally conspire to advise you to leave them
to the people just as they were. Their happiness depends
upon it; their allegiance to their new sovereign depends
upon it . . .

When gentlemen apply the word " assimilation " to
religion, to law, to civil laws, and to manners, I can easily
conceive it is not an undesirable object in policy, that
they should be so far assimilated. To a certain degree, I
can conceive that the government of the country, under
the present constitution, will look upon it to be their duty
to assimilate the people in language, manners and every
other respect in which they can be expected to hold a
more intimate connexion. But when that assimilation is
proposed to be carried into the law-form of the constitution, I cannot conceive the form of the British
constitution, as it stands at present, proper for them.
Upon this main principle, you ought to make a repartition of the sovereignty of the country between the King
and the people, of whom 558 are to be elected a parliament. On this principle, the sovereignty of this country
was intended to reside, and does, in fact, reside there.
But do you mean to vest the sovereignty of the province,
either by repartition or otherwise, in any other place
than in the House of Lords and Commons of Great
Britain? Yet, if you follow your assimilating idea, you
must do that. I only know that none of the charters
intended it. It is impossible for the King to have done
it—to have created the sovereign authority of governor,
council, and assembly, in any one of the provinces. In
point of fact, they have considered themselves, in more
views than I wish to draw into debate, masters of the
sovere:gn power. Is their money to be applied to support

the British empire? Are their forces to be applied to the support of the British empire? Are they content that the King, Lords, and Commons of Great Britain shall be the judges of the drawing forth of those forces, and the applying of that money to the protection of the British empire? I think I drew a degree of attention and conviction, when I stated it as an absurdity, that the sovereignty of the province should be divided between the governor, council, and assembly; and to be sure it is a grossness—it is making two allied kingdoms, totally out of our power, to act as a federal union if they please, and if they do not please, to act as an independent country—a federal condition pretty near the condition of the states of Germany. If you do not like that idea, in all the extent, in all the grossness of it, would you create a constitution in such a case which would make it, in fact, the very thing you deny in words?

The next thing that has been said is, that Englishmen carry over their constitution along with them; and in that respect it is a hard measure to take from them any of the English laws they carry over with them. I no more understand this proposition, especially as applied to the present subject, than I do the former. When the Crown of Great Britain makes a conquest of any foreign established country, if it be true that it is an article of humanity and justice to leave the country in possession of their laws, then, I say, if any English resort to the country, they do not carry the several ideas of laws that are to prevail the moment they go there: it would be just as wise to say, if an Englishman goes to Guernsey, the laws of the city of London were carried over with him. To take the laws as they stand has been allowed; to act according to those laws, and to be bound by their coercion, is a natural consequence. In this view, I think

35

the bill has done nothing obnoxious. I have no speculative opinions. I would have consulted the French habit
to a much greater extent, if it had been for me to have
framed the law.

COLONEL BARRÉ: I cannot help observing, that the
honourable and learned gentleman seems to be more
solicitous upon this occasion than the conquered inhabitants of that country, and, in some measure, more than
those who have been the conquerors of it. This proclamation, Sir, gave a certain form to the colony. It provided,
that the inhabitants should have an assembly, as well as
all the other royal governments, as soon as possible. The
proclamation held out this language, that " until such
assemblies could be called, all persons inhabiting in, or
resorting to, the said colonies, might confide in the royal
protection for the enjoyment of the benefit of the laws
of England." Under this proclamation, thus held out as
a solemn act to the people of that country, many Englishmen went, and settled in the heart of Canada: but their
rights, their privileges, were not thought worthy of the
honourable and learned gentleman's consideration; he
stood up only in defence of the Canadians: but there is
a very considerable number of men, no matter of what
description—they may have been poor bankrupts, but
they are English subjects, who have setled there under
the faith of this proclamation. The honourable and
learned gentleman was not precise in stating the limits
of our colonies. He seemed unwilling for the House to
think that any one of the colonies, especially Penn-
sylvania and Virginia, had a right to settle beyond the
Endless Mountains; as if the honourable and learned
gentleman could be ignorant of the fact, that many
thousands of English subjects are established some

hundred miles beyond the Endless Mountains, upon the very spot which you are now going to make a part of this country of Canada.

Sir, with respect to the Canadians themselves, the learned gentleman asks—what would you do with them? would you do the cruelest thing that ever was done to any conquered nation upon earth? would you take away their laws, their customs? Now, Sir, I never yet knew it was found a grievance to any nation, to give them the English laws, the English constitution. So far from it, the Canadians admired and revered those laws, as far as they could be made acquainted with them.

THE SOLICITOR-GENERAL (ALEXANDER WEDDERBURN): A great deal has been said with regard to the British subjects settled in Canada. Now, I confess, that the situation of the British settler is not the principal object of my attention. I do not wish to see Canada draw from this country any considerable number of her inhabitants. I think there ought to be no temptation held out to the subjects of England to quit their native soil, to increase colonies at the expence of this country. If persons have gone thither in the course of trade, they have gone without any intention of making it their permanent residence; and, in that case, it is no more a hardship to tell them, " this is the law of the land," than it would be to say so to a man whose affairs induced him to establish himself in Guernsey, or in any other part of North America. With regard to the English who have settled there, their number is very few. They are attached to the country either in point of commercial interest, or they are attached to it from the situations they hold under government. It is one object of this measure, that these persons should not settle in Canada. The subjects of this country, in Holland, in the Baltic, and in different parts of the world, where they may go to push their commercial views, look upon England as their home; and it should be our care to keep alive in their breasts this attachment to their native soil.

Mr. CHARLES FOX: It is not right for this country to originate and establish a constitution, in which there is not a spark or semblance of liberty. A learned gentleman has said, that by this means we should deter our own countrymen from settling there. Now, Sir, as it is my notion, that it is the policy of this country to induce Englishmen to mix as much as possible with the Canadians, I certainly must come to a different conclusion . . .

I cannot conceive why we should not give them the law of this country. If we gave them that law, it would be easy to alter it in many respects, so as to make it agreeable to them. That, Sir, I conceive it to be the duty of this country to do; and it is very easy to do it: but to go at once, and establish a perfectly despotic government, contrary to the genius and spirit of the British constitution, carries with it the appearance of a love of despotism, and a settled design to enslave the people of America, very unbecoming this country. My idea is, that America is not to be governed by force, but by affection and interest.

31 May 1774

Mr. EDMUND BURKE: When that country cannot be governed as a free country, I question whether this can. No free country can keep another country in slavery. The price they pay for it will be their own servitude. The constitution proposed is one which men never will, and never ought to bear. When we are sowing the seeds of despotism in Canada, let us bear in mind, that it is a growth which may afterwards extend to other countries. By being made perpetual, it is evident that this constitution is meant to be both an instrument of tyranny to the Canadians, and an example to others of what they have to expect; at some time or other it will come home to England. When it is proved that the laws of England could not govern Canada, it will be plain that some stronger power than the laws of England is necessary to govern this country. I shall give my first vote upon this bill, against the despotic government there; whether it is to be established for any length of time, or to be established at all by Parliament. When you cannot make a free government, you ought to leave a country to be governed by the force of necessity.

8 June 1774

LORD NORTH: Now, I ask, is it safe for this country—for we must consider this country—to put the principal power into the hands of an assembly of Roman Catholic new subjects? I agree with the honourable gentleman [Fox], that the Roman Catholics may be honest, able, worthy, sensible men, entertaining very correct notions of political liberty; but I must say, there is something in that religion, which makes it not prudent in a Protestant government, to establish an assembly consisting entirely of Roman Catholics. The honourable gentleman is of opinion, that more is to be dreaded from the seigneurs, than from those in the lower ranks. Sure I am, that the seigneurs, who are the great possessors of the lands, would be the persons who composed the assembly, and some of them will, I hope, be admitted to the legislative council; but then, the governor will choose those on whose fidelity he has the greatest reason to rely. They

will be removeable by the King in council, and will not
depend wholly upon the Roman Catholic electors, or be
removeable at their pleasure. It is not at present expedient to call an assembly. That is what the act says;
though it would be convenient that the Canadian laws
should be assimilated to those of this country, as far as
the laws of Great Britain admit, and that British
subjects should have something or other in their constitution preserved for them, which they will probably
lose when they cease to be governed entirely by British
laws. That it is desirable to give the Canadians a constitution in every respect like the constitution of Great
Britain, I will not say; but I earnestly hope that they
will, in the course of time, enjoy as much of our laws,
and as much of our constitution, as may be beneficial
for that country, and safe for this. But that time is not
yet come.

Sir Henry Cavendish, *Debates on the Canada Bill in* 1774 (ed.
J. Wright, 1839), pp. 30, 35–9, 57, 61–2, 89–90, 247–8.

2. EDMUND BURKE: Speech on Conciliation with America

House of Commons, 22 March 1775

PERHAPS, Sir, I am mistaken in my idea of an empire,
as distinguished from a single state or kingdom. But my
idea of it is this; that an empire is the aggregate of
many states under one common head; whether this head
be a monarch, or a presiding republick. It does, in such
constitutions, frequently happen (and nothing but the
dismal, cold, dead uniformity of servitude can prevent
its happening) that the subordinate parts have many
local privileges and immunities. Between these privileges and the supreme common authority the line may
be extremely nice. Of course disputes, often too, very

bitter disputes, and much ill blood, will arise. But though every privilege is an exemption (in the case) from the ordinary exercise of the supreme authority, it is no denial of it. The claim of a privilege seems rather, *ex vi termini*, to imply a superiour power. For to talk of the privileges of a state, or of a person, who has no superiour, is hardly any better than speaking nonsense. Now, in such unfortunate quarrels among the component parts of a great political union of communities, I can scarcely conceive any thing more completely imprudent, than for the head of the empire to insist, that, if any privilege is pleaded against his will, or his acts, his whole authority is denied; instantly to proclaim rebellion, to beat to arms, and to put the offending provinces under the ban. Will not this, Sir, very soon teach the provinces to make no distinctions on their part? Will it not teach them that the government, against which a claim of liberty is tantamount to high treason, is a government to which submission is equivalent to slavery? It may not always be quite convenient to impress dependent communities with such an idea.

My hold of the colonies is in the close affection which grows from common names, from kindred blood, from similar privileges, and equal protection. These are ties, which, though light as air, are as strong as links of iron. Let the colonies always keep the idea of their civil rights associated with your government;—they will cling and grapple to you; and no force under heaven will be of power to tear them from their allegiance. But let it be once understood, that your government may be one thing, and their privileges another; that these two things may exist without any mutual relation; the cement is gone; the cohesion is loosened; and every thing hastens to decay and dissolution. As long as you have the wisdom to keep the sovereign authority of this country as the sanctuary of liberty, the sacred temple consecrated to our common faith, wherever the chosen race and sons of England worship freedom, they will turn their faces towards you. The more they multiply, the more friends you will have; the more ardently they love liberty, the more perfect will be their obedience. Slavery they can have any where. It is a weed that grows in every soil. They may have it from Spain, they may have it from Prussia. But, until you become lost to all feeling of your true interest and your natural dignity, freedom they can have from none but you. This is the commodity of price, of which you have the monopoly. This is the true act of navigation, which binds to you the commerce of the colonies, and through them secures to you the wealth of the world. Deny them this participation of freedom, and you break that sole bond, which originally made, and must still preserve, the unity of the empire. Do not entertain so weak an imagination, as that your registers and your bonds, your affidavits and your sufferances, your cockets and your clearances, are what form the great securities of your commerce. Do not dream that your letters of office, and your instructions, and your suspending clauses, are the things that hold together the great contexture of this mysterious whole. These things do not make your government. Dead instruments, passive tools as they are, it is the spirit of the English communion that gives all their life and efficacy to them. It is the spirit of the English constitution, which, infused through the mighty mass, pervades, feeds, unites, invigorates, vivifies every part of the empire, even down to the minutest member . . .

All this, I know well enough, will sound wild and

chimerical to the profane herd of those vulgar and mechanical politicians, who have no place among us; a sort of people who think that nothing exists but what is gross and material; and who therefore, far from being qualified to be directors of the great movement of empire, are not fit to turn a wheel in the machine. But to men truly initiated and rightly taught, these ruling and master principles, which, in the opinion of such men as I have mentioned, have no substantial existence, are in truth every thing, and all in all. Magnanimity in politicks is not seldom the truest wisdom; and a great empire and little minds go ill together. If we are conscious of our situation, and glow with zeal to fill our places as becomes our station and ourselves, we ought to auspicate all our publick proceedings on America, with the old warning of the church, *Sursum corda!* We ought to elevate our minds to the greatness of that trust to which the order of Providence has called us. By adverting to the dignity of this high calling, our ancestors have turned a savage wilderness into a glorious empire: and have made the most extensive, and the only honourable conquests; not by destroying, but by promoting the wealth, the number, the happiness of the human race. Let us get an American revenue as we have got an American empire. English privileges have made it all that it is; English privileges alone will make it all it can be.

Edmund Burke, *Works* (1826), Vol. III, pp. 69–71, 123–5, 126–7.

3: ADAM SMITH. *An Inquiry into the Nature and Causes of the Wealth of Nations*
1776

Book IV, Chapter VII, Part III

To found a great empire for the sole purpose of raising up a people of customers, may at first sight appear a pro-

43

ject fit only for a nation of shopkeepers. It is, however, a project altogether unfit for a nation of shopkeepers; but extremely fit for a nation whose government is influenced by shopkeepers. Such statesmen, and such statesmen only, are capable of fancying that they will find some advantage in employing the blood and treasure of their fellow-citizens, to found and maintain such an empire. Say to a shopkeeper, Buy me a good estate, and I shall always buy my clothes at your shop, even though I should pay somewhat dearer than what I can have them for at other shops; and you will not find him very forward to embrace your proposal. But should any other person buy you such an estate, the shopkeeper would be much obliged to your benefactor if he would enjoin you to buy all your clothes at his shop. England purchased for some of her subjects, who found themselves uneasy at home, a great estate in a distant country. The price, indeed, was very small, and instead of thirty years purchase, the ordinary price of land in the present times, it amounted to little more than the expence of the different equipments which made the first discovery, reconnoitred the coast, and took a fictitious possession of the country. The land was good and of great extent, and the cultivators having plenty of good ground to work upon, and being for some time at liberty to sell their produce where they pleased, became in the course of little more than thirty or forty years (between 1620 and 1660) so numerous and thriving a people, that the shopkeepers and other traders of England wished to secure to themselves the monopoly of their custom. Without pretending, therefore, that they had paid any part, either of the original purchase-money, or of the subsequent expence of improvement, they petitioned the parliament that the cultivators of America might for the future be confined to their shop; first, for buying all the goods which they wanted from Europe; and, secondly, for selling all such parts of their own produce as those traders might find it convenient to buy. For they did not find it convenient to buy every part of it. Some parts of it imported into England might have interfered with some of the trades which they themselves carried on at home. Those particular parts of it, therefore, they were willing that the colonists should sell where they could; the farther off the better; and upon that account proposed that their market should be confined to the countries south of Cape Finisterre. A clause in the famous act of navigation established this truly shopkeeper proposal into law.

The maintenance of this monopoly has hitherto been the principal, or more properly perhaps the sole end and purpose of the dominion which Great Britain assumes over her colonies. In the exclusive trade, it is supposed, consists the great advantage of provinces, which have never yet afforded either revenue or military force for the support of the civil government, or the defence of the mother country. The monopoly is the principal badge of their dependency, and it is the sole fruit which has hitherto been gathered from that dependency. Whatever expence Great Britain has hitherto laid out in maintaining this dependency, has really been laid out in order to support this monopoly. The expence of the ordinary peace establishment of the colonies amounted, before the commencement of the present disturbances, to the pay of twenty regiments of foot; to the expence of the artillery, stores, and extraordinary provisions with which it was necessary to supply them; and to the expence of a very considerable naval force which was constantly kept up, in order to guard, from the smuggling vessels of other nations, the immense coast of North America, and

45

that of our West Indian islands. The whole expence of this peace establishment was a charge upon the revenue of Great Britain, and was, at the same time, the smallest part of what the dominion of the colonies has cost the mother country. If we would know the amount of the whole, we must add to the annual expence of this peace establishment the interest of the sums which, in consequence of her considering her colonies as provinces subject to her dominion, Great Britain has upon different occasions laid out upon their defence. We must add to it, in particular, the whole expence of the late war, and a great part of that of the war which preceded it. The late war was altogether a colony quarrel, and the whole expence of it, in whatever part of the world it may have been laid out, whether in Germany or the East Indies, ought justly to be stated to the account of the colonies. It amounted to more than ninety millions sterling, including not only the new debt which was contracted, but the two shillings in the pound additional land tax, and the sums which were every year borrowed from the sinking fund. The Spanish war which began in 1739, was principally a colony quarrel. Its principal object was to prevent the search of the colony ships which carried on a contraband trade with the Spanish main. The whole expence is, in reality, a bounty which has been given in order to support a monopoly. The pretended purpose of it was to encourage the manufactures, and to increase the commerce of Great Britain. But its real effect has been to raise the rate of mercantile profit, and to enable our merchants to turn into a branch of trade, of which the returns are more slow and distant than those of the greater part of other trades, a greater proportion of their capital than they otherwise would have done; two events which if a bounty could have prevented, it might perhaps have been very worth while to give such a bounty.

Under the present system of management, therefore, Great Britain derives nothing but loss from the dominion which she assumes over her colonies.

To propose that Great Britain should voluntarily give up all authority over her colonies, and leave them to elect their own magistrates, to enact their own laws, and to make peace and war as they might think proper, would be to propose such a measure as never was, and never will be adopted, by any nation in the world. No nation ever voluntarily gave up the dominion of any province, how troublesome soever it might be to govern it, and how small soever the revenue which it afforded might be in proportion to the expence which it occasioned. Such sacrifices, though they might frequently be agreeable to the interest, are always mortifying to the pride of every nation, and what is perhaps of still greater consequence, they are always contrary to the private interest of the governing part of it, who would thereby be deprived of the disposal of many places of trust and profit, of many opportunities of acquiring wealth and distinction, which the possession of the most turbulent, and, to the great body of the people, the most unprofitable province seldom fails to afford. The most visionary enthusiast would scarce be capable of proposing such a measure, with any serious hopes at least of its ever being adopted. If it was adopted, however, Great Britain would not only be immediately freed from the whole annual expence of the peace establishment of the colonies, but might settle with them such a treaty of commerce as would effectually secure to her a free trade, more advantageous to the great body of the people, though less so to the merchants, than the monopoly which she at present enjoys. By thus parting good friends, the natural affection of the colonies to the mother country, which, perhaps, our late dissensions have well nigh extinguished, would quickly revive. It might dispose them not only to respect, for whole centuries together, that treaty of commerce which they had concluded with us at parting, but to favour us in war as well as in trade, and, instead of turbulent and factious subjects, to become our most faithful, affectionate, and generous allies; and the same sort of parental affection on the one side, and filial respect on the other, might revive between Great Britain and her colonies, which used to subsist between those of ancient Greece and the mother city from which they descended.

Book V, Chapter I, Part III, Article 1st

Frequently a man of great, sometimes even a man of small fortune, is willing to purchase a thousand pounds share in India stock, merely for the influence which he expects to acquire by a vote in the court of proprietors. It gives him a share, though not in the plunder, yet in the appointment of the plunderers of India; the court of directors, though they make that appointment, being necessarily more or less under the influence of the proprietors, who not only elect those directors, but sometimes overrule the appointments of their servants in India. Provided he can enjoy this influence for a few years, and thereby provide for a certain number of his friends, he frequently cares little about the dividend; or even about the value of the stock upon which his vote is founded. About the prosperity of the great empire, in the government of which that vote gives him a share, he seldom cares at all. No other sovereigns ever were, or, from the nature of things, ever could be, so perfectly indifferent about the happiness or misery of their subjects, the improvement or waste of their dominions, the glory or disgrace of their administration; as, from irresistible moral causes, the greater part of the proprietors of such a mercantile company are, and necessarily must be.

Book V, Chapter III

The rulers of Great Britain have, for more than a century past, amused the people with the imagination that they possessed a great empire on the west side of the Atlantic. This empire, however, has hitherto existed in imagination only. It has hitherto been, not an empire, but the project of an empire; not a gold mine, but the project of a gold mine; a project which has cost, which continues to cost, and which, if pursued in the same way as it has been hitherto, is likely to cost, immense expence, without being likely to bring any profit; for the effects of the monopoly of the colony trade, it has been shewn, are, to the great body of the people, mere loss instead of profit. It is surely now time that our rulers should either realize this golden dream, in which they have been indulging themselves, perhaps, as well as the people; or, that they should awake from it themselves, and endeavour to awaken the people. If the project cannot be completed, it ought to be given up. If any of the provinces of the British empire cannot be made to contribute towards the support of the whole empire, it is surely time that Great Britain should free herself from the expence of defending those provinces in time of war. and of supporting any part of their civil or military establishments in time of peace, and endeavour to accommodate her future views and designs to the real mediocrity of her circumstances.

An Inquiry into the Nature and Causes of the Wealth of Nations (ed. Cannan, London, 1925), Vol. II. pp. 114–7, 243, 432–3.

4 : EDMUND BURKE. Speech on Fox's East India Bill

House of Commons, 1 December 1783

Parliament had begun to control the actions of the East India Company with Lord North's Regulating Act (1773). Defects in it and the controversy over the administration of Warren Hastings led to new Bills in 1783. Fox's government fell through George III's opposition to patronage provisions in this Bill but Pitt's Act (1784) was based on the same principle—that of placing the Company in direct and permanent subordination to a body representing the British Government.

THE rights of *men,* that is to say, the natural rights of mankind are indeed sacred things; and if any publick measure is proved mischievously to affect them, the objection ought to be fatal to that measure, even if no charter at all could be set up against it. If these natural rights are further affirmed and declared by express covenants, if they are clearly defined and secured against chicane, against power, and authority, by written instruments and positive engagements, they are in a still better condition: they partake not only of the sanctity of the object so secured, but of that solemn publick faith itself, which secures an object of such importance. Indeed this formal recognition, by the sovereign power, of an original right in the subject, can never be subverted, but by rooting up the holding, radical principles of government, and even of society itself. The charters, which we call by distinction *great,* are publick instruments of this nature; I mean the charter of king John and king Henry the third. The things secured by these instruments may, without any deceitful ambiguity, be very fitly called the *chartered rights of men.*

These charters have made the very name of a charter dear to the heart of every Englishman.—But, Sir, there

may be, and there are charters, not only different in
nature, but formed on principles the *very reverse* of
those of the great charter. Of this kind is the charter of
the East-India company. *Magna charta* is a charter to
restrain power, and to destroy monopoly. The East-
India charter is a charter to establish monopoly, and to
create power. Political power and commercial monopoly
are *not* the rights of men; and the rights to them derived
from charters, it is fallacious and sophistical to call " the
chartered rights of men." These chartered rights, (to
speak of such charters and of their effects in terms of
the greatest possible moderation) do at least suspend the
natural rights of mankind at large; and in their very
frame and constitution are liable to fall into a direct
violation of them.

It is a charter of this latter description (that is to say
a charter of power and monopoly) which is affected by
the bill before you. The bill, Sir, does, without question,
affect it; it does affect it essentially and substantially.
But having stated to you of what description the chartered rights are which this bill touches, I feel no difficulty
at all in acknowledging the existence of those chartered
rights, in their fullest extent. They belong to the company in the surest manner; and they are secured to that
body by every sort of publick sanction. They are stamped
by the faith of the king; they are stamped by the faith
of parliament; they have been bought for money, for
money honestly and fairly paid; they have been bought
for valuable consideration, over and over again. . . .

But granting all this, they must grant to me in my
turn, that all political power which is set over men, and
that all privilege claimed or exercised in exclusion of
them, being wholly artificial, and for so much a deroga-
tion from the natural equality of mankind at large, ought

to be some way or other exercised ultimately for their benefit.

If this is true with regard to every species of political dominion, and every description of commercial privilege, none of which can be original, self-derived rights, or grants for the mere private benefit of the holders, then such rights, or privileges, or whatever else you choose to call them, are all in the strictest sense a *trust;* and it is of the very essence of every trust to be rendered *accountable*; and even totally to *cease*, when it substantially varies from the purposes for which alone it could have a lawful existence.

This I conceive, Sir, to be true of trusts of power vested in the highest hands, and of such as seem to hold of no human creature. But about the application of this principle to subordinate, *derivative* trusts, I do not see how a controversy can be maintained. To whom then would I make the East-India company accountable? Why, to parliament, to be sure; to parliament, from which their trust was derived; to parliament, which alone is capable of comprehending the magnitude of its object, and its abuse; and alone capable of an effectual legislative remedy. The very charter, which is held out to exclude parliament from correcting malversation with regard to the high trust vested in the company, is the very thing which at once gives a title and imposes on us a duty to interfere with effect, wherever power and authority originating from ourselves are perverted from their purposes, and become instruments of wrong and violence.

If parliament, Sir, had nothing to do with this charter, we might have some sort of Epicurean excuse to stand aloof, indifferent spectators of what passes in the company's name in India and in London. But if we are the very cause of the evil, we are in a special manner engaged to the redress; and for us passively to bear with oppressions committed under the sanction of our own authority, is in truth and reason for this house to be an active accomplice in the abuse.

That the power, notoriously, grossly abused, has been bought from us is very certain. But this circumstance, which is urged against the bill, becomes an additional motive for our interference; lest we should be thought to have sold the blood of millions of men, for the base consideration of money. We sold, I admit, all that we had to sell; that is, our authority, not our controul. We had not a right to make a market of our duties.

I ground myself therefore on this principle—that if the abuse is proved, the contract is broken; and we re-enter into all our rights; that is, into the exercise of all our duties. Our own authority is indeed as much a trust originally, as the company's authority is a trust derivatively; and it is the use we make of the resumed power that must justify or condemn us in the resumption of it. When we have perfected the plan laid before us by the right honourable mover, the world will then see what it is we destroy, and what it is we create. By that test we stand or fall; and by that test I trust that it will be found in the issue, that we are going to supersede a charter abused to the full extent of all the powers which it could abuse, and exercised in the plentitude of despotism, tyranny, and corruption; and that in one and the same plan, we provide a real chartered security for the *rights of men,* cruelly violated under that charter.

This bill, and those connected with it, are intended to form the *magna charta* of Hindostan. Whatever the treaty of Westphalia is to the liberty of the princes and free cities of the empire, and to the three religions there

53

professed—Whatever the great charter, the statute of tallege, the petition of right, and the declaration of right, are to Great Britain, these bills are to the people of India. Of this benefit, I am certain, their condition is capable; and when I know that they are capable of more, my vote shall most assuredly be for our giving to the full extent of their capacity of receiving; and no charter of dominion shall stand as a bar in my way to their charter of safety and protection.

Edmund Burke, *Works* (1826), Vol. IV, pp. 8–14.

5: EDMUND BURKE. Speeches in the Impeachment of Warren Hastings

Warren Hastings was successively Governor and Governor-General of Bengal from 1772 to 1785. On return to England he was impeached and acquitted in a trial that lasted from 1788 to 1795, in which Burke led for the House of Commons. His view of Hastings persisted in the Whig tradition, to find expression in Macaulay's essay. The fact that subsequent historians have rescued Hastings from these attacks does not invalidate the importance of this trial, voted for by Wilberforce and Pitt, in establishing standards for British rulers in the Empire.

Opening Speech, 16 February 1788

MY Lords, we contend, that Mr. Hastings, as a British governour, ought to govern on British principles, not by British forms—God forbid; for, if ever there was a case, in which the letter kills and the spirit gives life, it would be an attempt to introduce British forms and the substance of despotick principles together into any country. No. We call for that spirit of equity, that spirit of justice, that spirit of protection, that spirit of lenity, which ought to characterize every British subject in power; and on these, and these principles only, he will be tried.

But he has told your lordships, in his defence, that actions in Asia do not bear the same moral qualities, which the same actions would bear in Europe.

My Lords, we positively deny that principle. I am authorized and called upon to deny it. And having stated at large what he means by saying, that the same actions have not the same qualities in Asia and in Europe, we are to let your lordships know, that these gentlemen have formed a plan of *geographical morality,* by which the duties of men, in publick and in private situations, are not to be governed by their relation to the great Governour of the Universe, or by their relation to mankind, but by climates, degrees of longitude, parallels not of life but of latitudes; as if, when you have crossed the equinoctial, all the virtues die, as they say some insects die when they cross the line; as if there were a kind of baptism, like that practised by seamen, by which they unbaptize themselves of all that they learned in Europe, and after which a new order and system of things commenced.

This geographical morality we do protest against. Mr. Hastings shall not screen himself under it; and on this point I hope and trust many words will not be necessary to satisfy your Lordships. But we think it necessary, in justification of ourselves, to declare, that the laws of morality are the same every where; and that there is no action, which would pass for an act of extortion, of peculation, of bribery, and of oppression in England, that is not an act of extortion, of peculation, of bribery, and oppression in Europe, Asia, Africa, and all the world over. This I contend for, not in the technical forms of it, but I contend for it in the substance.

7 May 1789

YOU now see some of the means, by which fortunes have been made, by certain persons in India; you see the confederacies they have formed with one another for their mutual concealment and mutual support; you will see how they reply to their own deceitful inquiries by fraudulent answers; you will see that Cheltenham calls upon Calcutta, as one deep calls upon another; and that the call, which is made for explanation, is answered in mystery: in short, you will see how the very constitution of their minds here developed.

And, now my Lords, in what a situation are we all placed? This prosecution of the Commons (I wish to have it understood, and I am sure I shall not be disclaimed in it) is a prosecution not only for the punishing a delinquent, a prosecution not merely for preventing this and that offence, but it is a great censorial prosecution, for the purpose of preserving the manners, characters, and virtues, that characterize the people of England. The situation in which we stand is dreadful. These people pour in upon us every day. They not only bring with them the wealth, which they have acquired, but they bring with them into our country the vices by which it was acquired. Formerly the people of England were censured, and, perhaps properly, with being a sullen, unsocial, cold, unpleasant race of men: and as inconstant as the climate in which they are born. These are the vices, which the enemies of the kingdom charged them with, and people are seldom charged with vices, of which they do not in some measure partake. But nobody refused them the character of being an open-hearted, candid, liberal, plain, sincere people; qualities, which would cancel a thousand faults, if they had them.

But if, by conniving at these frauds, you once teach the

56

people of England a concealing, narrow, suspicious, guarded conduct: if you teach them qualities directly the contrary to those by which they have hitherto been distinguished: if you make them a nation of concealers, a nation of dissemblers, a nation of liars, a nation of forgers; my Lords, if you, in one word, turn them into a people of *Banyans*, the character of England, that character, which more than our arms and more than our commerce has made us a great nation, the character of England will be gone and lost.

Our liberty is as much in danger as our honour and our national character. We, who here appear representing the Commons of England, are not wild enough not to tremble, both for ourselves and for our constituents, at the effect of riches: *"Opum metuenda potestas."* We dread the operation of money. Do we not know that there are many men who wait, and who indeed hardly wait, the event of this prosecution to let loose all the corrupt wealth of India, acquired by the oppression of that country, for the corruption of all the liberties of this: and to fill the Parliament with men, who are now the object of its indignation?—To-day, the Commons of Great Britain prosecute the delinquents of India.— To-morrow the delinquents of India may be the Commons of Great Britain. We know, I say, and feel the force of money; and we now call upon your Lordships for justice in this Cause of money. We call upon you for the preservation of our manners—of our virtues. We call upon you for our national character. We call upon you for our liberties; and hope that the freedom of the Commons will be preserved by the justice of the Lords.

Ibid., Vol. XIII, pp. 154–6, Vol. XIV, pp. 275–8.

Part II

BUILDERS OF THE SECOND EMPIRE

6: WARREN HASTINGS. Enclosure in a letter to Alexander Elliott

Fort William, Calcutta, 10 February 1777

THE dominion exercised by the British Empire in India is fraught with many radical and incurable defects, besides those to which all human institutions are liable, arising from the distance of its scene of operations, the impossibility of furnishing it at all times with those aids which it requires from home, and the difficulty of reconciling its primary exigencies with those which in all States ought to take place of every other concern, the interests of the people who are subjected to its authority. All that the wisest institutions can effect in such a system can only be to improve the advantages of a temporary possession, and to protract that decay, which sooner or later must end it.

Gleig, *Memoirs of Warren Hastings*, Vol. II, pp. 149–150.

7: JOHN GRAVES SIMCOE. Letter to Sir Joseph Banks

8 January 1791

The interest of this letter lies partly in its being from a father of one colony to the father of another. Simcoe had served in the American War of Independence, being invalided out in 1781 with the rank of colonel. Ten years later, after a year in Parliament, he was appointed first Lieutenant-Governor of Upper Canada where he illustrated by his practice and expression the 'assimilation' theories of the time.

I AM one of those who know all the consequences of our

late American dominions, and do not attempt to hide from myself the impending calamity in case of future war, because neither in council nor in the field did I contribute to their dismemberment. I would die by more than Indian torture to restore my King and his family to their just inheritance and to give my country that fair and natural accession of power which an union with their brethren could not fail to bestow and render permanent. Though a soldier, it is not by arms that I hope for this result; it is *volentes in populos* only, that such a renewal of empire can be desirable to His Majesty—and I think even now, (though I hold that the last supine five years and every hour that the Government is deferred detracts from our fair hopes) even now, this event may take place.

I mean to prepare for whatever convulsions may happen in the United States; and the method I propose is by establishing a free, honourable British Government, and a pure administration of its laws, which shall hold out to the solitary emigrant, and to the several states, advantages that the present form of government doth not and cannot permit them to enjoy. There are inherent defects in the congressional form of Government, the absolute prohibition of any order of nobility is a glaring one. The true New England Americans have as strong an aristocratical spirit as is to be found in Great Britain; nor are they anti-monarchical. I hope to have a hereditary council with some mark of nobility. . . .

Now, sir, not to trespass on your time, you will see how highly important it will be, that this colony, (which I mean to show forth with all the advantages of British protection as a better Government than the United States can possibly obtain) should in its very foundations provide for every assistance that can possibly be procured for the arts and sciences, and for every embellishment that hereafter may decorate and attract notice, and may point it out to the neighbouring States as a superior, more happy, and more polished form of Government. I would not in its infancy have a hut, nor in its maturity, a palace built without this design.

My friend, the Marquis of Buckingham, has suggested that Government ought to allow me a sum of money to be laid out for a Public library, to be composed of such books as might be useful to the colony. He instanced the encyclopaedia, extracts from which might occasionally be published in the newspapers. It is possible private donations might be obtained, and that it would become an object of Royal munificence.

If any botanical arrangement could take place, I conceive it might be highly useful, and might lead to the introduction of some commodities in that country which Great Britain now procures from other nations. Hemp and flax should be encouraged by Romulus. In the literary way I should be glad to lay the foundation stone of some society that I trust might hereafter conduce to the extension of science. Schools have been shamefully neglected—a college of a higher class would be eminently useful, and would give a tone of principles and of manners that would be of infinite support to Government.

Printed by Dr. H. Scadding (Toronto, 1890).

8: RICHARD, MARQUESS WELLESLEY.
Despatch to the Court of Directors of the East India Company

Fort William, Calcutta, 9 July 1800

The Governor-Generalship of Wellesley (1798–1805) was decisive in the extension of British power in India. His defeat of Tipu of

Mysore (1799) and the treaty of Bassein with the Mahrattas (1802) marked the necessity, as his young officers saw it, of going forward to the natural frontiers of India—disapproval at home led to Wellesley's recall but could only check the forward policy, drawn on by the anarchy of Central India.

WE feel that it would not only be impolitic, but highly immoral to suppose that Providence has admitted of the establishment of the British power over the finest provinces of India, with any other view than that of its being conducive to the happiness of the people, as well as to our national advantage.

In proportion as the policy and conduct of the British Government shall correspond with these beneficent intentions, we are persuaded that its power will acquire increasing stability.

Impressed with a deep sense of the justice and wisdom of these principles, we are confident that it will always be equally for the interests of the Company, and of the British nation, that they should constitute the basis of the system of our Indian Government; and that consistently with the considerations of a well regulated economy, we ought never to withhold that portion of the resources derived from these valuable possessions, which may be found indispensably necessary for dispensing to them the invaluable blessings of civil order and good government.

S. J. Owen, *A Selection from Wellesley's Despatches*, p. 687.

9: WILLIAM COBBETT. *Political Register*

16 April 1808

The builders of the Empire, in common with others of the class of " tax-eaters ", were constantly attacked by the Tory Radical,

Cobbett. He served in the army in Canada (for his opinions of which *vide* No. 18), and then emigrated to the United States where he wrote in defence of British policy. On return to England in 1800 he was welcomed by the Government but from about 1804 began to voice Radical opinions.

THE recent intelligence from India, or, " our Empire in the East," is of a gloomy complexion, in my sight, only inasmuch as it gives an account of the loss of a great number of English officers and soldiers. It may serve to make men reflect justly on the nature of the wars we carry on in India ; and may lead them to the conclusion, so much to be desired, namely, that the possession of that country is a terrible evil. This, it seems, is to be *the last* war ; but, we have been told the same thing for more than thirty years past. There is a constant, never-ceasing war in India. There is not always actual fighting ; but, there are always going on preparations for fighting ; What right, in God's name, what right have we to do this ? How is it possible for us to justify our conduct, upon any principle of morality ? Conquests in India are not at all necessary either to our safety or our comfort. There is no glory attending such conquests and their accompanying butcheries. We must be actuated by a shere love of gain ; a shere love of plunder. I really believe, that the history of the whole world does not afford an instance of a series of aggressions so completely unjustifiable and inexcusable.

Printed in *The Opinions of William Cobbett* (ed. G. D. H. and M. Cole, 1944), p. 258.

10 : THOMAS STAMFORD RAFFLES. Despatch to Lord Minto

Malacca, 10 June 1811

Minto from his appointment as Governor-General of India in

1807 had been planning to eliminate French influence in the Indian Ocean. The capture of Java was an essential part of the strategy. Raffles had been sent as " Agent to the Governor-General with the Malay States," to prepare the expedition at Malacca; on the conquest of Java be became its Governor. This is an extract from his report to Minto, the day before the first division of the transports sailed for Java. Raffles's hopes of a more permanent establishment in the island were dashed at the peace settlement when it was handed back to the Dutch. He was knighted by the Prince Regent in 1816, returning to the East to become the founder of the modern Singapore.

THE benefits which the Malay nations may derive from a close connexion with the British government and nation, are such as there is no probability of their ever deriving from the French or Dutch.

The doctrine that a colony should always be considered as a distant province of the mother country could never have been received by the Dutch, and the radical want of strength in the government of Batavia must always have prevented them from venturing to act upon it. Of course they must always have contemplated the prosperity of the eastern tribes with the invidious regret of a rival shopkeeper, and regarded their progress in civilization with the jealousy of a timorous despot, which in point of fact we know they actually did. The power of the English in the East enables them to employ a less timid policy; humanity imperiously requires that they should employ it, and fortunately their own interest coincides with these as an additional inducement. . . .

The propagation of Christianity among these islands is obviously liable to none of the objections which have been urged against it in our Indian possessions. A great proportion of the natives are still Pagans, under the influence of a wild, and almost unintelligible superstition, the principles of which are not recorded in books, but are handed down like stories of ghosts, fairies, and witches, with all the uncertainty of tradition. . . .

In these observations I have in some degree avoided alluding to the advantages which may be expected to accrue to the British nation itself, and also to the British possessions in India, from the acquisition of Java and the Eastern Isles, because I am persuaded that the real advantages which these countries possess will be found, under a liberal and enlightened system of management, vastly to exceed any expectations which may be formed in the present state of our information concerning them. In their present state, with the exception of Java, these countries are poor in respect of general wealth, and can only pay in rude produce for the articles which they require from other countries. The rude produce, however, of the Malay countries is of various kinds, some of which are extremely valuable, and equally calculated for the European, the Indian, and the China market. The intercourse between countries rich in manufacturing industry and countries rich in raw produce is universally admitted to be of equal benefit to both. 'In respect of the Malay islands, India must long be regarded as a manufacturing country, and is particularly fitted to supply a variety of articles in general request among the Malays, without interfering with the industry of the mother country. . . .

I have now only to congratulate your Lordship on the most splendid prospect which any administration has beheld since our first acquisition of India : the pacification of India completed, the tranquillity and prosperity of our eastern possessions secured, the total expulsion of the European enemy from the Eastern Seas, and the justice, humanity, and moderation of the British government, as much exemplified in fostering and leading on new races of subjects and allies in the career of improvement, as the undaunted courage and resolution of British soldiers in rescuing them from oppression.

Printed in *Memoir of Sir Stamford Raffles* (1830), pp. 76–7, 82, 83, 85.

11 : SIR THOMAS MUNRO. Minute on the Employment of Natives in the Public Service

31 December 1824

Sir Thomas Munro became Governor of Madras in 1820 after a distinguished military career in the Indian Army. He was one of an eminent group which carried out the reconstruction after the preceding wars: their names, Malcolm in Central India, Elphinstone in the Deccan, Metcalfe, Tod and Ochterlony in Rajputana, were long household words in these areas. Of them all Munro's influence has perhaps been the most lasting. The extract is a good example of the insight of his minutes into the problems of the country.

THERE is one great question to which we should look in all our arrangements: What is to be their final result on the character of the people? Is it to be raised, or is it to be lowered? Are we to be satisfied with merely securing our power and protecting the inhabitants, leaving them to sink gradually in character lower than at present; or are we to endeavour to raise their character, and to render them worthy of filling higher situations in the management of their country, and of devising plans for its improvement? It ought undoubtedly to be our aim to raise the minds of the natives, and to take care that whenever our connection with India might cease, it did not appear that the only fruit of our dominion there, had been to leave the people more abject and less able to govern themselves than when we found them. Many different plans may be suggested for the improvement of their character, but none of them can be successful, unless it be first laid down as a main principle of our policy, that the improvement must be made. This principle once established, we must trust to time and perseverance for realizing the object of it. We have had too little experience, and are too little acquainted with the natives, to be able to determine without trial what means would be most likely to facilitate their improvement. Various measures might be suggested, which might all probably be more or less useful; but no one appears to me so well calculated to insure success as that of endeavouring to give them a higher opinion of themselves, by placing more confidence in them, by employing them in important situations, and perhaps by rendering them eligible to almost every office under Government. It is not necessary at present to define the exact limit to which their eligibility should be carried, but there seems to be no reason why they should be excluded from any office for which they were qualified, without danger to the preservation of our own ascendency.

Liberal treatment has always been found the most effectual way of alleviating the character of many people, and we may be sure that it will produce a similar effect on that of the people of India. The change will no doubt be slow; but that is the very reason why no time should be lost in commencing the work. We should not be discouraged by difficulties; nor, because little progress may be made in our own time, abandon the enterprise as hopeless, and charge upon the obstinacy and bigotry of the natives the failure which has been occasioned solely by our own fickleness, in not pursuing steadily the only line of conduct on which any hope of success could be reasonably founded. We should make the same allowances for the Hindus as for other nations, and consider how slow the progress of improvement has been among the nations of Europe, and through what a long course of barbarous ages they had to pass before they attained their present state. When we compare other countries with England, we usually speak of England as she is now —we scarcely ever think of going back beyond the Reformation; and we are apt to regard every foreign country as ignorant and uncivilized, whose state of government does not in some degree approximate to our own, even though it should be higher than our own was at no very distant period.

We should look upon India, not as a temporary possession, but as one which is to be maintained permanently, until the natives shall in some future age have abandoned most of their superstitions and prejudices, and become sufficiently enlightened to frame a regular government for themselves, and to conduct and preserve it. Whenever such a time shall arrive, it will probably be best for both countries that the British control over India should be gradually withdrawn. That the desirable change here contemplated may in some after age be effected in India, there is no cause to despair. Such a change was at one time in Britain itself at least as hopeless as it is here. When we reflect how much the character of nations has always been influenced by that of governments, and that some, once the most cultivated, have sunk into barbarism, while others, formerly the rudest, have attained the highest point of civilization, we shall see no reason to doubt that if we pursue steadily the proper measures, we shall in time so far improve the character of our Indian subjects as to enable them to govern and protect themselves.

Sir Thomas Munro, Selection from his Minutes (ed. Arbuthnot, 1881), Vol. II, pp. 326–7.

12: THOMAS BABINGTON MACAULAY. Speech on the Government of India

House of Commons, 10 July 1833

The East India Company's Charter was renewed at twenty-yearly intervals from 1773 to 1853, thereby providing debates often of first importance on the principles and policy of British rule in India. (The debates of 1813 and 1853 are illustrated in Nos. 20 and 42.) The Act of 1833 took from the Company its last trade—that to China—leaving it as a purely administrative body in India.

Macaulay has been included in this section as he was appointed first Law Member of the Governor-General's Council in the changes subsequent on this Act.

THERE is . . . one part of the Bill on which . . . I feel myself irresistibly impelled to say a few words. I allude to that wise, that benevolent, that noble clause, which enacts that no native of our Indian Empire shall, by reason of his colour, his descent, or his religion, be incapable of holding office. At the risk of being called by that nickname which is regarded as the most opprobrious of all nicknames, by men of selfish hearts and contracted minds—at the risk of being called a philosopher—I must say that, to the last day of my life, I shall be proud of having been one of those who assisted in the framing of the Bill which contains that clause. We are told that the time can never come when the natives of India can be admitted to high civil and military office. We are told that this is the condition on which we hold our power. We are told, that we are bound to confer on our subjects—every benefit which they are capable of enjoying?—no—which it is in our power to confer on them?—no—but which we can confer on them without hazard to our own domination. Against that proposition I solemnly protest as inconsistent alike with sound policy and sound morality.

I am far, very far, from wishing to proceed hastily in this most delicate matter. I feel that, for the good of India itself, the admission of natives to high office must be effected by slow degrees. But that, when the fulness of time is come, when the interest of India requires the change, we ought to refuse to make that change lest we should endanger our own power—this is a doctrine which I cannot think of without indignation. Governments, like men, may buy existence too dear. "Propter vitam vivendi perdere causas," is a despicable policy either in individuals or in states. In the present case, such a policy would be not only despicable, but absurd. The mere extent of empire is not necessarily an advantage. To many governments it has been cumbersome; to some it has been fatal. It will be allowed by every statesman of our time, that the prosperity of a community is made up of the prosperity of those who compose the community, and that it is the most childish ambition to covet dominion which adds to no man's comfort or security. To the great trading nation, to the great manufacturing nation, no progress which any portion of the human race can make in knowledge, in taste for the conveniences of life, or in the wealth by which those conveniences are produced, can be matter of indifference. It is scarcely possible to calculate the benefits which we might derive from the diffusion of European civilisation among the vast population of the East. It would be, on the most selfish view of the case, far better for us that the people of India were well governed and independent of us, than ill governed and subject to us—that they were ruled by their own kings, but wearing our broad cloth, and working with our cutlery, than that they were performing their salams to English collectors and English Magistrates, but were too ignorant to value, or too poor to buy, English manufactures. To trade with civilized men is infinitely more profitable than to govern savages. That would, indeed, be a doting wisdom, which, in order that India might remain a dependency, would make it. an useless and costly dependency—which would keep a hundred millions of men from being our customers in order that they might continue to be our slaves.

It was, as Bernier tells us, the practice of the miserable tyrants whom he found in India, when they dreaded the capacity and spirit of some distinguished subject, and yet could not venture to murder him, to administer to him a daily dose of the pousta, a preparation of opium, the effect of which was in a few months to destroy all the bodily and mental powers of the wretch who was drugged with it, and to turn him into an helpless idiot. That detestable artifice, more horrible than assassination itself, was worthy of those who employed it. It is no model for the English nation. We shall never consent to administer the pousta to a whole community—to stupify and paralyse a great people whom God has committed to our charge for the wretched purpose of rendering them more amenable to our control. What is that power worth which is founded on vice, on ignorance, and on misery—which we can hold only by violating the most sacred duties which as governors we owe to the governed —which as a people blessed with far more than an ordinary measure of political liberty and of intellectual light—we owe to a race debased by three thousand years of despotism and priestcraft? We are free, we are civilized, to little purpose, if we grudge to any portion of the human race an equal measure of freedom and civilization.

Are we to keep the people of India ignorant in order that we may keep them submissive? Or do we think that we can give them knowledge without awakening ambition? Or do we mean to awaken ambition and to provide it with no legitimate vent? Who will answer any of these questions in the affirmative? Yet one of them must be answered in the affirmative, by every person who maintains that we ought permanently to exclude the natives from high office. I have no fears. The path of duty is plain before us: and it is also the path of wisdom, of national prosperity, of national honour.

The destinies of our Indian empire are covered with thick darkness. It is difficult to form any conjecture as to the fate reserved for a state which resembles no other in history, and which forms by itself a separate class of political phenomena. The laws which regulate its growth and its decay are still unknown to us. It may be that the public mind of India may expand under our system till it has outgrown that system; that by good government we may educate our subjects into a capacity for better government, that, having become instructed in European knowledge, they may, in some future age, demand European institutions. Whether such a day will ever come I know not. But never will I attempt to avert or to retard it. Whenever it comes, it will be the proudest day in English history. To have found a great people sunk in the lowest depths of slavery and superstition, to have so ruled them as to have made them desirous and capable of all the privileges of citizens would indeed be a title to glory all our own. The sceptre may pass away from us. Unforeseen accidents may derange our most profound schemes of policy. Victory may be inconstant to our arms. But there are triumphs which are followed by no reverses. There is an empire exempt from all natural causes of decay. Those triumphs are the pacific triumphs of reason over barbarism; that empire is the imperishable empire of our arts and our morals, our literature and our laws.

Hansard, Third Series, Vol. XIX, cs. 534–6.

Part III

ECONOMISTS AND RADICALS

13: JEREMY BENTHAM. *Manual of Political Economy*

1798

From a hostility to empire which he displayed in addressing the French Convention in 1793 under the title " Emancipate your Colonies" Bentham gradually changed until in 1831 he drew up a scheme for Wakefield for the formation of a joint-stock colonization society.

LET us, however, see the consequences which we ought to draw from these data.

1. Ought we not to form any colonial establishment? Certainly not with the intention of enriching the mother-country: it is always a certain expense, for a contingent and far distant profit. But we have seen that, as a means of relieving the population—of preventing its excess, by providing a vent for those who find themselves over-burthened upon their native soil, colonization offers an advantageous resource; and when it is well conducted, and free from any regulations which may hinder its prosperity, there may result from it a new people, with whom we shall possess all the connexions of language, of social habits, of natural and political ties.

2. Ought colonies already possessed to be emancipated? Yes, certainly; if we only consider the saving of the expenses of their government, and the superior advantages of a free commerce. But it is necessary to examine what is due to colonial establishments—to a family which has been created, and which ought not to be abandoned. Can they maintain themselves? Will not

their internal tranquillity be interrupted? Will not one class of the inhabitants be sacrificed to another? for example, the free men to the slaves, or the slaves to the free men? Is it not necessary that they should be protected and directed, in their condition of comparative weakness and ignorance? Is not their present state of dependence their safeguard against anarchy, murder, and pillage? Such are the points of view under which this question ought to be considered.

When we shall have ceased to consider colonies with the greedy eyes of fiscality, the greater number of these inconveniences will cease of themselves. Let governments lay aside all false mercantile notions, and all jealousy of their subjects, and everything which renders their yoke burthensome will fall at once: there will no longer be any reason to fear hostile dispositions and wars for independence. If wisdom alone were listened to, the ordinary object of contention would be reversed—the mother-country would desire to see her children powerful, that they might become free, and the colonies would fear the loss of that tutelary authority which gave them internal tranquillity and security against external foes.

The Works of Jeremy Bentham (ed. Bowring, 1843), Vol. III, pp. 56–7.

14: HENRY PETER BROUGHAM. *An Inquiry into the Colonial Policy of the European Powers*

1803

While these are not the views that Brougham was later to expound on Colonies (cf. No. 25), these extracts are included to show how slight an influence Adam Smith could have on a young man who the previous year had been welcomed into the select band establishing the *Edinburgh Review*, the Whigs' most powerful journal. Mercantilism was not antiquated in 1803.

THE commerce which a country carries on with its colonies, is, in every respect, a home trade. The stock and the industry engaged in it, are employed for the purpose of circulating the surplus produce of the different parts of the same extensive empire, subject to one government, inhabited by the same people, and ruled, in general, by the same system of laws.

Every operation of this traffic replaces two capitals, the employment and distribution of which, puts in motion, and supports the labour of the different members of the same state. The trade of London, or Liverpool, with the countries round the Baltic and Mediterranean, replaces, indeed, two capitals; but one of these only is British:—the other puts in motion the industry of foreigners; of Spaniards, for example; or of Russians. The trade, on the other hand, which the same towns carry on with the British West Indies, replaces two capitals, both of which are British; and supports the industry of British subjects, in the same manner with the trade which those towns carry on between themselves, or with Edinburgh and Dublin.

In like manner, the profits of a colonial trade are all accumulated in the hands of the same people, and tend to enrich and aggrandize the same nation. The increasing wealth of Russia or Spain, can never benefit Great Britain, unless by the increasing demand for her produce which it may occasion. On the contrary, it may, and often is, turned against her wealth and power. The riches of the colonies have certainly the same tendency to widen the market for British produce, and can never injure the wealth or power of the mother country: on the contrary, such an aggrandizement of the colonies, is, in fact, an increase of the British empire, to whose general resources they will always be made to contri-

bute, like the contiguous districts, when they have sufficiently acquired the means.

The similarity of manners, of government, above all,
of language, offers many inducements to change of residence. With the bulk of mankind, the opening to capital,
industry, or talents, afforded by a foreign country, never
enters into the calculation; while the difference of
language presents an obstacle scarcely to be surmounted.
Even if the language is the same, the difference of
government is of vast importance to the views, more
especially of capitalists, and almost equally of men who
look forward to the acquisition of stock: and although
the security afforded may be equal, perhaps superior, to
what their own government holds out, the chance of a
rupture is a consideration of great weight with men who
mean only to change their abode, in order to revisit that
country to which their hearts cling. The possession, then,
of remote territories, understocked with capital and
hands, is the only thing which can secure to the popula-
lation of a country, those advantages derived from an
easy outlet, or prospect of outlet, to those persons who
may be ill provided for at home.

Now, the long voyage has another, and a very material
advantage. Whether the distant market be a home or a
foreign one; and whether it be more or less remote than
twice the distance of the other markets with the profits
of which we may compare its returns, it encourages a
breed of men essentially necessary to every member of
the European commonwealth, which would engage in an
extensive foreign traffic of any description whatever—I
mean, the breed of seamen. The coasting trade is, indeed,
an excellent nursery: but it is in no country sufficient to

form a navy, not even in Great Britain, however extensive her sea-coast, and her internal commerce may be. The commerce of the nearer countries in Europe, however enlarged, although the whole capital employed in the colonial trade were turned into it, would still be inadequate.

The larger size of the vessels employed in the distant trade, is also an advantage to the navy of the state. . . . The large merchantmen are always ready for being armed in war: some of them may be equipped as frigates, and a few of them even taken into the line. We may therefore rest assured, that the commerce with distant countries employs more seamen and vessels fit for the service of the state, in proportion to the tonnage, than the trade with countries less remote.

The colony trade has this very great advantage, in common with the coasting trade, that the sailors which it employs are seldom or never in a foreign port. They are, of consequence, much less exposed to the danger of deserting into foreign service; vacancies in their number are more easily, and better filled up, not by foreigners, but by other inhabitants of the same country; and they are always in some part of the empire, where their services may be needed for the military operations of the state. The seamen required for the navy, upon any emergency, cannot be procured from the vessels engaged in a trade that requires them to remain in a foreign country—in the Gulph of Finland, for example, or the Levant. In this case, government must wait for their return. But those employed in the colony trade are either in some port of the mother country, or of the colonies; on both of which stations their services may be required for the ships of war.

We are desired, with no small appearance of triumph, to view the history of the last century; and to mark the manifold wars which the balancing system produced; the various intrigues to which it gave rise; the destructive conquests of which it furnished the pretext; and the national catastrophes which it could not avert. But had it not been for the wholesome jealousy of rival neighbours, which modern politicians have learned to cherish, how many conquests and changes of dominion would have taken place, instead of wars, in which a few useless lives were lost, and some superfluous millions were squandered? How many fair portions of the globe might have been deluged in blood, instead of some hundreds of sailors fighting harmlessly on the barren plains of the ocean, and some thousands of soldiers carrying on a scientific, and regular, and quiet system of warfare, in countries set apart for the purpose, and resorted to as the *arena* where the disputes of nations may be determined?

Henry Peter Brougham, *An Inquiry into the Colonial Policy of the European Powers* (London, 1803), Vol. I, pp. 148–50, 166, 174–5, 180, 189, Vol. II pp. 197–8.

15: JAMES MILL. Article *Colony*

Supplement to the *Encyclopaedia Britannica*, 1824

Between 1816 and 1823 James Mill contributed a series of articles to the *Encyclopaedia Britannica* which were subsequently reprinted in an undated volume of *Essays*. Together they form a useful view of Utilitarian ideas. The importance of Bentham and Mill lies in their influence on the Colonial Reformers; " they have been the teachers of the teachers," as John Stuart Mill put it.

IF an assembly of ingenious men, in the character of legislators, had sitten down to devise a method of dealing with delinquents, which, while it had some appearance of securing society from the crimes of the detected individual, should be, to the greatest possible degree, devoid, both of the reality and even the appearance of any efficacy, by its example, of deterring other men from the pursuit of similar courses, they could not have devised any thing better calculated for that preposterous end than the colony of New South Wales. Nothing can operate where it does not exist. The men to be operated upon are in England; the example which should operate is in New South Wales. Much more might be said, but it is unnecessary. In the great majority of cases, a voyage to New South Wales has not even the appearance of a punishment. Men of that description have neither friends nor affections. They leave nobody or thing whom they like, and nobody who likes them. What is it to such men that they are for a while, or for ever, taken away from England, along, very frequently, with the only sort of persons with whom they have any connection, the companions of their debaucheries and of their crimes?

It never ought to be forgotten, that, in every country, there is " a Few ", and there is " a Many "; that in all countries in which the government is not very good, the interest of " the Few " prevails over the interest of " the Many ", and is promoted at their expence. " The Few " is the part that governs; ". the Many " the part that is governed. It is according to the interest of " the Few " that colonies should be cultivated. This, if it is true, accounts for the attachment which most of the countries, that is, of the governments of modern Europe, have displayed to colonies. In what way it is true, a short explanation will sufficiently disclose.

Sancho Panza, had a scheme for deriving advantage from the government of an island. He would sell the people for slaves, and put the money in his pocket. "The Few," in some countries, find in colonies, a thing which is very dear to them; they find, the one part of them, the precious matter with which to influence; the other, the precious matter with which *to be* influenced;—the one, the precious matter with which to make political dependents; the other, the precious matter with which they are made political dependents; — the one, the precious matter by which they augment their power; the other, the precious matter by which they augment their riches. Both portions of the "ruling Few", therefore, find their account in the possession of colonies. There is not one of the colonies but what augments the number of places. There are governorships and judgeships, and a long train of *et ceteras*; and above all, there is not one of them but what requires an additional number of troops, and an additional portion of navy,—that is of great importance. In every additional portion of army and navy, beside the glory of the thing, there are generalships, and colonelships, and captainships, and lieutenantships, and in the equipping and supplying of additional portions of army and navy, there are always gains, which may be thrown in the way of a friend. All this is enough to account for a very considerable quantity of affection maintained towards colonies. . . .

Of the proposition, that colonies are a grand source of wars, and of additional expence in wars; that expence, by which the ruling few always profit at the cost of the subject many; it is not probable that much of proof will be required.

With regard to additional expence, it can hardly appear to be less than self-evident. Whenever a war breaks out, additional troops, and an additional portion of navy, are always required for the protection of the

colonies. Even during peace, the colonies afford the pretext for a large portion of the peace establishment, as it
is called,—that is, a mass of warlike apparatus and
expence, which would be burdensome even in a season
of war. How much the cost amounts to, of a small additional portion, not to speak of a large additional portion,
of army and navy, Englishmen have had experience to
instruct them ; and how great the mischief which is done
by every particle of unnecessary expence, they are daily
becoming more and more capable of seeing and understanding.

That the colonies multiply exceedingly the causes and
pretexts of war, is matter of history; and might have
been foreseen, before reaping the fruits of bitter experience. Whatever brings you in contact with a greater
number of states, increases, in the same proportion, those
clashings of interest and pride out of which the pretexts for war are frequently created. It would exhibit a
result, which probably would surprise a good many
readers, if any body would examine all the wars which
have afflicted this country, from the time when she first
began to have colonies, and show how very great a proportion of them have grown out of colony disputes.

Supplement to 4th, 5th and 6th editions of the *Encyclopaedia
Britannica* (1824), pp. 263, 272–3.

16: WILLIAM HUSKISSON. Speech in the House of Commons

21 March 1825

Huskisson as President of the Board of Trade, 1823–7, continued
his predecessor's policy of freeing the restraints of the Navigation
Laws; his was a policy of Imperial Preference, not of Free Trade.
As James Stephen said, he brought " a dominant understanding "

to his time as Secretary of War and the Colonies, September 1827–May 1828. His attitude may be further studied in A. Brady, *William Huskisson and Liberal Reform.*

I CANNOT doubt, that without any other encouragement than freedom of trade, and a lenient administration, these [i.e. North American] Provinces will, henceforward, make the most rapid strides towards prosperity;— that connecting their prosperity with the liberal treatment of the Mother Country, they will neither look with envy at the growth of other States on the same Continent, nor wish for the dissolution of old, and the formation of new, political connexions. With a tariff of duties, accounted for to their own treasury, and moreover far lighter than those paid by their neighbours,—with a trade as free,—with their shipping in possession of greater privileges,—themselves in the enjoyment of the same civil rights,—they will not be easily moved to acts by which all these advantages may be placed in jeopardy or danger. Such a course is not in human nature. At any rate, let us, as the parent state, fulfil our duties with all proper kindness and liberality. This is true wisdom; affording us, on the one hand, the best chance of perpetuating a solid and useful connexion, and on the other, the best hope if (which God avert!) in the progress of human events, that connexion is ever to be dissolved, that the separation may not be embittered by acrimony and bloodshed; and the certain consolation that, however brought about, it will not have been hastened or provoked, by vexatious interference or oppressive pretensions on our part. In addition, therefore, to all the advantages which the prosperity of our North American Colonies must reflect upon our own prosperity, I consider that, by extending to them this participation of the

commercial facilities and privileges which we enjoy, we
shall unite the mutual interests, and draw closer the
bonds of harmony and good understanding, between us
and these valuable dependencies.

Huskisson, *Speeches* (1831 ed.), Vol. II, pp. 321–2.

17: WILLIAM HUSKISSON. Speech on moving
for a Select Committee on the Civil Government of
Canada

House of Commons, 2 May 1828

SIR, I should now have concluded all that I feel it necessary to state to the House on the present occasion, if I
had not witnessed in some quarters, and I may say in
some degree in this House, a disposition to think that all
enquiry and concern about Canada are unnecessary, and
that the public interest of this country would be best
consulted by our at once relinquishing all controul and
dominion over these possessions. Sir, it is very easy, but I
must say it is the proof of a very shallow mind, to lay
down a rule of this sort. In British America there are
nearly a million of our fellow-subjects, born like ourselves in allegiance to the Crown of this country, anxious
to remain in that allegiance,—fulfilling all the duties of
it, and having as good a right as ourselves to claim for
their persons and property the protection which is the
consequence of that allegiance. Is this country, without
necessity, without that right being challenged by any
one, to incur the indelible disgrace of withdrawing
that protection? In contemplating such a question, I will
not allow myself to say one word of the advantages,
naval, commercial, and political, which we derive from
our connexion with our colonies. But I may be allowed
to speak of the political character of the country—of

the moral impression throughout the world of such an abandonment as is here proposed. I may be allowed to say, that England cannot afford to be little. She must be what she is, or nothing. It is not Canada estimated in pounds, shillings, and pence—but the proudest trophies of British valour, but the character of British faith, but the honour of the British name, which we shall cast off, if upon such considerations as I have heard, we cast off Canada from our protection. We cannot part with our dominions there, without doing an injustice to their fidelity and tried attachment, and tarnishing the national honour. We are not, Sir, at liberty to forego the high and important duties imposed on us by our relative situation towards those colonies. It is a country where no distinctions prevail, such as disturb some of our other territorial possessions abroad. There are no distinctions of castes, no slavery, which tend to engender dissention and disaffection. We have every where displayed marks of a paternal government, and planted improvement, not only on our colonies there, but wherever our empire is acknowledged.

Sir, England is the parent of many flourishing colonies —one of them is become an empire among the most powerful in the world. In every quarter of the globe we have planted the seeds of freedom, civilization, and Christianity. To every quarter of the globe we have carried the language, the free institutions, the system of laws, which prevail in this country;—in every quarter they are fructifying and making progress; and if it be said by some selfish calculator, that we have done all this at the expense of sacrifices which we ought not to have made, my answer is,—in spite of these sacrifices, we are still the first and happiest people in the old world; and, whilst this is our lot, let us rejoice rather

in that rich harvest of glory, which must belong to a
nation that has laid the foundation of similar happiness
and prosperity to other nations, kindred in blood, in
habits, and in feelings to ourselves.
Ibid., Vol. III, pp. 286–7.

18: WILLIAM COBBETT. *Rural Rides*

19 April 1830

THERE is at Hull one farmer going who is seventy years
of age; but who takes out five sons and fifteen hundred
pounds! Brave and sensible old man! and good and
affectionate father! He is performing a truly parental
and sacred duty; and he will die with the blessing of his
sons on his head, for having rescued them from this scene
of slavery, misery, cruelty, and crime. Come, then,
Wilmot Horton, with your sensible associates, Burdett
and Poulett Thomson; come into Lincolnshire, Nor-
folk, and Yorkshire; come and bring Parson Malthus
along with you; regale your sight with this delightful
" stream of emigration "; congratulate the " greatest
captain of the age," and your brethren of the Collective: congratulate the " noblest assembly of free men,"
on these the happy effects of their measures. Oh! no,
Wilmot! Oh! no, generous and sensible Burdett, it is not
the aged, the infirm, the halt, the blind, and the idiots
that go: it is the youth, the strength, the wealth, and the
spirit that will no longer brook hunger and thirst, in order
that the maws of the tax-eaters and Jews may be
crammed. You want the Irish to go, and so they will *at
our expense,* and all the bad of them, to be kept at our
expense on the rocks and swamps of Nova Scotia and
Canada. You have no money to send them away with:
the tax-eaters want it all; and thanks to the "improvements of the age," the steam-boats will continue to bring

THE CONCEPT OF EMPIRE

them in shoals in pursuit of the orts of the food that their task-masters have taken away from them. . . .

From the Thames, and from the several ports down the Channel, about two thousand have gone this spring. All the flower of the labourers of the east of Sussex and west of Kent will be culled out and sent off in a short time. From Glasgow the sensible Scotch are pouring out amain. Those that are poor and cannot pay their passages, or can rake together only a trifle, are going to a rascally heap of sand and rock and swamp, called Prince Edward's Island, in the horrible Gulf of St. Lawrence; but when the American vessels come over with Indian corn and flour and pork and beef and poultry and eggs and butter and cabbages and green pease and asparagus for the soldier-officers and other tax-eaters that we support upon that lump of worthlessness; for the lump itself bears nothing but potatoes; when these vessels come, which they are continually doing, winter and summer; towards the fall, with apples and pears and melons and cucumbers; and, in short, everlastingly coming and taking away the amount of taxes raised in England; when these vessels return, the sensible Scotch will go back in them for a dollar a head, till at last not a man of them will be left but the bed-ridden. Those villainous colonies are held for no earthly purpose but that of furnishing a pretence of giving money to the relations and dependents of the aristocracy; and they are the nicest channels in the world through which to send English taxes to enrich and strengthen the United States. Withdraw the English taxes, and, except in a small part in Canada, the whole of those horrible regions would be left to the bears and the savages in the course of a year.

W. Cobbett, *Rural Rides* (Everyman edition 1941), Vol. II, pp. 258–9.

19: RICHARD WHATELY. *Remarks on Transportation and on a recent defence of the system; in a second letter to Earl Grey*

1834

Before his elevation to the Archbishopric of Dublin in 1831 Whately had been for two years Drummond Professor of Political Economy at Oxford. In churchmanship an anti-Evangelical, his ideas on transportation spring more from the economic side of his thought, paralleling in many of his arguments Bentham and James Mill.

THE settlers accordingly, and others connected with the Colony, led by a sort of patriotic feeling for that Colony, to plead the cause of what they consider its good, (which, if it were real, ought not to demand the sacrifice of *our* good) are perpetually losing sight of that which is, naturally, a very subordinate object at least to them, though to us it ought to be primary,—the efficacy of Transportation in the diminution of crime, *here*. They feel called on indeed to say something from time to time, in its defence in that point of view; shifting their ground backwards and forwards, between the *reformation* of criminals and the *prevention* of offences; but it is evidently the prosperity of the *Colony* that really occupies the chief part of their attention. One out of many indications of this, is their strong and often repeated disparagement of the judgment of all who have not *been on the spot*. We, it seems, cannot possibly be acquainted with the details of the system:—we are destitute of experience:—our knowledge must be imperfect and inaccurate:—in short, we ought to have no voice in the question.

Now admitting all this;—which would be admitting far too much; since I have stated nothing but on the evidence of those who have been there, confirmed by the admissions of the advocates themselves;—but admitting all this local ignorance, it is evident that the whole argument proceeds on the supposition, that the *Colony is the only thing* to be attended to. The settlers, we will suppose, must know best what benefits the Colony; but they cannot surely be the sole judges as to what are the secondary punishments that operate best for this country.

One of the writers before me recommends Transportation, not on the ground of what it has hitherto been, but of what it may *hereafter* become, under the operation of some new regulation. The others also recommend it, deprecating these very regulations, and reverting to what it *has* been, but is likely to be no longer. Neither party seems to speak in the present tense, but the one in the past and the other in the future. But supposing these advocates were agreed in their views, as much as they manifestly disagree, still, *we* also should be allowed to form our own judgments on the system, as far as relates to *this* country. It is only by making the Colony the primary, and indeed sole object, that they can maintain their *exclusive* claim to *practical knowledge* and experience.

When the advantages of any foreign commerce, that to China for instance—are discussed, British manufacturers and tradesmen are accustomed to speak of their experience respecting the demand in England for Chinese commodities, and the demand for ours as exports to China. Now would it not be strange for any one to put them all to silence, by saying, " You can know nothing about the matter, because you have never been in China?" They would answer, " The residents in China may be the best judges of the benefit of the trade to *that* country, but *we* must surely know something of its effects at home: and, to the British nation, *this* is the important point."

So in the present case also, it is the effect of Transportation, here, as a mode of secondary punishment, that is confessedly the important consideration.

Remarks on Transportation (1834), pp. 93–6.

Part IV

THE EVANGELICALS

20: WILLIAM WILBERFORCE. Speech on the East India Company's Charter Bill

House of Commons, 1 July 1813

After his success in ending the slave trade (1807) Wilberforce's second Parliamentary campaign was for Christian influence upon India. Evangelical pressure led to the provision in this Act that the Government of India was to make a grant of not less than £10,000 for education; that missionaries were to be admitted under licence. The declaration of the Act, "it is the duty of this country to promote the interests and happiness of the native inhabitants of India," owes something to the same influence but the other expressions of the period should not be overlooked (cf. Wellesley in No. 8).

I FRANKLY acknowledge that I have long thought that we hold our East Indian possessions by a very precarious tenure. This is a topic on which it would be painful to expatiate, and perhaps imprudent to be particular; but the most cursory survey of the circumstances of our East Indian empire must be sufficient, in the minds of all who are ever so little read in the page of history, to justify the suspicion which I now intimate.

On the most superficial view, what a sight does that empire exhibit to us! A little island obtaining and keeping possession of immense regions, and of a population of sixty millions that inhabit them, at the distance of half the globe from it! of inhabitants differing from us as widely as human differences can go! differences exterior and interior—differences physical, moral, social and domestic—in points of religion, morals, institutions, language, manners, customs, climate, colour, in short in almost every possible particular that human experience can suggest, or human imagination devise! Such, Sir, is the partnership which we have formed; such rather the body with which we are incorporated, nay, almost assimilated and identified. Our oriental empire indeed is now a vast edifice; but the lofty and spacious fabric rests on the surface of the earth, without foundations. The trunk of the tree is of prodigious dimensions; and there is an exterior of gigantic strength. It has spread its branches widely around it, and there is an increasing abundance of foliage and of fruit; but the mighty mass rests on the ground merely by its superincumbent weight, instead of having shot its roots into the soil, and incorporated itself with the parent earth beneath it. Who does not know that the first great storm probably would lay such a giant prostrate?

This, Sir, I fear, is but too just a representation of the state of our East Indian empire. ... In truth, Sir, are we at this time of day still to be taught that most important lesson, that no government can be really secure which does not rest on the affections of the governed; or at least on their persuasion that its maintenance and preservation are in some degree connected with their own well-being? And did we want the papers on the table to inform us, as, however, in more than one place, they do inform us, that, notwithstanding the vast improvements we have introduced among the people of India, and the equity and humanity with which our government is administered, the native population is not attached to us? It might easily be shewn also, that many of the peculiar institutions of India, more especially that of its castes, greatly favours the transference of dominion from one conqueror to another. Then, the situation and neighbourhood of India! Regions which have been again and again the prey of those vast Tartar hordes which at different times have descended like some mountain torrent, and have swept all before them with resistless fury! Sir, would we render ourselves really secure against all such attacks, as well as against any, less perhaps to be dreaded, which our great European enemy may make upon us in that quarter, let us endeavour to strike our roots into the soil, by the gradual introduction and establishment of our own principles and opinions; of our own laws, institutions, and manners; above all, as the source of every other improvement, of our religion, and consequently of our morals. Why, Sir, if it were only that we should thereby render the subjects of our Asiatic empire a distinct and peculiar people; that we should create a sort of moral and political basis in the vast expanse of the Asiatic regions, and amidst the unnumbered myriads of its population, by this change we should render our East Indian dominions more secure, merely from the natural desire which men feel to preserve their own institutions, solely because they are their own, from invaders who would destroy them. But far more than this;—are we so little aware of the vast superiority even of European laws and institutions, and far more of British laws and institutions, over those of Asia, as not to be prepared to predict with confidence, that the Indian community which should have exchanged its dark and bloody superstitions for the genial influence of Christian light and truth, would have experienced such an increase of civil order and security; of social pleasures and domestic comforts, as to be desirous of preserving the blessings it should have acquired; and can we doubt that it would be bound even by the ties of gratitude to those who had been the honoured instruments of communicating them?

21: WILLIAM WILBERFORCE. *An Appeal to the Religion, Justice, and Humanity of the Inhabitants of the British Empire, In behalf of the Negro Slaves in the West Indies*

1823

AND now, without a further or more particular delineation of the slavery of the British colonies, what a system do we behold!! Is it too much to affirm, that there never was, certainly never before in a Christian country, a mass of such aggravated enormities?

That such a system should so long have been suffered to exist in any part of the British Empire will appear, to our posterity, almost incredible. It had, indeed, been less surprising, if its seat had been in regions, like those of Hindostan, for instance, where a vast population had come into our hands in all the full-blown enormity of heathen institutions; where the bloody superstitions, and the unnatural cruelties and immoralities of paganism, had established themselves in entire authority, and had produced their natural effects in the depravity and moral degradation of the species; though even in such a case as that, our excuse would hold good no longer than for the period which might be necessary for reforming the native abuses by those mild and reasonable means which alone are acknowledged to be just in principle, or practically effectual to their purpose. But that in communities formed from their very origin by a Christian people, and in colonies containing no Pagan inhabitants but those whom we ourselves have compulsorily brought into it,—inhabitants, too, who, from all the circumstances of their case, had the strongest possible claims on us, both for the reparation of their wrongs, and the relief of their miseries,—such a system should have been continued for two centuries, and by people who may, nevertheless, I trust, be affirmed to be the most moral and humane of nations, is one of those anomalies which, if it does not stagger the belief, will, at least, excite the astonishment of future ages.

William Wilberforce, *An Appeal* . . . (1823), pp. 32–3.

22: REPORT OF THE PARLIAMENTARY SELECT COMMITTEE ON ABORIGINES (BRITISH SETTLEMENTS)

1837

This report was very largely the work of Buxton, (q.v. No. 24), in the obtaining of the Committee, its Chairmanship, and the actual writing of the Report. Included among the members of the Committee was Gladstone.

GREAT BRITAIN has, in former times, countenanced evils of great magnitude,—slavery and the slave-trade; but for these she has made some atonement; for the latter, by abandoning the traffic; for the former, by the sacrifice of 20 millions of money. But for these offences there was this apology; they were evils of an ancient date, a kind of prescription might be pleaded for them, and great interests were entwined with them.

An evil remains very similar in character, and not altogether unfit to be compared with them in the amount of misery it produces. The oppression of the natives of barbarous countries is a practice which pleads no claim to indulgence; it is an evil of chiefly recent origin, imperceptible and unallowed in its growth; it never has had even the colour of sanction from the legislature of this country; no vested rights are associated with it, and we have not the poor excuse that it contributes to any interest of the state. On the contrary, in point of economy, of security, of commerce, of reputation, it is a short-sighted and disastrous policy. As far as it has prevailed, it has been a burthen on the empire. It has thrown impediments in the way of successful colonization ; it has engendered wars, in which great expenses were necessarily incurred, and no reputation could be won ; and it has banished from our confines, or exterminated, the natives, who might have been profitable workmen, good customers, and good neighbours. These unhappy results have not flowed from any determination on the part of the government of this country to deal hardly with those who are in a less advanced state of society ; but they seem to have arisen from ignorance, from the difficulty which distance interposes in checking the cupidity and punishing the crimes of that adventurous class of Europeans who lead the way in penetrating the territory of uncivilized man, and from the system of dealing with the rights of the natives. Many reasons unite for apprehending that the evils which we have described will increase if the duty of coming to a solemn determination as to the policy we shall adopt towards ruder nations be now neglected ; the chief of these reasons is, the national necessity of finding some outlet for the superabundant population of Great Britain and Ireland. It is to be feared that, in the pursuit of this benevolent and laudable object, the rights of those who have not the means of advocating their interests or exciting sympathy for their sufferings, may be disregarded.

This, then, appears to be the moment for the nation to declare, that with all its desire to give encouragement to emigration, and to find a soil to which our surplus population may retreat, it will tolerate no scheme which implies violence or fraud in taking possession of such a

territory; that it will no longer subject itself to the guilt
of conniving at oppression, and that it will take upon
itself the task of defending those who are too weak and
too ignorant to defend themselves.

Your Committee have hitherto relied chiefly on arguments, showing that no national interest, even in its
narrowest sense, is subserved by encroachments on the
territory or disregard of the rights of the aboriginal
inhabitants of barbarous countries; but they feel it their
duty to add, that there is a class of motives of a higher
order which conduce to the same conclusion.

The British empire has been signally blessed by
Providence; and her eminence, her strength, her wealth,
her prosperity, her intellectual, her moral and her
religious advantages, are so many reasons for peculiar
obedience to the laws of Him who guides the destiny of
nations. These were given for some higher purpose than
commercial prosperity and military renown. " It is not
to be doubted that this country has been invested with
wealth and power, with arts and knowledge, with the
sway of distant lands, and the mastery of the restless
waters, for some great and important purpose in the
government of the world. Can we suppose otherwise
than that it is our office to carry civilization and
humanity, peace and good government, and, above all,
the knowledge of the true God, to the uttermost ends of
the earth?"[1] He who has made Great Britain what she is,
will inquire at our hands how we have employed the
influence He has lent to us in our dealings with the
untutored and defenceless savage; whether it has been
engaged in seizing their lands, warring upon their people,
and transplanting unknown disease, and deeper degrada-

[1] Rev. Mr. Whewell's Sermon before the Trinity Board (note in the report).

tion, through the remote regions of the earth; or whether
we have, as far as we have been able, informed their
ignorance, and invited and afforded them the opportunity of becoming partakers of that civilization, that
innocent commerce, that knowledge and that faith with
which it has pleased a gracious Providence to bless our
own country.

Reports from Committees, Vol. VII (1837), pp. 75–6.

23 : Letters to Lord Glenelg, Secretary of State for the Colonies, on the New Zealand Association

1837

The duel of pamphlets in 1837 over the New Zealand Association is one action in the constant battle in Imperial history
between settlers and native interests, showing the pressures
brought on the home government. Wakefield (q.v. No. 26), had
formed the Association to forward his plans of systematic
colonisation in New Zealand, where the Church Missionary
Society had been active since 1814. Dandeson Coates was their
lay secretary (1830–46) and powerful organiser. In Glenelg he
was addressing a member of the Society's committee. It was
the Colonial Office's failure to act that provoked Molesworth's
motion of censure on Glenelg (No. 27).

DANDESON COATES

IT is too high wrought, too Utopian, to believe that a mis-
cellaneous body of men will expatriate themselves, to a
savage land at the antipodes, merely out of a benevolent
regard to the civilization and moral improvement of the
Natives. This point must be made unequivocally clear;
for distrust of the real motives of the whole scheme cannot be excluded from the minds of impartial by-
standers. . . .

Knowing, as I do know, that it is not without difficulty
that the Missionaries have been able, on some occasions,

to obtain a sufficiency of land for their objects, the peculiar character of which were well understood by the Natives, I hold it to be in the highest degree improbable that tracts of sufficient extent and entireness could be acquired by the Association for their Settlements; and I have the strongest persuasion, that a " cession of sovereignty " will not be voluntarily made by the Chiefs of New Zealand. It is a fact, fully established by the intercourse of the Missionaries with the Natives, that extreme jealousy is entertained by them of being deprived of their independence and sovereignty, by their intercourse with White People. They are fully aware of the effects of Colonization in New South Wales upon the Aborigines of that country; and point to the fact, as a justification of their own distrust and anxiety on this subject. Let, therefore, the Association make the Natives clearly understand, that they surrender their sovereignty over the portions of territory ceded for the location of the Settlements—and this they are bound to do, on the principle laid down by themselves, that " it is unjust and cruel to lead savage or semi-barbarous men into engagements which they do not perfectly comprehend "[1]—and a stop must inevitably be put, *in limine,* to this Utopian scheme.

But, I ask, is it practicable to put savage or semi-barbarous men fully in possession of the consequences of such a transfer of their lands to the Association, as that contemplated? The very state of barbarism in which the Natives are found, would, I apprehend, render it quite impossible to make them fully comprehend the ultimate consequences to themselves of such an arrangement. The ignorance, too, of the Natives of the English language,

[1] Statement of the objects of the New Zealand Association (note in original).

and the rudeness and poverty of their own, would form very serious obstacles to their entering into so serious a bargain as that proposed by the Association, with a clear comprehension of its import.

The Mission of the Church Missionary Society has, under the blessing of Almighty God, risen to its present hopeful and promising state, not only without the intervention of coercive power, but, I very believe, because the Missionaries have had it not;—for it is the possession of coercive power on the part of Colonists which is the occasion of collision and bloodshed. Where this is possessed, it will most certainly, sooner or later, be used in furtherance of the interests or security of the possessor. The Missionary, on the other hand, has simply the religious and social good of the people in view; and for success rests, under God, on the substantial blessings which he has it in his power to impart, and on his own prudence, forbearance, and moderation, totally exclusive of human power. He, therefore, is in a state of constant dependence on the Chiefs; and can maintain his position, and advance his object, only by the influence which he acquires from his character and labours. . . .

Wherever the Missionary goes, even among strange Tribes, he is not only safe, but his presence is hailed with joy, as a harbinger of good; for HE is known to be A MAN OF PEACE. Throughout the whole course of the Society's operations in New Zealand, extending now through nearly a quarter of a century, no serious personal injury has been suffered by any single Missionary at the hands of the Natives. How is this remarkable difference, between Missionary intercourse with an uncivilized people, and that of Colonists, to be accounted for, if it be not found in the fundamentally and essen-

tially different principles on which they severally proceed; and on the possession of coercive power by the
Colonists, and the entire absence of it in the Missionaries?

Dandeson Coates, *The Principles, Objects, and Plan of the
New-Zealand Association Examined, in a letter to the Right Hon.
Lord Glenelg, Secretary of State for the Colonies* (1837), pp. 13,
16–7, 39–41.

EDWARD GIBBON WAKEFIELD
12 December 1837

THE British colonization that is going on in New Zealand,
is of the most disorderly, the most licentious kind. But is
it, on that account, less injurious to the natives? On the
contrary, it is more injurious. This appears to be the very
worst of all systems, or rather sorts of colonization. . . .

Even if not one more Englishman should emigrate to
New Zealand, either from England or the convict
colonies, yet, in the course of time, those islands would
be colonized by the rapidly-increasing offspring of
missionaries and other married settlers. But, unless
some law be passed to prevent it, more Englishmen will
settle in New Zealand. The missionaries have so far
humanized the natives as to render the country very
attractive to such British settlers as have no object but
gain. The natives have acquired numerous wants which
can no otherwise be supplied than by exchange with
Europeans; and they encourage Europeans to settle
amongst them, by readily selling their land, and flax, and
timber, and by labouring for wages in fishing, building,
agriculture, and the collection of spontaneous produce.
Every year sees an increase in the number of British
Settlers, possessed of capital, and engaging in production
and trade. Not less than four hundred vessels are sup-

posed to anchor in the harbours of New Zealand during a twelvemonth. The number of runaway-convicts and runaway-sailors is visibly increasing, and cannot but increase still further with the undisturbed residence of so many of that class of people in the islands. The agricultural and commercial advantages of New Zealand, and the improved temper of the natives towards foreigners, having been recently made public in England, long-forgotten schemes of private settlement have been revived; and there can be no doubt that unless Parliament interfere to forbid it, numbers will seek to share in the high profits of agriculture and trade, which, it has now been made plain, even by the success of missionaries in their secular pursuits, that fine country yields to well-directed enterprise. It were idle to suppose that Parliament will remove the actual British Colonists of New Zealand, or even forbid emigration to that country. New Zealand, therefore, must be colonized in one way or another. . . .

Something must be done. This will be admitted by everybody. The only question is,—What is best to be done? . . .

Surely, if there were an established authority in New Zealand, competent to stop lawless British colonization by convicts or other desperadoes; with a well-protected religious establishment, having at its head an able and zealous bishop; surely, in that case, the large expenditure of the Society would be far more productive. Nay, missionaries themselves, my lord, are not exempt from that law of fallible human-nature, which makes authority and subordination indispensable to an efficient performance of duty. When the New Zealand chiefs, Honghi and Wycato, begged for twenty English soldiers to protect their own countrymen the English settlers at the Bay

of Islands, they shrewdly added a wish for "three officers
to keep the soldiers in order." Those savages, as we call
them, would at once have perceived the utility of a
bishop,—of a sufficient spiritual authority on the spot—
for giving greater effect to the labours of the *Church*
missionaries. At present, (I say it with unaffected serious-
ness) Mr. Coates is the English bishop of New Zealand.
But neither a bishop, nor any other chief, can exercise
perfect control over subordinates at an immense distance; still less if he have many other duties to perform,
and other distant places to attend to. A bishop *on the
spot* would be all in all for the Church of England in
New Zealand.

E. G. Wakefield, *Mr. Dandeson Coates, and the New Zealand
Association; in a letter to the Right Hon. Lord Glenelg* (1837),
pp. 5, 7–8, 11–2, 24–5.

24: SIR THOMAS FOWELL BUXTON.
The African Slave Trade and its Remedy

1839

Buxton led the Evangelicals from 1823 in the struggle against
slavery. Such was his influence in the thirties that *The Times*
called it " the era of Sir Fowell Buxton ". The solution offered
here was the civilisation of Africa, " Christianity and Commerce ".
The immediate plans crashed in the fiasco of the Niger expedition
of 1841.

A NOBLER achievement now invites us. I believe that
Great Britain can, if she will, under the favour of the
Almighty, confer a blessing on the human race. It may
be that at her bidding a thousand nations now steeped in
wretchedness, in brutal ignorance, in devouring superstition, possessing but the one trade, and that one the
foulest evil that ever blighted public prosperity, or

poisoned domestic peace, shall, under British tuition, emerge from their debasement, enjoy a long line of blessings—education, agriculture, commerce, peace, industry, and the wealth that springs from it; and, far above all, shall willingly receive that religion which, while it confers innumerable temporal blessings, opens the way to an eternal futurity of happiness.

I have already confessed that I am not experienced or skilful in matters which touch the commercial part of the question. I tread this ground with diffidence. I say no more, than that it appears to me that the soil in Africa being rich, and the people being found upon it, it is not advisable to carry them to a distance. It is possible, however, that some fallacy, unsuspected by me, may lurk under my theory, if theory of mine it can be called; but when I come to humanity, justice, and the duties of Christian men, I stand upon a rock. It may be, or it may not, that while we act under the impulse of charity to the most afflicted of mankind, we are also obeying the dictates of the most far-sighted policy, and the most refined ambition. It may prove, or it may not, that while we are leading Africa to grow at home, cheaper sugar than Brazil, and cheaper cotton than the United States, we are renovating the very sinews of our national strength. Be this as it may, without doubt it is the duty of Great Britain to employ the influence and the strength which God has given her, in raising Africa from the dust, and enabling her, out of her own resources, to beat down Slavery and the Slave Trade.

The African Slave Trade and its Remedy (2nd ed. 1840), pp. 528–9.

PART V

THE CANADA DEBATES OF 1838

25: THE CANADA DEBATES OF 1838

The news of the rebellions in the Provinces of Upper and Lower Canada in the autumn of 1837 reached London as Parliament was adjourning for the Christmas recess. It re-assembled on 16 January 1838 to debate a bill " to make temporary provision for the government of Lower Canada ". The previous day Durham had agreed to Melbourne's request that he should go to Canada as Governor-General under the new Act with the powers of a virtual dictator. His Radical sympathies modified some of the Radical opposition to such a proposal but the debates illustrate the growth of the feeling that separation was inevitable. (For Lord John Russell see No. 46, Brougham, No. 14 and Molesworth, No. 27.)

House of Commons, 16 January 1838

LORD JOHN RUSSELL: Although, I repeat, that I am not prepared to give immediate independence, this I will say, that if the time were come at which such an important change might be safely and advantageously made, I should, by no means, be indisposed to give the 1,400,000 of our present fellow-subjects who are living in the provinces of North America a participation in the perfect freedom enjoyed by the mother country. If it were a fit time, if circumstances of all kinds were such as to render such an arrangement desirable, I think that our colonies might with propriety be severed from us, and formed into a separate and distinct state, in alliance, offensive and defensive, with this country. . . . Of this I am sure, that if things had arrived at the state which I have described, if the time for such a separation had arrived, (which I utterly deny) we should then have as allies men influenced by the most amiable and affectionate feelings towards the mother country; not men who would wish to see the British arms defeated, or who would entertain the aspiration that the power of Great Britain might sink into insignificance and contempt. On the contrary, I am convinced that we should find in them men who would cheer on the efforts of this great empire, who would reverence our character, and share our triumphs. Until such a time, however, shall arrive, until separation shall be the mutual interest of the British colonies and the British empire, we will not consent that these provinces shall lose British protection, in addition to the privileges which they enjoy in common with their fellow-subjects.

(c. 41)

SIR ROBERT PEEL: The main question before the House, however, was, if it was fitting that the House of Commons should assure Her Majesty of its cordial support in putting down this revolt; and he must say, that he never felt more sincerely that he was right than when, without passion, and after great deliberation, and not without a cautious forecast of all the probable consequences, he came to the conclusion of offering to the Crown his assurances of cordial support in attempting, at any hazard, to suppress this revolt. The hon. Gentleman who had last spoken [Grote], had suggested considerations which he admitted to be of great importance. He said, that the majority of the people of Canada were disaffected to the British Government, and he contended that therefore they ought to be released from their allegiance. The hon. Gentleman stated, that the more conciliatory the intentions of the colonial Government had been, the greater had been their failure, and the greater were the apprehensions that it would be

116

impossible to establish mutual goodwill and harmony in the relations between the colony and the parent state. He admitted the importance of these suggestions, but at the same time he must be permitted to ask, whether the principles which the hon. Gentleman had laid down, were to be applied to the whole empire. Let not the House forget, that we had an extended colonial empire, including India, including Europe. Let them not forget the extent to which this principle, if admitted, might be applied. Let it be laid down, then, as a principle, that the first expression of dissatisfaction with our Government, and the first instance of resistance to our authority, was to be a signal for abandoning our claim to superiority. To put the strongest case, suppose Canada were an island; could we say, that after possession of the colony for seventy years, gained by a series of brilliant conquests, and after we had at least intended to do justice, that we ought to relinquish our sovereignty, because it was dissatisfied with our Government? If we laid down that principle, could it be limited to colonies? Could it not be applied to integral parts of the empire? Why might it not be extended to a part of England, if that part expressed itself dissatisfied with the rule of England? The fact of dissatisfaction with our Government, as the hon. Gentleman contended, showed that the colony had been misgoverned, and then, he asked, what was the good of ruling over discontented subjects. Why, if we were to act on such a rule of public conduct, the glory of England would, in ten years, be utterly annihilated. The great influence which we possessed, owing to our vast colonial establishments, and the great power which we derived from our navy, which, as the noble Lord [Russell] had observed, was supported by our commercial marine, would soon pass away; and England, from the foremost rank among the nations of the earth, would descend to the situation of a subordinate and a fifth-rate power. Suppose that doctrine be applied to an island not connected with the British empire, would it even then be applicable to Canada? He thought not; for there appeared no reason for believing, that the dissatisfaction of Canada was so fixed, so deeply rooted, as to despair of effecting an ultimate arrangement.

(cs. 69–70)

House of Lords, 18 January 1838

LORD BROUGHAM: Not only do I consider the possession as worth no breach of the Constitution—no violation of the principles of justice—good God!—what possession can ever be of a value to justify a price like that!—but in a national view, I really hold those colonies to be worth nothing. The only interest we have in the matter, concerns the mode in which a separation, sooner or later inevitable, shall take place. The only question worth considering, as far as our national interest is concerned, is whether that separation shall be effected amicably or with hostile feelings, unless in so far as the honour of the country is involved. But I am not so romantic as to suppose, that any nation will ever be willing to give up an extended dominion, how unprofitable, nay, how burthensome soever it may be to hold it. Such possessions, above all, are not likely to be surrendered to dictation and force. The feelings of national pride and honour are averse to yielding in these circumstances; but I do venture to hope, that when all feelings of pride and honour are saved—when resentment and passion has cooled—when the wrong-doers on either side are forgiven—when the reign of law is restored; that justice will be tempered with mercy, the foundation for an amicable separation laid, and an estimate calmly made of the profit and the loss which result from our North American dominions. I am well assured that we shall then find them very little worth the cost they have entailed on us, in men, in money, and in injuries to our trade; nay, that their separation will be even now a positive gain, so it be but effected on friendly terms, and succeeded by an amicable intercourse.

(cs. 213–4)

VISCOUNT MELBOURNE: My noble friend (Brougham) concluded his speech with some observations on the general state of Canada, and the advantage it was of to this country; and as to some of his remarks, I must own, my Lords, that to an observer of the present day only, and who looks alone to the present state of Europe, I am not disposed to say that there is not some appearance of truth in the noble and learned Lord's observations; but these are matters of vast and grave importance, and ought not to be incidentally discussed. We have been told, my Lords, that these provinces contain within them materials from which might be formed a great empire; that they have vast harbours, immense natural resources, and that they are rich in mineral and vegetable products; and that it is not known of what influence they might become as a separate country. But, my Lords, it is not known how valuable all these resources may become in the hands of England herself, and our present proceedings not only involve the interests of the colonies themselves and of England also, but the honour and integrity of this country, its interest among nations, and its character as a great empire. This question also involves, my Lords, the future welfare as well as the present security and tranquillity of these colonies. It is of great importance, therefore, that we should not listen to vague theories or fanciful suggestions.

(c. 223)

House of Commons, 22 January 1838

MR. J. A. ROEBUCK (Agent for the Lower Canada Assembly, presenting a petition against the Bill): I entreat this House to view the consequences that will naturally result from this disastrous question. I see on the other side of the St. Lawrence a nation now so powerful that we can hardly measure its extent; a nation, that has now dominion from Florida to the Lakes of Canada, and which, if we are wise, we shall take especial care has no increase of territory. If we are wise, we shall see and arrange all matters in Canada, and in our other North American possessions, so as to prepare them when a separation shall come, as come it must, to be an independent nation. But if you treat them thus as you are now treating them, all their hopes will be centered in America, and unhappily all their alliances will be American; and when we lose Canada, as lose her one day or other we shall, she will merge in the United States, and then we shall see that nation stretching its power from the Gulf of Mexico to the northern pole, with their fleets in every sea, and her insolent dominion, over-riding every power: for men, whether under good or bad institutions, if you make them irresponsible, will be unjust. Then, in your turn, you will have to meet the injustice of too powerful America, in like manner as Canada has now to meet the injustice of too powerful England.

(cs. 309–310)

House of Commons, 23 January 1838

SIR WILLIAM MOLESWORTH: But it should be remarked that of all the high functionaries the Colonial

Secretary was the one least exposed to effective responsibility, because the people of a mother country are necessarily uninterested and unacquainted with the affairs of their remote dependencies. Therefore it was only on extraordinary occasions that the public attention could be directed from matters of nearer interest to colonial concerns: it was rarely that the Colonial Office could be made to feel the weight of public opinion, and to fear censure and exposure. Where, however, responsibility was wanting, the experience of all ages had proved, that abuses would exist, and continue to exist, unredressed, until at last they reached that amount which induced them no longer to trust to prayer and humble petition, but raise the cry of war, and have recourse to arms. Such had been the case of Canada. In that province for the last thirty years acknowledged abuses had existed; acknowledged by Committees, and by Members of every party in the House of Commons. Great changes had taken place in the Government of this country, yet no changes had taken place in the administration of colonial affairs. The same odious system of colonial misgovernment which was pursued by the Tories had been acted upon by the Whigs. The causes for the continuance of the same colonial system under Ministers of the most adverse principles were easily to be explained. The Colonial Secretary seldom remained long enough in his office to become acquainted with the concerns of the numerous colonies which he governed. In the last ten years there had been no less than eight different Colonial Secretaries. They had seldom, therefore, the time, and still more seldom the inclination, to make themselves acquainted with the complicated details of their office; their ignorance rendered them mere tools in the hands of the Permanent Under-Secretaries and other clerks. It was in the dark recesses of the Colonial Office—in those dens of peculation and plunder —it was there that the real and irresponsible rulers of the millions of inhabitants of our colonies were to be found. Men utterly unknown to fame, but for whom, he trusted, some time or other, a day of reckoning would come, when they would be dragged before the public, and punished for their evil deeds. These were the men who, shielded by irresponsibility, and hidden from the public gaze, continued the same system of misgovernment under every party which alternately presided over the destinies of the empire. By that misgovernment they drove the colonies to desperation—they connived at every description of abuse, because they profited by abuse—they defended every species of corruption, because they gained by corruption. These men he now denounced as the originators and perpetrators of those grievances in Canada, the evil effects of which this country had already begun to experience. He trusted the experience thus gained would convince the people of the necessity of a sweeping reform in the Colonial Office.

(cs. 384–6)

MR. W. E. GLADSTONE: In the infancy of a country it was far better that it should be connected with an old nation, where capital existed in abundance, where the habits of men had been matured by the influence of long-established civilization, and the resources of social life had been fully called into action, than that it should be left to struggle unaided with the difficulties inseparable from an early stage of society. Such had been the case of Canada, and what was the real rate of her progress which had been reported as so slow? If compared with the United States, its advance in prosperity was found to be even more rapid. In 1775 the population of Canada was but 60,000. It now amounted to 600,000, having been multiplied tenfold since that year. At the commencement of the American war, the population of the United States was 2,500,000, and now amounted to 15,000,000, having increased six-fold. How did these facts agree with the statements of the advocates of the insurgents, who attempted to persuade the world that Canada had made no progress and had derived no benefits from its connexion with this country. Did hon. Gentlemen recollect the progress which New South Wales had made, notwithstanding the peculiar disadvantages under which it laboured? Against these facts it was impossible to contend, and he was justified in dismissing at once the supposition that the progress of Canada had been retarded by its subjection to Britain.

(c. 428)

LORD JOHN RUSSELL: Having acquired large possessions by various wars and by the efforts of powerful men from Cromwell to Marlborough, and from Marlborough to Wellington, it was desirable carefully to consider the peculiar usages, the peculiar wants, the religious habits, and the peculiar aptitudes of the people over whom they ruled, so as to take such measures as would be best calculated to conciliate their good opinion. When revolutions were to be quelled, let the necessary measures for quelling them be adopted—but when a permanent Government was to be established, let everything be done to ascertain the just expectations and wishes of the people, and let not this country, for paltry objects of its own, impose upon them institutions which might prove unpalatable or intolerant. This was the aim which he had in view with respect to Canada, and to all the other

North American provinces. They were not to be governed in the same manner as islands in the Mediterranean or our dominions in the east; but by making such temporary changes and ameliorations as from time to time the circumstances might call for—such changes as might suit the habits of the persons to be governed, and at the same time that they did honour to the mother country prove advantageous to the colonies, so that the name of the mother country might not suffer, nor the empire be diminished. This was the end to which he looked in sending out the instructions by Lord Durham, and those were the objects which he wished that noble Lord to have in view before he transmitted his plan to this country.

(cs. 468–9)

Hansard, Third Series, Vol. XL.

PART VI

THE COLONIAL REFORMERS

26: EDWARD GIBBON WAKEFIELD. *A Letter from Sydney*

1829

The leader of the so-called Colonial Reformers of 1830, Edward Gibbon Wakefield, wrote this *Letter from Sydney* in Newgate prison without ever having seen a Colony. He had been sentenced for abducting an heiress, his second elopement. This escapade meant that Parliament was closed to him; his political activity was confined to influence; much of his writing was carried out under assumed names. This appeared as the work of a young settler in New South Wales offering the novel solution of systematic emigration for the problem of the chronic labour shortage that led many Australians to desire the continuance of transportation (cf. No. 19). Both here and in his later writings (*England and America* (1834) and *A View of the Art of Colonization* (No. 34)) Wakefield goes on to discuss the whole problem of the colonial relationship.

He accompanied Durham to Canada as unofficial adviser in 1838, later buying land there and being elected to the second Canadian Parliament for a French constituency. In the end he followed the Otago and Canterbury settlers to New Zealand where he died in 1862.

If an Englishman who ardently desires the greatest good of his country—Mr. Wilmot Horton, for instance—were offered the gratification of one wish, however extravagant, for what would he ask? For an immense gold mine? For the destruction of his natural enemies, the French? For an earthquake to swallow up troublesome Ireland? Oh no!—for none of these would he ask. If his character were more remarkable for justice than humanity, he might, perhaps, be tempted to wish for a straightforward Catholic Relief Bill; but, on the whole, he would, I think, wish for the power to increase the territory of Britain according to the wants of the people. And, in making this choice of blessings, he would not be actuated by any ambitious views with reference to the territorial extent of his country. His sole object would be to put an end to that portion of crime and misery which in Britain is produced by an excess of people in proportion to territory; and he would not care, therefore, whether the increase of territory, having that effect, should take place near to or at a distance from Britain.

The colonies . . . would no longer be new societies, strictly speaking. They would be so many *extensions* of an old society. Pursue that idea, and you will see that emigration from Britain would not be confined to Paupers, passing by the free bridge. We (I speak in the name of the colonists) should acquire wealth rapidly. Such of us as are landowners must have good incomes, without trouble; for remember that, though the tax upon rent would take something from us, it would only take a part from what it would first bestow! How many ready-made articles, both useful and ornamental, should we import from England, for which, now, we have not the means to pay? Let me enumerate a few of them—farming bailiffs, surveyors, builders, architects and engineers; mineralogists, practical miners, botanists and chemists; printers, schoolmasters and schoolmistresses, booksellers, authors, publishers, and even reviewers; merchants, to supply us with English goods, and to take our surplus produce; bankers, underwriters, life-insurers, and clerks innumerable; actors, surgeons, and physicians; lawyers, clergymen, singers, music and dancing masters, milliners and other female artists, and at least, one good Political

Economist at each settlement, to prevent us from devising an Australasian tariff. Most of these emigrants would call themselves ladies and gentlemen, and would object to pass by the bridge of charity. Consequently we could not force them to preserve an equal sexual proportion; but if an excessive number of males should emigrate, they would create, here, a demand for females, and a supply would immediately follow by the bridge. Moreover, as the value of all land purchased of the government must necessarily rise somewhat above the amount of the purchase-money; and as portions, on or near to which towns would grow up, must rise in value considerably above the government price, the purchase of waste land would be an excellent employment of capital. Much of the surplus capital of Britain, therefore, might be so invested, instead of being given away to monks in Spain and to Tartars in South America. Some of the persons, who should invest their money in this manner, would emigrate along with it, in order to become the leading men of civilized Australasia.

The system in question would tend more than any thing to preserve an intimate connection between the colony and the mother country. In fact, the mother country and the colony would become partners in a new trade—the creation of happy human beings; one country furnishing the raw material—that is, the land, the dust of which man is made; the other furnishing the machinery—that is, men and women, to convert the unpeopled soil into living images of God. In this honourable, and, we may say, even glorious copartnership, the interest of the mother country would be greater than that of the colony; and a rupture of their connection would, therefore, be most injurious to the former. If the system of

free migration should be destroyed by a war of independence, the colony might still pursue the system of
restriction, and so preserve all the desirable attributes of
an old people; but in that case, the mother country
would lose a given portion of the means by which she
had enjoyed the one great good that belongs to new
countries—the power of supplying a constant increase
of territory according to the wants of the people. The
mother country, therefore, in governing the colony,
would consult the greatest advantage of the colonists, in
order to preserve their friendship; and the colonists,
having much to lose, and being incapable of dispersion,
would feel a wholesome dread of war. The colonists,
being an instructed and civilized people, would be as well
qualified to govern themselves as the people of Britain;
and, being a wealthy people, they would be able, without
going to war, to assert the birth-right of all British
subjects—to enforce in the British Parliament, against a
bad British ministry, their claim to equality before the
law. Qualified, entitled, and powerful to govern themselves, they might either take a share in framing the
general laws of the empire, by means of their representatives in the British Parliament; or, if a mean jealousy on
the part of Englishmen should prevent such an arrangement, they might frame their own laws, in a Colonial
Assembly, under the eye of a viceroy, incapable of
wrong, and possessing a veto like the king of England,
but whose secretaries, like the ministers of England,
should be responsible to the people! At all events, they
must be governed, by whatever machinery, with a view
to their good and their contentment, which is the greatest
good, instead of to the satisfaction of their governors
only. This would render them happy in a most intimate
connexion with their mother country; and the American

war of independence would no longer be a favourite theme in the still dependent colonies of Britain. Mutual dependence would prevent oppression on the one part, and on the other, a wish for independence; reciprocity of interest would occasion mutual good will; there would no longer be injurious distinctions, or malignant jealousies, or vulgar hatred between British subjects, wherever born; and Britain would become the centre of the most extensive, the most civilized, and, above all, the happiest empire in the world.

A Letter from Sydney (1829), pp. 180–1, 186–8, 196–9.

27: SIR WILLIAM MOLESWORTH. Speech in moving a vote of censure on Lord Glenelg's Colonial Administration

House of Commons, 6 March 1838

Molesworth (1810-55) who had been sent down from Cambridge for challenging his tutor to a duel, was the leading spokesman of the Colonial Reformers in the Commons in the thirties. He was Chairman of the Select Committee on Transportation that reported in 1837. His attacks on the Colonial Office continued until he himself became Secretary of State in Palmerston's government in July 1855; he died suddenly in October of the same year.

THE saying, "Emancipate your colonies," means with those who employ it most emphatically, a great deal more than the mere words convey. It is used, by some at least, to express an opinion that a country like this would be better without colonies, and even that it would have been better for us if we had never had colonies. From this sentiment, notwithstanding my respect for some who entertain it, I venture to disagree altogether. What! are we to repent of having planted the thirteen English colonies of North America, which have expanded into one of the greatest, most prosperous, and happiest nations that the world ever saw? Are we to regret that the more northern deserts of the American continent, which constitute her Majesty's possessions in that quarter of the globe, are in the course of being reclaimed, cultivated, and filled with inhabitants of our race, whose industry finds an ample reward, and who, having wants like our own, require objects that are produced here, and thus furnish us with continually increasing markets in which to sell the produce of our domestic industry? Is it a pity that our numerous and profitable markets in the West Indies should ever have existed? Should we despond over our mighty empire in the East, which has brought to us—let those deny it who would deny the shining of the sun at noon—an incalculable tribute of wealth? Is our extraordinary trade with the infant colonies of Australasia an evil or a good? Sir, for my part, I can see no necessary evil, but do see vast and inevitable good, in the possession of colonies. . . .

Those who cry " Emancipate your colonies " appear to have seen nothing but the abuses and evils; they have imagined that colonies and jobbing, colonial trade and colonial monopoly, were synonymous terms. Nor is this to be wondered at, perhaps; for it should be recollected that, until of late years, it was generally and seriously believed that a colonial trade was of no value, unless it was in some way or another a monopoly trade; and secondly, that colonial misgovernment has been far greater and far more obvious in the present generation than it was before. I mean by this to infer that the most enlightened men are apt—and by reason of their hostility to the old system of colonial monopoly—to undervalue and disparage colonial trade itself, confounding the

uses with the abuses, which last had got full possession of
their minds; and in the next place, that since we lost, by
maltreating them, our colonies in North America, and
since we set up in Downing Street a Colonial Office to
conquer and to govern the colonies of other nations;
since, in a word, we abandoned the old system of Chartered Colonies and adopted the new one of Crown
Colonies; since we exchanged our ancient and successful
system of colonising—that of allowing to the colony a
large share of local self-government,—since we have
pursued the Spanish system of governing in all things
from a distance by a Council of the Indies in Downing
Street,—the government of our colonies has been far
more objectionable, more ignorant, necessarily so on
account of the great distance between the subjects and
the seat of all authority; more oppressive, insomuch as
local power has been confided to strangers, who have no
permanent interest in, or sympathy with, the colony;
and, lastly, more injurious to us at home, by furnishing
a larger amount of Government patronage, or, in other
words, larger means of parliamentary corruption. A new
dislike to the old system of colonial trade, and an impression made by the new system of colonial government,
under which the evils and abuses, necessarily belonging
to all governments from a distance, had increased and
become more obvious—these I believe to be at the
bottom of the opinion, which condemns as mischievous
and absurd the old fashioned, but (as it appears to me)
sound opinion which is expressed by the cry "Ships,
colonies, and commerce." Instead of wishing to separate
from our colonies, or to avert the establishment of new
ones, I would say distinguish between the evil and the
good; remove the evil, but preserve the good; do not
"Emancipate your colonies," but multiply them, and

improve—reform your system of colonial government.
Selected Speeches of Sir William Molesworth (ed. H. E. Egerton,
1903), pp. 2–3, 10–11.

28: JOHN GEORGE LAMBTON, EARL OF DURHAM. *Report on the Affairs of British North America*

1839

THROUGHOUT the whole of the North American Provinces there prevails among the British population an affection for the mother country, and a preference for its institutions, which a wise and firm policy, on the part of the Imperial Government, may make the foundation of a safe, honourable and enduring connexion. But even this feeling may be impaired, and I must warn those in whose hands the disposal of their destinies rests, that a blind reliance on the all-enduring loyalty of our countrymen may be carried too far. It is not politic to waste and cramp their resources, and to allow the backwardness of the British Provinces every where to present a melancholy contrast to the progress and prosperity of the United States. Throughout the course of the preceding pages, I have constantly had occasion to refer to this contrast . . . It is no true loyalty to hide from Your Majesty's knowledge the existence of an evil which it is in Your Majesty's power, as it is Your Majesty's benevolent pleasure, to remove. For the possibility of reform is yet afforded by the patient and fervent attachment which Your Majesty's English subjects in all these Provinces still feel to their allegiance and their mother country. Calm reflection and loyal confidence have retained these feelings unimpaired, even by the fearful drawback of the general belief that every man's

134

property is of less value on the British than on the opposite side of the boundary. It is time to reward this noble confidence, by showing that men have not indulged in vain the hope that there is a power in British institutions to rectify existing evils, and to produce in their place a well-being which no other dominion could give. It is not in the terrors of the law, or in the might of armies, that the secure and honourable bond of connexion is to be found. It exists in the beneficial operation of those British institutions which link the utmost development of freedom and civilization with the stable authority of an hereditary monarchy, and which, if rightly organized and fairly administered in the Colonies, as in Great Britain, would render a change of institutions only an additional evil to the loss of the protection and commerce of the British Empire.

I am, in truth, so far from believing that the increased power and weight that would be given to these Colonies by union would endanger their connexion with the Empire, that I look to it as the only means of fostering such a national feeling throughout them as would effectually counterbalance whatever tendencies may now exist towards separation. No large community of free and intelligent men will long feel contented with a political system which places them, because it places their country, in a position of inferiority to their neighbours. The colonist of Great Britain is linked, it is true, to a mighty Empire; and the glories of its history, the visible signs of its present power, and the civilization of its people, are calculated to raise and gratify his national pride. But he feels also, that his link to that Empire is one of remote dependence; he catches but passing and inadequate glimpses of its power and prosperity; he knows that in its government he and his countrymen have no voice. While his neighbour on the other side of the frontier assumes importance, from the notion that his vote exercises some influence on the councils, and that he himself has some share in the onward progress of a mighty nation, the colonist feels the deadening influence of the narrow and subordinate community to which he belongs. In his own, and in the surrounding Colonies, he finds petty objects occupying petty, stationary and divided societies; and it is only when the chances of an uncertain and tardy communication bring intelligence of what has passed a month before on the other side of the Atlantic, that he is reminded of the Empire with which he is connected. But the influence of the United States surrounds him on every side, and is for ever present. . . . It stamps, on all the habits and opinions of the surrounding countries, the common characteristics of the thoughts, feelings and customs of the American people. Such is necessarily the influence which a great nation exercises on the small communities which surround it. Its thoughts and manners subjugate them, even when nominally independent of its authority. If we wish to prevent the extension of this influence, it can only be done by raising up for the North American colonist some nationality of his own; by elevating these small and unimportant communities into a society having some objects of a national importance; and by thus giving their inhabitants a country which they will be unwilling to see absorbed even into one more powerful.

It is by a sound system of colonization that we can render these extensive regions available for the benefit of the British people. The mismanagement by which the resources of our Colonies have hitherto been wasted, has, I know, produced in the public mind too much of a disposition to regard them as mere sources of corruption and loss, and to entertain, with too much complacency, the idea of abandoning them as useless. I cannot participate in the notion that it is the part either of prudence or of honour to abandon our countrymen when our government of them has plunged them into disorder, or our territory, when we discover that we have not turned it to proper account. The experiment of keeping colonies and governing them well, ought at least to have a trial, ere we abandon for ever the vast dominion which might supply the wants of our surplus population, and raise up millions of fresh consumers of our manufactures, and producers of a supply for our wants.

Lord Durham's Report (ed. Lucas, Oxford 1912), Vol. II, pp. 262–4, 310–2, 331.

29: CHARLES BULLER. *Responsible Government for Colonies*

1840

Buller (1806–48) was Durham's Chief Secretary in the mission to Canada of 1838, and he was widely credited at the time with writing the report. While Durham's own authorship is now conceded, Buller's influence on phrases and thought is clear and he did write the report on Public Lands and Emigration in the appendices. He held minor offices, with an understanding that he would assist in colonial matters, in Russell's government of 1846, until his sudden death in 1848.

IT is in order that our Colonies may long continue connected with the empire, and be the source to us of those advantages which we believe to be the fruit of wise colonization, that we think that their dependence should be held by a very loose rein. It is in order to keep

colonies, and to profit by them, that we would insist on
their being allowed to manage their own internal affairs,
and that the interference of the Imperial Government
should be confined to the very few points on which
Imperial interests are affected by what passes in the
Colonies. . . .

We want colonies in order to have customers for our
trade and a field for our surplus capital and labour.
These are the sole objects for which we maintain
colonies, and for securing which we are obliged to keep
up our dominion over them. We are under the necessity
of governing them, and of protecting them by our fleets
and armies, solely in order that we may be sure of trading with them, and sending our emigrants to them. We
need interfere with them solely in order to secure an
advantageous trade, a ready access to our emigrants, and
such a disposal of the lands of the colony as shall promote emigration into it.

In speculating on questions of Colonial government,
we must be allowed to assume that the colony does not
desire the severance of its connexion with Great Britain.
Of course, it can be of no use to devise a means of
trusting it with a limited portion of power if we suppose
its desire to be to use that power for the purpose of destroying whatever institutions may be framed for it.
Assuming, therefore, that the people of the colony
desire to be connected with Britain, on what may fairly
be considered the necessary terms of Colonial dependence, we can see no reason for apprehending that giving
an Assembly control over one portion of the policy and
composition of the Executive, would enable it to
encroach on that which is expressly reserved from it. The
general control proposed would in no wise, as we have

shown, extend to the excepted departments. And though the Assembly might still, as it now does, be inclined to usurp authority by having recourse to extreme measures, we feel very confident that the Colonial public would be far less inclined to subject itself to the evils incidental to such a contest, when the object in dispute was thus narrowed by general and liberal concessions on the part of the Mother-country.

Printed in E. M. Wrong, *Charles Buller and Responsible Government* (Oxford 1926), pp. 109, 110, 133–4.

30: THOMAS CARLYLE. *Past and Present*

1843

Carlyle has been considered by some the founder of British Imperialism, yet his references to the Colonies are but scattered and in much he only echoes the Colonial Reformers, of whom Charles Buller had been his pupil. His contempt for democracy voiced itself in demands for active Governors such as the colonists abhorred, while his attacks on the separatist economists' thought is shown in that section (No. 41).

WHY should there not be an 'Emigration Service,' and Secretary, with adjuncts, with funds, forces, idle Navy-ships, and ever-increasing apparatus; in fine an *effective system* of Emigration; so that . . . every honest willing Workman who found England too strait, and the 'Organisation of Labour' not yet sufficiently advanced, might find likewise a bridge built to carry him into new Western Lands, there to 'organise' with more elbow-room some labour for himself? There to be a real blessing, raising new corn for us, purchasing new webs and new hatchets from us; leaving us at least in peace; —instead of staying here to be a Physical-Force

Chartist, unblessed and no blessing! Is it not scandalous to consider that a Prime Minister could raise within the year, as I have seen it done, a Hundred and Twenty Millions Sterling to shoot the French; and we are stopt short for want of the hundredth part of that to keep the English living? The bodies of the English living, and the souls of the English living:—these two 'Services,' an Education Service and an Emigration Service, these with others will actually have to be organised!

A free bridge for Emigrants: why, we should then be on a par with America itself, the most favoured of all lands that have no government; and we should have, besides, so many traditions and mementos of priceless things which America has cast away. We could proceed deliberately to 'organise Labour,' not doomed to perish unless we effected it within year and day;—every willing Worker that proved superfluous, finding a bridge ready for him. This verily will have to be done; the Time is big with this. Our little Isle is grown too narrow for us; but the world is wide enough yet for another Six Thousand Years. England's sure markets will be among new Colonies of Englishmen in all quarters of the Globe. All men trade with all men, when mutually convenient; and are even bound to do it by the Maker of men. Our friends of China, who guiltily refused to trade, in these circumstances,—had we not to argue with them, in cannon-shot at last, and convince them that they ought to trade! 'Hostile Tariffs' will arise, to shut us out; and then again will fall, to let us in: but the Sons of England, speakers of the English language were it nothing more, will in all times have the ineradicable predisposition to trade with England. Mycale was the *Pan-Ionion*, rendezvous of all the tribes of Ion, for old Greece: why should not London long continue the *All-Saxon-home*, rendezvous of all the 'Children of the Harz-Rock,' arriving, in select samples, from the Antipodes and elsewhere, by steam and otherwise, to the ' season ' here!— What a Future; wide as the world, if we have the heart and heroism for it,—which, by Heaven's blessing we shall.

T. Carlyle, *Past and Present*, Bk. IV. ch. III (1897 ed.) pp. 266–8.

31 : CHARLES BULLER. Speech in moving a motion on Systematic Colonization

House of Commons, 6 April 1843

SOME improvement of their condition you must secure for the people, and you must secure it before long. But that you will never do until, by laying open a wider field of employment, you can succeed in diminishing that terrible competition of capital with capital and labour with labour, which is the permanent cause of distress. It is with this view that I propose that you should investigate the efficacy of colonization, as a remedy against the distress of the country. I say as a remedy, because I do not bring it forward as a panacea—as the only, as an infallible, remedy for every ill—but as one among many remedies, which would be valuable, even if they could not go the length of entirely removing distress, provided they enabled us to render its recurrence less frequent, its operation less intense, and its pressure less severe. I say distinctly that you will not effect your purpose of permanently and fully bettering the condition of the people, unless you apply a variety of remedies directed to the various disorders of their present state. But confining myself to the economical evil that arises solely from that one cause, of which I have laboured to describe the operation, namely, the competition both of capital and labour in a restrictive field, I propose colonization as a means of remedying that evil by enlarging the field of employment. . . .

Sir, in the principles and objects of the friends of Free-trade I fully concur. I not only think that we ought to do what they propose, but I am ready to admit that the first and most simple and most effectual mode of enlarging the field of employment is by trading on the freest terms with all the existing markets in the world. I propose colonization as subsidiary to Free-trade; as an additional mode of carrying out the same principles, and attaining the same object. You advocates of Free-trade wish to bring food to the people. I suggest to you at the same time to take your people to the food. You wish to get fresh markets by removing the barriers which now keep you from those that exist throughout the world. I call upon you, in addition, to get fresh markets, by calling them into existence in parts of the world which might be made to teem with valuable customers . . . I must not, therefore, be understood to propose colonization as a substitute for Free-trade. I do not vaunt its efficacy as superior; indeed I admit that its efficacy in extending employment must be slower. But, on the other hand, it will probably be surer; and will be liable to no such interruptions from the caprice of others, as trade with foreign nations must always be subject to. I grant that the restrictive policy of other nations is, in great measure, to be ascribed to the influence of our example; and I am inclined to concur in the hope that the relaxation of our commercial system will be the signal for freedom of trade in many other countries. But still we are not sure how soon this effect may be produced; how long an experience may be required to convince our neighbours of the injurious operation of monopoly; or how soon or how often the policy of protection may reappear in some shape or other, whether finding favour with the fantastic minds of statesmen, or the capricious feelings of nations, or dictated by political views totally independent of merely economical considerations. But of the legislature of your own colonies—of the fiscal policy of the different portions of your own empire—you can always make sure, and may rely upon being met by no hostile tariffs on their part.

Hansard, Third Series, Vol. LXVIII, cs. 499–51.

32: EDWARD GIBBON WAKEFIELD.
Sir Charles Metcalfe in Canada

Article in *Fisher's Colonial Magazine*, July 1844

IT was long held that Colonies must necessarily separate from the Mother Country, whenever they arrive at that stage of improvement which may enable them to assert their independence; and many yet take it for granted that they always will. But upon what sort of ground, I feel bound to ask, does this notion rest? All depends upon the temper of mind in which they may be when they reach this stage. Will they wish for separation, or will they not, is the question? What right have we to presume, as a matter of course, that they will seek so great a change, whether they have or have not any real reason to be dissatisfied with their actual condition? It is nothing to say that in this or that instance, ancient or modern, Colonies have in fact desired and gained for themselves independent nationality. In every one of these cases there has been an obvious cause for their having done so, in the injustice or folly with which they have been treated. Colonists carry with them from home just as strong a feeling of attachment to that home as those who stay there cherish; nay, the very leave-taking tends to make the feeling, for their after-life, the deeper. The memory of the heart deals always far more with its sunshine than with its clouds. To their dying day, the old country is emphatically 'home'. They seldom or never fail to teach the lesson to their children; and their children and their children's children are seldom or never slow to learn it. The instinct of country of the natives of a Colony must point to the land of their birth, the only country they have personally known; but the old-country remains the home of their traditions, the father-land whose institutions and glories they love to dwell upon as still their own. Why is it that this lesson of attachment has so often been unlearned? Why, indeed, but because powerful influences have been wantonly called into play, to counteract the otherwise natural tendency of things? The Colonial tie has been made irksome to Colonists, in spite of all that education and habit have done to make them cling to it. They have been treated as an inferior class in the distribution of the honours and emoluments of the state; almost any man of metropolitan birth being preferred in practice to almost any man of provincial origin. They have been thwarted as regards the conduct of their own affairs,—their local government systematically carried on, under the auspices of the parent state, just as they would not have had it carried on if they could have helped it. Metropolitan law-makers have sacrificed their interests to some imagined interest of the Mother Country, or sought (for sometimes, as in 1776, the folly was even carried to this last extravagance) to deprive them arbi-

trarily of rights, which they valued too highly to endure
to see taken from them. Causes like these there have
always been, to account for colonial disaffection, wherever it has existed. Is it in the nature of things, that they
must always be in operation wherever colonies are to be
found? If so, then indeed we may hold that colonies
cannot possibly be retained in their connexion with the
parent-state; but surely, not otherwise.

The wide Continents we are colonizing promise at
some distant day to maintain communities too powerful for the precise colonial relation, . . . to continue for
ever to subsist between them and the people of these
Islands. But that period is distant, though inevitable.
All we can certainly know is that it will come; that at
some future time our Colonies, powerful as the Parent
State or more so, must either, thanks to mismanagement, have become independent states more likely to
be its enemies than its hearty friends, or else, through
a wise foresight, have been kept closely bound to it,—
confederacy, in some shape, by degrees taking the place
of the old bond of union,—the British nation continuing still united, so far as perpetual peace, mutual good
understanding, freedom of commerce, and identity
of foreign policy, can unite it,—these Islands still its
Metropolis, though their people be no longer the
admitted holders of its whole Imperial power. All we
can do is to take care of the present and near future.
The future that is far off will take good care of itself.
For this age and the next it is enough to know that
Colonies, built up by our own people, and gifted
with our own free institutions, must be bound, alike by
the natural feelings and the commercial wants of their
people, to ourselves and our policy, no less than to our

trade; that neither the one tie nor the other need we, nor yet if we are wise shall we, ever let go or loosen.

Printed in E. M. Wrong, *Charles Buller and Responsible Government* (Oxford, 1926), pp. 176–8, 351–2.

33: JOHN STUART MILL. *Principles of Political Economy*
1848

The closeness of Mill to the Colonial Reformers is seen in that he was numbered among them in 1830, while Charles Buller and Molesworth were considered to be of the group of the philosophic Radicals. In 1838 he supported Durham in Canada in two articles. As a clerk at the East India House, Mill was in touch with Imperial affairs (*vide* No. 37).

IF it is desirable, as no one will deny it to be, that the planting of colonies should be conducted, not with an exclusive view to the private interests of the first founders, but with a deliberate regard to the permanent welfare of the nations afterwards to arise from these small beginnings; such regard can only be secured by placing the enterprise, from its commencement, under regulations constructed with the foresight and enlarged views of philosophical legislators; and the government alone has power either to frame such regulations, or to enforce their observance.

The question of government intervention in the work of Colonization involves the future and permanent interests of civilization itself, and far outstretches the comparatively narrow limits of purely economical considerations. But even with a view to those considerations alone, the removal of population from the overcrowded to the unoccupied parts of the earth's surface is one of those works of eminent social usefulness, which most require, and which at the same time best repay, the intervention of government.

To appreciate the benefits of colonization, it should be considered in its relation, not to a single country, but to the collective economical interests of the human race. The question is in general treated too exclusively as one of distribution; of relieving one labour market and supplying another. It is this, but it is also a question of production, and of the most efficient employment of the productive resources of the world. Much has been said of the good economy of importing commodities from the place where they can be bought cheapest; while the good economy of producing them where they can be produced cheapest is comparatively little thought of. If to carry consumable goods from the places where they are super-abundant to those where they are scarce is a good pecuniary speculation, is it not an equally good speculation to do the same thing with regard to labour and instruments? The exportation of labourers and capital from old to new countries, from a place where their productive power is less to a place where it is greater, increases by so much the aggregate produce of the labour and capital of the world. It adds to the joint wealth of the old and the new country, what amounts in a short period to many times the mere cost of effecting the transport. There needs be no hesitation in affirming that Colonization, in the present state of the world, is the best affair of business, in which the capital of an old and wealthy country can engage.

J. S. Mill, *Principles of Political Economy* (ed. Ashley), Bk. V, ch. XI, sec. 14, pp. 970–1.

34: EDWARD GIBBON WAKEFIELD. *A View of the Art of Colonization*

1849

IF ever the Colonial Office originates a scheme of policy, it seldom pursues it consistently to the end. It sets off in one direction, and takes another the moment some interest, or clique, or association in this country strongly objects to the first course. At one time, the West-India Body in England suggests what it shall do; at another, the Anti-Slavery Society impels it. To-day its measures originate with some Canada merchants in London; to-morrow it abandons those measures, and pursues others of an opposite tendency at the instance of some London newspaper. At the instigation of a missionary society it all but made New Zealand a convict colony of France; and then yielding to the remonstrances of a joint-stock company, it established the British sovereignty which it had just before loudly repudiated. For awhile the Company led it to favour colonization; but ere long the anti-colonizing views of the Society again prevailed with it; and of late years its policy as to New Zealand has been an alternation of shuttlecock flights between the battledores of Salisbury-Square and Broad-Street-Buildings. It even yields to individual pressure, such as no other department would heed or feel; such as no domestic government would tolerate. Conscious of feebleness arising from the want of a public on the spot to sustain it in doing right and prevent it from doing wrong—fully aware of its own unpopularity as a bureaucratic institution in a free country — well acquainted with the facilities which the free press and the free institutions of this country afford for pressing it disagreeably—the Colonial Office but faintly resists anybody who may choose to make a business of pressing it. A list of the individuals who have made this their business during the last twenty years, would not be very short, and might be given with chapter and verse for what each of them successfully pressed it to do, undo, or leave undone. The whole would form a book of directions for future meddlers in colonial affairs. They would learn from its pages how easy it is for even the most obscure person, if he resides here and sets about the work in earnest, to prompt or thwart the policies of the Colonial Office, to suggest or overturn its decisions, to get its servants appointed or recalled, and to give the great bureaucracy more trouble in a year than it ever spontaneously bestowed on the colonies in five. Verily the Colonial Office would be at least more self-impelled if it were seated in Russia or St. Helena.

Between the municipal and republican principles there is no connexion whatever. Is there a country in the world where the monarchical principle is more cherished than in Great Britain? Yet there is no country in the world where the municipal principle, as a delegation of authority for limited purposes, has been so largely carried into effect. What the form of government may be in a municipal dependency, is a matter wholly independent of the municipal character of the government. Municipal, applying the word to colonies, signifies nothing but local ...

But supposing it admitted that the municipal system has no tendency to republicanism, and produces loyalty rather than disaffection—that it is the strongest cement of an empire composed of divers communities—yet the questions may be asked, Would you deprive the imperial power of all local control in the colonies? would you

149

make them wholly independent states within their own bounds, reserving only such allegiance to the empire as would prevent them from being independent, or foreign states? Certainly not. On the contrary, I, for one, am of opinion, that if colonization were systematically conducted with a view to the advantage of the mother-country, the control of the imperial power ought to be much greater, and the connexion between the colonies and the centre far more intimate than either has ever yet been. I regard the waste but partially-occupied territories which this nation has acquired by costly efforts, as a valuable national property, which we have every right in justice, and are bound by every consideration of prudence, to use for the greatest benefit of the people of this country: and instead of leaving colonies to take what form a thousand accidents may determine, and to grow up as cast-aways till they are strong enough to become enemies, I think that the imperial power ought to mould them into the forms most agreeable to itself, and to bind them to this kingdom by indissoluble ties.

E. G. Wakefield, *A View of the Art of Colonization* (1849), pp. 236–7, 271–2, 275–6.

35: WILLIAM EWART GLADSTONE. Speech in the House of Commons

21 May 1852

Gladstone was Under-Secretary for War and the Colonies in 1835 and Secretary from 1845 to 1846. He acknowledged the influence on his colonial ideas of Molesworth and Wakefield and the latter considered this speech of such importance that he printed it as a pamphlet. See P. Knaplund, *Gladstone and Britain's Imperial Policy* (London 1927).

You have implanted a principle, if not of absolute, yet

of comparative feebleness in your distant settlements.
You have brought upon yourselves enormous expense;
and, by depriving them of the fulness of political freedom, you have deprived them of the greatest attraction
which they could possibly hold out to the best part of
your population to emigrate; because Englishmen do
not love to emigrate to countries where they cannot enjoy
the political franchises which they enjoy at home, and
where the regulation of their interests will be committed
to the hands of a Government which, however mild and
equitable, must still be called in principle despotic.
Whatever we may say as to despotism—and I am not
given to take an over severe view of despotism, where it
is adapted to the habits of a country and its social state
—yet as regards freeborn Englishmen, such a system is
most monstrous and most irrational; and the consequence has been that there is a subject of complaint
present and familiar to us all, namely this, that you have
been unable to get the superior classes of the community
to emigrate; for the high-minded, well-educated men,
who would have been themselves the centres of a valuable social influence, have been reluctant to leave the
shores of England, because they were unwilling to forfeit
the advantages of a state of high civilisation, and to
incur a certain deprivation of the great bulk of their
political liberties. And thus our modern colonists, instead
of remaining, as formerly, in continuous and hereditary
possession of their liberties, after quitting the mother
country, instead of keeping them and handing them on
as the regular and unquestioned heritage of their
children in another hemisphere, go out to Australia or
New Zealand to be deprived of these liberties, and then
perhaps, after fifteen, or twenty, or thirty years' waiting,
or yet more, to have a portion given back to them with

THE CONCEPT OF EMPIRE

great and magnificent language about the liberality of
Parliament in conceding free institutions; while during
the whole of that interval they are condemned to hear
the whole of the miserable jargon which has grown into
use about training them for free institutions, and fitting
them for the privileges thus conferred; whereas, in point
of fact, so far from thus training and fitting them, every
year and every month during which they are kept out
of the possession and familiar use of such institutions,
and retained under the administration of a despotic
Government, renders them less fit for free institutions,
and the consequence is that the introduction of them at
length is attended with great embarrassments; liberty
comes to them as a novelty; its working is something
strange and unknown, attended with hazard, uncertainty,
and excitement; and thus you have inconvenient or disastrous consequences brought upon you by your own
fault, which you might have avoided if you had only
followed that which in this case no one need be ashamed
of holding up to commendation as the wisdom of your
ancestors—if you had only walked in the path they
had struck out for your guidance. Let the people you
send out to colonise a distant land take root unmolested
in their new ground as the seed of a future community,
as the natural and living centre around which population
is to grow; and instead of training them for free institutions, rely upon it that the best training they can have is
the training they have already received before they left
your shores, and while they are still British citizens; let
them carry their freedom with them, even as they carry
their agricultural implements, or anything else necessary
to establish them in their new abodes; so let them hold
it for themselves, and so let them transmit it to their
children. This is the true secret of subduing the difficulties of colonisation.   152

The principles upon which our Colonial administration was once conducted have been precisely reversed. Our colonies have come to be looked upon as being, not municipalities endowed with external freedom, but petty States. If you had only kept to the fundamental idea of your forefathers, that these were municipal bodies founded within the shadow and cincture of your imperial powers—that it was your business to impose on them such positive restraints as you thought necessary, and having done so, to leave them free in everything else —all those principles, instead of being reversed, would have survived in full vigour—you would have saved millions, I was going to say countless millions, to your exchequer; but you would have done something far more important by planting societies more worthy by far of the source from which they sprung; for no man can read the history of the great American revolution without seeing that 100 years ago your colonies such as they then were, with the institutions they then possessed, and the political relations in which they then stood to the mother country, bred and reared men of mental stature and power such as far surpassed anything that colonial life is now commonly considered to be capable of producing.

Hansard, Third Series, Vol. CXXI, cs. 954–6, 959.

36: W. E. GLADSTONE. Address to the Mechanics Institute, Chester

12 November 1855

THE material advantages of colonial enterprise and trade, though inferior to those of extended trade at home, present some recommendations that foreign trade does not possess. But these are incidental differences. Every legitimate, that is unforced, extension of trade is beneficial; and there is no doubt that as regards the trade and employment of the people, the possession of colonies like those of England, which are peopled by the spontaneous operation of natural causes—that is to say, by the free judgment of the people, each man carrying his labour or his capital to the market where he thinks he may get the best price for either—there is no doubt that, in a material point of view, the possession of such colonies is eminently beneficial, not because it creates a more profitable trade than other trades, but because it creates a perfectly new trade, and a trade which would not otherwise exist.

But I do not concede that the material benefit of colonies is the only consideration which we are able to plead. Their moral and social advantage is a very great one. If we are asked why, on these grounds, it is desirable that colonies should be founded and possessed, I answer by asking another question—Why is it desirable that your population at home should increase? Why is it that you rejoice, always presuming that the increase of population goes hand in hand with equally favourable or more favourable conditions of existence for the mass of the people—why is it that you rejoice in an increase of population at home? Because an increase of population is an increase of power, an increase of strength and stability to the state, and because it multiplies the number of people who, as we hope, are living under good laws, and belong to a country to which it is an honour and an advantage to belong. That is the great moral benefit that attends the foundation of British colonies. We think that our country is a country blessed with laws and a constitution that are eminently beneficial to mankind, and if so, what can be more to be desired than that we should have the means of reproducing in different portions of the globe something as like as may be to that country which we honour and revere? I think it is in a work by Mr. Roebuck that the expression is used, " that the object of colonisation is the creation of so many happy Englands." It is the reproduction of the image and likeness of England—the reproduction of a country in which liberty is reconciled with order, in which ancient institutions stand in harmony with popular freedom, and a full recognition of popular rights, and in which religion and law have found one of their most favoured homes. Well, as it is the destiny of man to live in society, under laws and institutions, it is desirable that he should live under good laws and institutions; but if we suppose the case of a country with very bad institutions, colonisation of such a country would be a curse to mankind instead of a blessing, and the reproduction of its tyranny on other shores would not be a cause, in a social or moral point of view, for satisfaction. It is because we feel convinced that our constitution is a blessing to us, and will be a blessing to our posterity, as it has been to our forefathers, that we are desirous of extending its influence, and that it should not be confined within the narrow borders of this little island; but that if it please Providence to create openings for us upon the broad fields of distant continents, we should avail ourselves in reason and moderation of those openings to reproduce the copy of those laws and institutions, those habits and national characteristics, which have made England so famous as she is.

It is now, then, coming to be understood that the affairs of the colonies are best transacted and provided for by the colonists themselves, as the affairs of England are best transacted by Englishmen. And upon this understanding we act more and more, and with still increasing advantage. We do not attempt to force English institutions on the colonies. But then it will be asked, " do you not intend to have English institutions in the colonies?" Certainly, by all means let us have English institutions in the colonies to the utmost extent to which their circumstances render possible. The main question is, who is to be judge of that extension? Now, I say we are not good judges whether laws useful and convenient to this country ought to prevail in the colonies or not; we are not such good judges of this as the colonies themselves. But more, I say this—experience has proved that if you want to strengthen the connexion between the colonies and this country—if you want to increase the resemblance between the colonies and this country—if you want to see British law held in respect and British institutions adopted and beloved in the colonies, never associate with them the hated name of force and coercion exercised by us, at a distance, over their rising fortunes. Govern them upon a principle of freedom—let them not feel any yoke upon their necks— let them understand that the relations between you and them are relations of affection; even in the matter of continuing the connexion, let the colonists be the judges, for they are the best judges, as to whether they ought to continue to be with you or not, and rely upon it you will reap a rich reward in the possession of that affection unbroken and unbounded in all the influence which the possession of such colonies will give you, and in all the grandeur which it will add to your renown. Defend them against aggression from without—regulate their foreign relations (these things belong to the colonial connexion, but of the duration of that connexion let them be the judges)—and I predict that if you leave them that freedom of judgment it is hard to say when the day will come when they will wish to separate from the great name of England. Depend upon it they covet a share in that name. You will find in that feeling of theirs the greatest security for the connexion. You may learn from the London booksellers that the greatest purchasers of books relating to old English history now are the Americans. The Americans who come over to this country seek out and visit the scenes where the most remarkable events in British history have occurred ; they cannot forget that they are the descendants of the men who have made that history just as much as you are. Make the name of England yet more and more an object of desire to the colonies. Their natural disposition is to love and revere it, and that reverence is by far the best security you can have for their continuing not only to be subjects of the crown—not only to render it allegiance, but to render it that allegiance which is the most precious of all—the allegiance which proceeds from the depths of the heart of man.

Printed in Knaplund, *Gladstone and Britain's Imperial Policy* (London, 1927), pp. 201–3, 224–6.

37 : JOHN STUART MILL. *Considerations on Representative Government*

1861

THOUGH Great Britain could do perfectly well without her colonies, and though on every principle of morality and justice she ought to consent to their separation, should the time come when, after full trial of the best form of union, they deliberately desire to be dissevered ;

there are strong reasons for maintaining the present slight bonds of connexion, so long as not disagreeable to the feelings of either party. It is a step, as far as it goes, towards universal peace, and general friendly co-operation among nations. It renders war impossible among a large number of otherwise independent communities; and moreover hinders any of them from being absorbed into a foreign state, and becoming a source of additional aggressive strength to some rival power, either more despotic or closer at hand, which might not always be so unambitious or so pacific as Great Britain. It at least keeps the markets of the different countries open to one another, and prevents that mutual exclusion by hostile tariffs, which none of the great communities of mankind, except England, have yet completely outgrown. And in the case of the British possessions it has the advantage, specially valuable at the present time, of adding to the moral influence, and weight in the councils of the world, of the Power which, of all in existence, best understands liberty—and whatever may have been its errors in the past, has attained to more of conscience and moral principle in its dealings with foreigners, than any other great nation seems either to conceive as possible, or recognise as desirable. Since, then, the union can only continue, while it does continue, on the footing of an unequal federation, it is important to consider by what means this small amount of inequality can be prevented from being either onerous or humiliating to the communities occupying the less exalted position.

The only inferiority necessarily inherent in the case is, that the mother country decides, both for the colonies and for herself, on questions of peace and war. They gain, in return, the obligation on the mother country to repel aggressions directed against them; but, except when the minor community is so weak that the protection of a stronger power is indispensable to it, reciprocity of obligation is not a full equivalent for non-admission to a voice in the deliberations. It is essential, therefore, that in all wars, save those which, like the Caffre or New Zealand wars, are incurred for the sake of the particular colony, the colonists should not (without their own voluntary request) be called on to contribute anything to the expense, except what may be required for the specific local defence of their own ports, shores, and frontiers against invasion. Moreover, as the mother country claims the privilege, at her sole discretion, of taking measures or pursuing a policy which may expose them to attack, it is just that she should undertake a considerable portion of the cost of their military defence even in time of peace; the whole of it, so far as it depends upon a standing army.

In the following passages on India, Mill speaks with the authority of one who had worked up from being a clerk under his father James Mill at the East India House in 1823 to become chief of the office in 1856. He drew up the Company's petition to Parliament against the Act of 1858 ending the Company's rule in India, and retired on pension, declining to serve on the new Council for India under the Government.

The government of a people by itself has a meaning, and a reality; but such a thing as government of one people by another, does not and cannot exist. One people may keep another as a warren or preserve for its own use, a place to make money in, a human cattle farm to be worked for the profit of its own inhabitants. But if the good of the governed is the proper business of a government, it is utterly impossible that a people should directly attend to it. The utmost they can do is to give some of their best men a commission to look after it; to whom the opinion of their own country can neither be much of a guide in the performance of their duty, nor a competent judge of the mode in which it has been performed. Let anyone consider how the English themselves would be governed, if they knew and cared no more about their own affairs, than they know and care about the affairs of the Hindoos. Even this comparison gives no adequate idea of the state of the case: for a people thus indifferent to politics altogether, would probably be simply acquiescent, and let the government alone: whereas in the case of India, a politically active people like the English, amidst habitual acquiescence, are every now and then interfering, and almost always in the wrong place. The real causes which determine the prosperity or wretchedness, the improvement or deterioration, of the Hindoos, are too far off to be within their ken. They have not the knowledge necessary for suspecting the existence of those causes, much less for judging of their operation. . . .

While responsibility to the governed is the greatest of all securities for good government, responsibility to somebody else not only has no such tendency, but is as likely to produce evil as good. The responsibility of the British rulers of India to the British nation is chiefly useful because, when any acts of the government are called in question, it ensures publicity and discussion. . . .

It is not by attempting to rule directly a country like India, but by giving it good rulers, that the English people can do their duty to that country; and they can scarcely give it a worse one than an English Cabinet Minister, who is thinking of English, not Indian politics; who seldom remains long enough in office to acquire an intelligent interest in so complicated a subject; upon whom the factitious public opinion got up in Parliament, consisting of two or three fluent speakers, acts with as much force as if it were genuine; while he is under none of the influences of training and position which would lead or qualify him to form an honest opinion of his own. A free country which attempts to govern a distant dependency, inhabited by a dissimilar people, by means of a branch of its own executive, will almost inevitably fail. The only mode which has any chance of tolerable success, is to govern through a delegated body, of a comparatively permanent character; allowing only a right of inspection, and a negative voice, to the changeable Administration of the State. Such a body did exist in the case of India; and I fear that both India and England will pay a severe penalty for the shortsighted policy by which this intermediate instrument of government was done away with.

J. S. Mill, *Considerations on Representative Government* (1900 ed.), pp. 133, 135–6, 138.

Part VII

MID-CENTURY SEPARATISM

38: RICHARD COBDEN. England, Ireland and America

1835

This book was published after Cobden's first visit to America and was his first publication in his crusade for free trade which continued until his death in 1865. On the Empire he maintained the Radical and economist traditions of Cobbett and James Mill. The thought of his *How Wars are Got up in India* (1853) should be compared with that of Cobbett (No. 9).

WE are aware that no power was ever yet known, voluntarily, to give up the dominion over a part of its territory. But if it could be made manifest to the trading and industrious portion of this nation, who have no honours, or interested ambition of any kind, at stake in the matter, that, whilst our dependencies are supported at an expense to them, in direct taxation, of more than five millions annually, they serve but as gorgeous and ponderous appendages to swell our ostensible grandeur, but, in reality, to complicate and magnify our government expenditure, without improving our balance of trade—surely, under such circumstances, it would become at least a question for anxious inquiry with a people so overwhelmed with debt, whether those colonies should not be suffered to support and defend themselves, as separate and independent existences.

Adam Smith, more than sixty years ago, promulgated his doubts of the wisdom and profitableness of our colonial policy; at a time, be it well remembered, when we were excluded, by the mother countries, from the

South American markets, and when our West Indian possessions appeared to superficial minds an indispensable source of vast wealth to the British empire. Had he lived to our day, to behold the United States of America, after freeing themselves from the dominion of the mother country, become our largest and most friendly commercial connection—had he lived also to behold the free states of South America only prevented from outstripping in magnitude all our other customers by the fetters which an absurd law of exclusive dealing with those very West Indian Colonies has imposed on our commerce—how fully must his opinions have coincided with all that we have urged on this subject!

The Political Writings of Richard Cobden (ed. Ridgway, 1868), Vol. I, pp. 30–1.

39: GEORGE CORNEWALL LEWIS. *An Essay on the Government of Dependencies*

1841

This book was of wide influence in mid-century separatist thought (cf. James Stephen in Nos. 50 and 51), providing political reasons to parallel the economic ones of Cobden and the Manchester School for accepting the ending of Empire. Cornewall Lewis's only acquaintance with the Colonies was as joint commissioner to enquire into the affairs of Malta, 1836–8. He entered Parliament in 1847, was Chancellor of the Exchequer 1855–8, Home Secretary 1859–61, and Secretary for War from then until his death in 1863. He succeeded to the baronetcy on his father's death in 1855.

IT is . . . conceivable that, in a given case, the dominant country might perceive that it derives no benefit from the possession of a dependency, and that the dependency is able and willing to form an independent state; and

166

that, consequently, a dominant country might abandon its authority over a dependency for want of a sufficient inducement to retain it. A dominant country might, for example, see that the dependency contributes nothing to its military defence, or to the expenses of the supreme government; that it adds nothing, as a dependency, to the productive resources or commercial facilities of the dominant country; that it is a constant source of expense to the supreme government, is likely to engender many economical evils, and may even involve the dominant country in war on its account. It might, moreover, perceive that the dependency is sufficiently populous and wealthy to form an independent state, and that the people of the dependency desire independence.

If a dominant country understood the true nature of the advantages arising from the relation of supremacy and dependence to the related communities, it would voluntarily recognize the legal independence of such of its own dependencies as were fit for independence; it would, by its political arrangements, study to prepare for independence those which were still unable to stand alone; and it would seek to promote colonization for the purpose of extending its trade rather than its empire, and without attempting to maintain the dependence of its colonies beyond the time when they need its protection.

The practical difficulties and inconveniences inherent in the government of dependencies . . . are necessary or natural consequences of the relation of supremacy and dependence, and of the imperfect though necessary expedient of a subordinate government. Now if a dependency is considered as in training for ultimate independence, the difficulties naturally incident to its government, if they do not vanish, are nevertheless greatly reduced. If a dependency were so considered, the free and forcible action of its local institutions would be encouraged as an unmixed good, not discouraged as a source of strife with the dominant country, and of vain resistance to its power; and all precautions on the part of the supreme government for the purpose of preventing the people of the dependency from regarding their subordinate government as virtually supreme, would be needless. If a dependency be distant, if its territory be large, and its population numerous; and if the powers of its local subordinate government reside, to a considerable extent, in a body chosen by the inhabitants; it is difficult for the dominant country to prevent it from forming habits and opinions which are scarcely consistent with its virtual dependence. But if such a dependency be regarded as in training for independence, the local popular institutions leading to, and implying, self-government, may be allowed to have free play, and the interferences of the dominant country with the political affairs of the country may cease almost insensibly.

Admitting the impossibility of the prevailing opinions concerning the advantages of extensive empire being so far modified as to permit a dominant country to take such a view of its political relations with its dependencies as that now indicated, it is proved by the example of England that the dominant country may concede virtual independence to a dependency, by establishing in it a system of popular self-government, and by abstaining almost constantly from any interference with its internal affairs.

Such a relation of the dominant country and the dependency as has been described in the preceding paragraph seems, however, scarcely consistent with the duration of the dependence of the latter for any considerable period. At all events the long duration of its dependence under such circumstances implies as much moderation and rationality on both sides as would be implied on the side of the dominant country by a voluntary cession of its authority over the dependency.

It is obvious to remark, that the dominant country ought not to abandon its authority over a dependency, unless the people of the dependency consent to the cession, and are capable of forming an independent community. It is bound morally, not to throw off a helpless dependency, although the possession of it should promise no advantage to itself.

Sir George Cornewall Lewis, *An Essay on the Government of Dependencies* (1841), pp. 333–5.

40: RICHARD COBDEN. Speech at Manchester

10 January 1849

WE are told we must keep up enormous armaments, because we have got so many colonies. People tell me I want to abandon our colonies; but I say, do you intend to hold your colonies by the sword, by armies, and ships of war? That is not a permanent hold upon them. I want to retain them by their affections. If you tell me that our soldiers are kept for their police, I answer, the English people cannot afford to pay for their police. The inhabitants of those colonies are a great deal better off than the mass of the people of England—they are in the possession of a vast deal more of the comforts of life than the bulk of those paying taxes here; they have very few of those taxes that plague us here so much—excise, stamps, and taxes, those fiscal impediments which beset you every day in your callings, are hardly known in our colonies. Our colonies are very able to protect themselves. Every man among them has his fowling-piece, and, if any savages come to attack them, they can defend themselves. They have another guarantee—if civilised men treat savages like men, there is never any occasion to quarrel with them. With regard to our navy, they tell us it is necessary because of our trade with the colonies. I should have thought it was just that trade which wanted no navy at all. It is a sort of coasting trade; our ships are at home when they get to our colonies. We don't want any navy to protect our trade with America, which is a colony emancipated; and we may thank our stars it has broke loose; it never would have been such a customer if the aristocracy of England had held that field of patronage for their younger sons. You don't want a ship of war to protect your trade with the United States; and last year you exported to them 10,900,000*l.* of your produce, more by upwards of a million than you exported to all your colonies together, India excepted.

Speeches of Richard Cobden (ed. John Bright and Thorold Rogers, 1880), pp. 148–9.

41 : THOMAS CARLYLE. *Latter-Day Pamphlets No. IV : The New Downing Street*

15 April 1850

MISERABLER theory than that of money on the ledger being the primary rule for Empires, or for any higher entity than City owls and their mice-catching, cannot well be propounded. And I would by no means advise Felicissimus, ill at ease on his high-trotting and now justly impatient Sleswicker, to let the poor horse in its desperation go in that direction for a momentary solace. If by

lumber-log Governors, by Godfrey's-cordial Constitutions or otherwise, he contrive to cut off the Colonies or
any real right the big British Empire has in her Colonies,
both he and the British Empire will bitterly repent it one
day! The Sleswicker, relieved in ledger for a moment,
will find that it is wounded in heart and honour forever;
and the turning of its wild forehoofs upon Felicissimus
as he lies in the ditch combed off, is not a thing I like to
think of! Britain, whether it be known to Felicissimus or
not, has other tasks appointed her in God's Universe than
the making of money; and woe will betide her if she
forget those other withal. Tasks, colonial and domestic,
which are of an eternally *divine* nature, and compared
with which all money, and all that is procurable by
money, are in strict arithmetic an imponderable quantity, have been assigned this Nation; and they also at last
are coming upon her again, clamorous, abstruse, inevitable, much to her bewilderment just now!

This poor Nation, painfully dark about said tasks and
the way of doing them, means to keep its Colonies nevertheless, as things which somehow or other must have a
value, were it better seen into. They are portions of the
general Earth, where the children of Britain now dwell;
where the gods have so far sanctioned their endeavour,
as to say that they have a right to dwell. England will
not readily admit that her own children are worth nothing but to be flung out of doors! England looking on her
Colonies can say: " Here are lands and seas, spice-lands,
corn-lands, timber-lands, overarched by zodiacs and
stars, clasped by many-sounding seas; wide spaces of the
Maker's building, fit for the cradle yet of mighty Nations
and their sciences and Heroisms. Fertile continents still
inhabited by wild beasts are mine, into which all the distressed populations of Europe might pour themselves,

and make at once an Old World and a New World human. By the eternal fiat of the gods, this must yet one day be; this, by all the Divine Silences that rule this Universe, silent to fools, eloquent and awful to the hearts of the wise, is incessantly at this moment, and at all moments, commanded to begin to be. Unspeakable deliverance, and new destiny of thousandfold expanded manfulness for all men, dawns out of the Future here. To me has fallen the godlike task of initiating all that: of me and of my Colonies, the abstruse Future asks, Are you wise enough for so sublime a destiny? Are you too foolish?

T. Carlyle, *Latter-Day Pamphlets No. IV: The New Downing Street* (1850), pp. 31–2.

42: JOHN BRIGHT. Speech on India

House of Commons, 3 June 1853

Of the two leaders of the Manchester School Bright's reactions to the Empire were the more complex. While agreeing with Cobden on the white Empire he accepted the fact of obligations to India and to the native peoples of South Africa. This led to Gladstone's offer of the Secretaryship of State for India in 1868, which, however, Bright refused, accepting instead the Presidency of the Board of Trade.

I RECOLLECT having heard the noble Lord the Member for Tiverton (Viscount Palmerston) deliver in this House one of the best speeches I ever listened to. On that occasion the noble Lord gloried in the proud name of England, and, pointing to the security with which an Englishman might travel abroad, he triumphed in the idea that his countrymen might exclaim, in the spirit of the ancient Roman, *Civis Romanus sum.* Let us not resemble the Romans merely in our national privileges and personal security. The Romans were great conquerors, but where they conquered, they governed wisely. The nations they conquered were impressed so indelibly with the intellectual character of their masters, that, after fourteen centuries of decadence, the traces of civilisation are still distinguishable. Why should not we act a similar part in India? There never was a more docile people, never a more tractable nation. The opportunity is present, and the power is not wanting. Let us abandon the policy of aggression, and confine ourselves to a territory ten times the size of France, with a population four times as numerous as that of the United Kingdom. Surely that is enough to satisfy the most gluttonous appetite for glory and supremacy. Educate the people of India, govern them wisely, and gradually the distinctions of caste will disappear, and they will look upon us rather as benefactors than as conquerors. And if we desire to see Christianity, in some form, professed in that country, we shall sooner attain our object by setting the example of a high-toned Christian morality, than by any other means we can employ.

Speeches on Questions of Public Policy by John Bright (ed. Thorold Rogers, 1868), I, pp. 32–3.

43: RICHARD COBDEN. Letters on India

16 October 1857. Unfortunately for me I can't even co-operate with those who seek to 'reform' India, for I have no faith in the power of England to govern that country at all permanently; and though I should like to see the Company abolished—because that is a screen between the English nation and a full sight of its awful responsibilities—yet I do not believe in the possibility of the Crown governing India under the control of Parliament. If the House of Commons were to renounce all responsibility for domestic legislation, and give itself exclusively to the task of governing one hundred millions of Asiatics, it would fail. Hindoostan must be ruled by those who live on that side of the globe. Its people will prefer to be ruled badly—*according to our notions*—by its own colour, kith and kin, than to submit to the humiliation of being better governed by a succession of transient intruders from the antipodes.

16 May 1858. I am afraid our national character is being deteriorated, and our love of freedom in danger of being impaired by what is passing in India. Is it possible that we can play the part of despot and butcher there without finding our character deteriorated at home? Were not the ancient Greeks and Romans corrupted and demoralized by their Asiatic conquests, and may we not share their fate, though in a different way? Then comes the question which you have so ably put in your letter. 'What possible benefit can we derive from our Indian conquests?' I confess I take a gloomy view of our prospects in that quarter. The English people will not give up Hindoostan, any more than they did North America, without years of exhausting war.

It is more and more my conviction that the task of governing *despotically* 150 millions of people at a distance of twelve thousand miles cannot be executed by a constitutional Government. It ought to be done, if at all, by a despot, whose rule is concentrated, and less liable to personal changes than our representative forms admit. With a change of Government every six or twelve months it is impossible that we can have a continuous plan or a real responsibility.

Printed in J. Morley, *Life of Cobden* (1881), Vol. II, pp. 207, 216–7.

44: ANTHONY TROLLOPE. *The West Indies and the Spanish Main*

1859

Trollope, as a Post Office official, was sent on missions in 1858 to Egypt and the West Indies. After the second he produced this volume which he regarded as " the best book that has come from my pen." (*Autobiography*).

THE present position and prospects of the children of Great Britain are sufficiently noble, and sufficiently extended. One need not begrudge to others their limited share in the population and government of the world's welfare. While so large a part of North America and Australia remain still savage—waiting the white man's foot—waiting, in fact, for the foot of the Englishman, there can be no reason why we should doom our children to swelter and grow pale within the tropics. A certain work has been ours to do there, a certain amount of re- maining work it is still probably our lot to complete. But when that is done; when civilization, commerce, and education shall have been spread; when sufficient of our blood shall have been infused into the veins of those children of the sun; then, I think, we may be ready, without stain to our patriotism, to take off our hats and bid farewell to the West Indies.

And be it remembered that I am here speaking of the · general ascendancy, not of the political power of these coloured races. It may be that after all we shall still have to send out some white Governor with a white aide-de- camp and a white private secretary—some three or four unfortunate white men to support the dignity of the throne of Queen Victoria's great-grandchild's grand- child. Such may be, or may not be. To my thinking, it would be more for our honour that it should not be so. If the honour, glory, and well-being of the child be dear to the parents, Great Britain should surely be more proud of the United States than of any of her colonies.

We Britishers have a noble mission. The word I know is unpopular, for it has been foully misused; but it is in itself a good word, and none other will supply its place. We have a noble mission, but we are never content with it. It is not enough for us to beget nations, civilize countries, and instruct in truth and knowledge the dominant races of the coming ages. All this will not suffice unless also we can maintain a king over them! What is it to us, or even to them, who may be their king or ruler—or, to speak with a nearer approach to sense, from what source they be governed—so long as they be happy, prosperous, and good? And yet there are men mad enough to regret the United States! Many men are mad enough to look forward with anything but composure to the inevitable, happily inevitable day, when Australia shall follow in the same path.

We have risen so high that we almost boast to have placed ourselves above national glory. The welfare of the coming world is now the proper care of the Anglo-Saxon race.

A. Trollope, *The West Indies and the Spanish Main* (4th ed., 1860), pp. 83–5.

PART VIII

OFFICIAL OPINION: RESPONSIBLE POLITICIANS

45: LORD EDWARD GEORGE GEOFFREY SMITH STANLEY. Speech in the House of Commons

30 May 1844

Stanley, later Prime Minister as Lord Derby, was Secretary for War and the Colonies 1833-4 and 1841-5. He once wittily called the joint department, as it was until 1854, " the office at war with all the colonies ". He had been responsible for the Act of Emancipation of 1833 while a Whig, but has been chosen here and in extract No. 48 as typical of responsible Conservative opinion.

SIR, I do not underrate the importance of Canada to the empire. I do not look on it as a source of strength in war —it is more likely to be a source of weakness. It would give us little or no support in an European war, and in case of a war with the United States, which God forbid, it would be our most vulnerable point. In a military point of view, therefore, Canada adds little to the strength of the empire. Indirectly, the connection strengthens us by forming a nursery for our seamen; and, in a commercial point of view, it is of great importance to us, as giving us a command over the inlet and outlet to a great Continent, through a mighty river, which is one of the finest water communications on the globe. Commercially and politically, then, I will not deny that it is of great importance to us; but if the connection be of importance to this country, I ask the hon. and learned Gentleman [Roebuck], whether, in his judgment, it is not infinitely more advantageous to the population of Canada? Are they slight advantages which the people of Canada derive from it? They enjoy as free a Government, and, I venture to say, the lightest taxation of any people on the inhabited globe. They have perfect religious freedom. They have, at no cost to themselves, the naval and military protection of one of the mightiest powers. They have annually an immense expenditure in the shape of Commissariat and other establishments distributed over their territory. They have been enabled during the last year to borrow (while the United States are unable to obtain money at 6 per cent) from their connection with this country and nothing else, for the improvement of their internal communications, a million and a half at little, if at all, exceeding $3\frac{1}{2}$ per cent. Canada has an immense indirect expenditure from the establishment of British merchants, and the investment of British capital. I have stated already she has the protection of this country. She has also for her produce (and no inconsiderable addition has lately been made to this advantage) the exclusive benefit of a free admission to the richest market in the world. These are the advantages which Canada possesses through her connection with this country; these are the advantages which Canada must be prepared to sacrifice if a separation should unhappily result. It is for Canada well to consider whether the price she has to pay in the slight and all but nominal subordination to this country is too high a price for the protection, advantages, and substantial benefits conferred on her. But Canada must not expect, as the hon. and learned Gentleman seems to think she has a right to expect, that she can at once enjoy the unlimited and entire independence of a separate republic, and the advantages derived from British protection and commerce. I believe the mass of the people of Canada are cordially attached to this country. I believe, when they seriously consider the results of the alternative I have put, they will follow, not the advice of the unprincipled demagogues—bad, rash, and interested counsellors, but take as their guide the liberal, sound, and honest views of the Governor General.[1] I am persuaded, that by the exercise of sound sense and discretion, the people of Canada may long continue to enjoy the advantages she now possesses ; and that in connection with, rather than in subordination to this country, she may assume the position of a thriving and happy Colony.

Hansard, Third Series, Vol. LXXV, cs. 59–61.

46: LORD JOHN RUSSELL. Speech in the House of Commons

8 February 1850

Russell was Secretary for War and the Colonies 1839–41 and Prime Minister 1846–52 and 1865–6. His approach to the problem of responsible government for the Colonies was essentially pragmatic (cf. p. 8 and No. 49). His general policy was set forth in this important speech. It provoked a hostile reaction in Canada because of the mention at the end of the distant possibility of separation. (Elgin commented on this " sting in the tail " in a dispatch to Grey, reprinted in Jack Simmons, *From Empire to Commonwealth* (1949).

In the controversy of 1869–70 Russell showed hostility to Gladstone's policy which seemed to him to lead to separation.

I COME now to a question which has been much agitated, and which has found supporters of very considerable ability—namely, that we should no longer think it worth our while to maintain our colonial empire. I say, in the first place, with regard to this proposal, that I consider it to be our bounden duty to maintain the colonies which have been placed under our own charge. I think we cannot get rid of the obligation and responsibility to govern

[1] Sir Charles Metcalfe (ed.).

those colonies for their benefit, and I trust we may be the instruments of improving and civilising those portions of the world in which they are situated. In the next place, I say that there are many reasons why we should consider that our colonies form part of the strength of the empire. I think that, in peace as well as in war, it is a question of the utmost importance whether we should retain these supports of the imperial authority of this country, or whether we should be deprived of them.

I would observe, further, that there are in some of these colonies native races which we have been able, in a certain degree, to civilise, and which we have brought in order and subjection to authority. There is now in one of our recent colonies a most remarkable race, I mean the population of New Zealand, which not many years ago was given up to practices the most abhorrent to humanity, but which, from intercourse and communication with our countrymen, appears to be far more capable of civilisation than almost any of the savage races with which we have come in contact. There is also another race, the natives of the district of Natal, in Africa, which shows every sign of docility and fitness for learning the arts of civilised life. There are other people, also, who, if they were abandoned by us, would undoubtedly relapse into their savage habits, and who would probably commence a war of races with the few Europeans who would be left in command of them; and we should thus give up parts of the world which have been reclaimed from barbarism to most cruel and desolating warfare.

But there are other matters relating to the imperial authority, and to the security of this country which cannot be lost sight of in considering the value of our colonies. Every one will admit the value of that commerce which penetrates to every part of the globe; and many of those colonies give harbours and security to that trade, which are most useful in time of peace, but are absolutely necessary in time of war. I think that the persons who talk about giving up the colonies, without much investigating the subject, do not consider what would be the probable result with respect to a great number of those colonies. It is easy to say, that because the United States have formed a prosperous, and civilised, and free community, and that because they are not only great customers for our goods, but also receive our emigrants, other colonies might take the same course with equal advantage. But many of our colonies would be wholly unable to do so, not having the means of preserving anything like independence or security amidst the savage races by which they are surrounded. What, then, would they do? If they were abandoned by Great Britain, they would most naturally and justly apply to some other country for protection. The Cape of Good Hope would apply to Holland; the Mauritius to France; other colonies would apply to other States, and they would say, "We have been abandoned by those to whom we were bound by allegiance; protection is now taken from us, and we ask you to become our protectors, and to receive our allegiance." Who can doubt that other countries would readily afford the protection so asked, and that they would become strong on what would be our weakness?

Sir, if this scheme is not consistent either with our honour or with our policy, there are others which have been proposed which I think equally objectionable. One is, that we should altogether abandon any share in the government of our colonies, and that we should likewise refuse them any means of defence. I think, Sir, that such a system would very soon lead to the same result as the proposal I have just noticed. These colonies would say, " If we are not to be defended—if we are to receive no support from Great Britain—let us look for other protectors; let us ask other States if they will assist us with their arms, and protect us against any attacks which may be made upon us."

Hansard, Third Series, Vol. CVIII, cs. 545–7.

47 : HENRY GEORGE, EARL GREY. *The Colonial Policy of Lord John Russell's Administration*

1853

Grey's Secretaryship for War and the Colonies (1846–52) is of first importance for the implementation of the Durham Report in the granting of responsible government to the colonies. He defended the whole of his policy in two volumes in the form of letters to Russell, from which these extracts are taken.

I CONSIDER, then, that the British Colonial Empire ought to be maintained, principally because I do not consider that the Nation would be justified in throwing off the responsibility it has incurred by the acquisition of this dominion, and because I believe that much of the power and influence of this Country depends upon its having large Colonial possessions in different parts of the world.

The possession of a number of steady and faithful allies, in various quarters of the globe, will surely be admitted to add greatly to the strength of any nation; while no alliance between independent states can be so close and intimate as the connection which unites the Colonies to the United Kingdom as parts of the Great British Empire. Nor ought it to be forgotten, that the power of a nation does not depend merely on the amount of physical force it can command, but rests, in no small degree, upon opinion and moral influence: in this respect British power would be diminished by the loss of our Colonies, to a degree which it would be difficult to estimate. Hence, if it is an advantage, not for the sake of domineering over other countries but with a view to our own security, to form part of a powerful nation rather than of a weak one (and, considering the many examples we have seen of the injustice to which weak ones are compelled to submit, this can hardly admit of a question), it seems to follow, that the tie which binds together all the different and distant portions of the British Empire, so that their united strength may be wielded for their common protection, must be regarded as an object of extreme importance to the interests of the Mother-country and her dependencies. To the latter it is no doubt of far greater importance than to the former, because, while still forming comparatively small and weak communities, they enjoy, in return for their allegiance to the British Crown, all the security and consideration which belongs to them as members of one of the most powerful States in the world. No foreign Power ventures to attack or interfere with the smallest of them, while every Colonist carries with him, to the remotest quarters of the globe which he may visit in trading or other pursuits, that protection which the character of a British subject everywhere confers, and can depend, in any difficulties, or under any oppression to which he may be exposed, on the assistance of Her Majesty's diplomatic and consular servants, supported, if necessary, by the whole power of the Empire.

But I should regard it as a very unworthy mode of considering this subject, if it were to be looked at with a view only to the interests of this Country, as that word is usually understood. I conceive that, by the acquisition of its Colonial dominions, the Nation has acquired a responsibility of the highest kind, which it is not at liberty to throw off. The authority of the British Crown is at this moment the most powerful instrument, under Providence, of maintaining peace and order in many extensive regions of the earth, and thereby assists in diffusing amongst millions of the human race, the blessings of Christianity and civilization. Supposing it were clear (which I am far from admitting) that a reduction of our national expenditure (otherwise impracticable), to the extent of a few hundred thousands a year, could be effected by withdrawing our authority and protection from our numerous Colonies, should we be justified, for the sake of such a saving, in taking this step, and thus abandoning the duty which seems to have been cast upon us?

It is to be remembered, that if we adopted this policy we must be prepared for very serious consequences, which would undoubtedly result from it. Some few only of these I will mention. No one acquainted with the actual state of society in the West India islands, and the feelings prevalent among the different classes of their inhabitants, can doubt that, if they were left, unaided by us, to settle amongst themselves in whose hands power should be placed, a fearful war of colour would probably soon break out, by which the germs of improvement now existing there would be destroyed, and civilization would be thrown back for centuries. In Ceylon a similar result would follow; its native races are utterly incapable of governing themselves, and yet they certainly would not submit to be ruled by the mere handful of Europeans who have settled among them, if this small body were unsupported by British power. The great wealth which within the last few years has been created in this island would be destroyed, and the most hopeless anarchy would take place of that security which now exists, and under the shelter of which such promising signs of improvement are beginning to appear. Even in New Zealand, although I have little doubt that the Colonists of European descent would be found capable of establishing a government, under which they might eventually rise to prosperity, yet we could scarcely hope to see this effected without a series of contests with the native inhabitants, in which the latter would in the end be destroyed, but not until they had inflicted and suffered an almost equal amount of misery. On the West Coast of Africa there is at this moment a far more encouraging prospect than at any previous time; the efforts which have been so long made to improve the negro race seem to be at length beginning to produce important results, and a great change for the better may be looked for. But if we take up a new policy, and abandon our positions on the African coast, the Slave Trade will again revive in the extensive territory within reach of our settlements, where it has now been extirpated, and has given place to a legitimate commerce, which is daily becoming more important.

To say nothing of higher motives, and of the duty which I conceive to be no less obligatory upon nations than upon individuals, of using the power and the advantage entrusted to them by Providence to advance the welfare of mankind, I would ask whether, even in mere money, there would not be something to set off against the saving of expense from the abandonment of our Colonies? On the other side of the account we have to put the destruction of British property which would thus be occasioned, and the annihilation of lucrative branches of our commerce, by allowing anarchy and bloodshed to arrest the peaceful industry which now creates the means of paying for the British goods consumed daily in larger quantities, by the numerous and various populations now emerging from barbarism under our protection.

It is true there are several of our Colonies to which the last observations do not directly apply; but the policy of abandoning a part of our Colonial Empire could scarcely be adopted, without giving so great a shock to the feeling of confidence and security in the remainder, as greatly to increase the difficulty of maintaining it; and I must add, that it appears to me very doubtful whether even the Colonies most capable of governing themselves, and which have no uncivilized tribes to deal with, from whom any danger could be apprehended, would not for some time have much difficulty in maintaining their present state of tranquillity and security, both externally and internally, if their connection with the Mother-country were suddenly dissolved.

In New South Wales, for instance, the interference of the Home Government in the internal administration of the Colony is exceedingly slight; but, slight as it is, it may be questioned whether, without it, the conflict of interests and opinions between different classes of the inhabitants and between different districts would not be likely to lead to very dangerous struggles; while in their relations with each other it would be still more likely that the different Australian Colonies would be involved in difficulties, if they ceased to be all placed under the supreme authority of the Imperial Government.

I have thought it necessary to state thus strongly my dissent from the views of those who wish to dismember the British Empire by abandoning the Colonies, because it is impossible not to observe that this policy—unworthy of a great Nation, and unwise as I consider it to be—is not only openly advocated by one active party in the country, but is also hardly less effectually supported by persons occupying an important position in Parliament, and who, while they hesitate to avow their adherence to it, hold language which obviously leads in the same direction, and advocate measures the adoption of which would inevitably bring about this result.

If the reasons which I have just stated for maintaining the connection between this Country and the British Colonies are admitted to be sound, it will follow as a necessary inference, that two very plain rules as to the terms on which that connection should be continued may be laid down. In the first place, I think it will clearly follow that this Country has no interest whatever in exercising any greater influence in the internal affairs of the Colonies, than is indispensable either for the purpose of preventing any one Colony from adopting measures injurious to another, or to the Empire at large; or else for the promotion of the internal good government of the Colonies, by assisting the inhabitants to govern themselves when sufficiently civilized to do so with advantage, and by providing a just and impartial administration for those of which the population is too ignorant and unenlightened to manage its own affairs. While it was our policy to maintain a monopoly of the trade of the Colonies, it was necessary for the Home Government to exercise a considerable control over their internal administration, because otherwise this monopoly would certainly have been evaded; and accordingly it will be found, on looking back at the earlier history of our Colonies, (especially those which now constitute the

United States,) that the interference of the servants of the Crown in their internal affairs, and the differences which that interference occasioned, arose almost entirely from the endeavour to uphold the commercial system then in force. The abandonment of that system has removed the necessity for this interference. Secondly, I think it will follow, that when this Country no longer attempts either to levy a commercial tribute from the Colonies by a system of restriction, nor to interfere need-lessly in their internal affairs, it has a right to expect that they should take upon themselves a larger proportion than heretofore of the expenses incurred for their advantage.

Both the Mother-country and the Colonies are deeply interested in preventing the improper and premature alienation of Colonial lands; since it is the interest of both, that every possible facility should be given to those who may be disposed to leave this country for the purpose of seeking a new home in our Colonial dominions. And it is on this account, that it seems to me both just and wise that the Imperial Government and Legislature should not, at too early a period, transfer to the local Authorities the power of determining under what regulations the Crown lands in the Colonies should be disposed of. These lands constitute a vast estate, which has been acquired, and to which all the value it possesses has been given, by the very large expense which has been incurred by the Mother-country in establishing, maintaining, and protecting its Colonies. This estate the Crown holds as trustee for the benefit of all its subjects, not merely of the few thousands who may at this moment inhabit a particular Colony, but of the whole British people, whether resident at home or in the Colonies; and it is the duty of the servants of the Crown, and of Parliament, to take care that the magnificent property thus held in trust for the good of the whole Empire, shall be wisely and carefully administered with a view to that object, and not improvidently wasted, or sacrificed to the rapacity of a few individuals. But if the power of altering the regulations under which the Crown lands are disposed of, were given too soon to every Colonial Legislature, nothing is more probable than that the small society of a young Colony might think it for their interest to share among them, to the exclusion of the other inhabitants of the Empire, the lands which properly belong to all; and it is still more probable that, in such a Colony, a few rapacious speculators might have sufficient influence to carry changes, which would conduce to their personal gain, under the plausible but delusive pretence of promoting the interests of their fellow-colonists.

The Colonial Policy of Lord John Russell's Administration, Vol. I, pp. 11–18, 318–9.

48: EDWARD GEORGE GEOFFREY SMITH STANLEY, EARL OF DERBY. Speech in the House of Lords

29 June 1854

I KNOW that there are those who treat lightly the separation of the Colonies from the mother-country; but, for my own part, I am one of those who would deeply regret that separation, although in the course of time I anticipate it, as the natural result of the growth and progress of democratic principles. I anticipate that the time will come when the great North American Federation, if I may so call it—the great aggregate of the North American Colonies—will take upon itself the entire and independent control of their own affairs, and will be, if not nominally separate, at all events practically and virtually separate, and independent alike of Parliament, of the Government, and of the Crown. I trust, however, that even in such a state of things that great federation will remain in perfect harmony with this country, bound by ties of loyalty to the same Sovereign, although that sovereignty may be but nominal. . . .

I have dreamed—perhaps it was only a dream—that the time would come when, exercising a perfect control over their own internal affairs, Parliament abandoning its right to interfere in their legislation, these great and important colonies, combined together, should form a monarchical Government, presided over either by a permanent viceroy, or, as an independent Sovereign, by one nearly and closely allied to the present Royal family of this country. I have believed that in such a manner it would be possible to uphold the monarchical principle, to establish upon that great continent a monarchy free as that of this country, even freer still with regard to the popular influence exercised, but yet a monarchy worthy of the name, and not a mere empty shadow. I can hardly believe that under such a system the friendly connection and close intimacy between the Colonies and the mother-country would in any way be affected; but, on the contrary, I feel convinced that the change to which I have referred would be productive of nothing, for years and years to come, but mutual harmony and friendship, increased and cemented as that friendship would be by mutual appreciation of the great and substantial benefits conferred by a free and regulated monarchy.

Hansard, Third Series, Vol. CXXXIV, cs. 844–5.

49: JOHN, EARL RUSSELL. Introduction to his
Speeches and Despatches

1870

I GAVE still stronger assurances [than to New Zealand] to
the British Provinces of North America, pledging to
them the word of the Queen, that so long as they desired
to remain her subjects, they should receive the support
of the Crown, and be defended as a part of the British
dominions.

A faint-hearted Government in Great Britain may
break these pledges, and depart from this policy. But
from the day when they do so the Decline and Fall of
British Empire may be dated.

At the same time I do not think that the relations of
the Colonies to the Mother Country, can be kept up precisely in their present form.

There is uneasiness growing up on both sides; the
Colonies doubting as to the protection they may receive,
and Great Britain complaining of the cost of the Naval
and Military expenses incurred in defence of colonial
interests, whenever they are in danger.

I am disposed to believe, that if a Congress, or Assembly representing Great Britain and her Dependencies,
could be convoked from time to time, to sit for some
months in the Autumn, arrangements reciprocally beneficial might be made.

Mr. Baldwin, who had taken a prominent part in
Canadian politics, came to England while Lord Glenelg
was Secretary of State for the Colonies, and by his desire
discussed with me the question of responsible government. I raised the objection that a responsible ministry
in Canada might object to take part with England in a
foreign war, in which she might be engaged.

Mr. Baldwin, who was a man of sense and ability, assured me that the Canadians had no such pretensions. They wished to manage their own local affairs, and had no desire to diminish the authority, or dim the lustre of the Crown of England in her external affairs.

With this assurance I was satisfied; and when I held the seals I practically acted upon it, though I did not concur in the theory. In 1854, I proposed to the House of Commons, on the part of the government of Lord Aberdeen, to give free scope to the legislature of Canada in ecclesiastical affairs, and I have seen no reason to regret this policy.

It is the fashion to say that those Colonies which have adopted British institutions, whose ministers resign on a vote of want of confidence, and whose laws are framed on a British type, are virtually independent, and have no right to look for British protection. In my opinion nothing could be meaner in spirit, nothing less wise in policy, than such assertions.

There was a time when we might have stood alone as the United Kingdom of England, Scotland and Ireland. That time has passed. We conquered and peopled Canada, we took possession of the whole of Australia, Van Dieman's Land and New Zealand. We have annexed India to the Crown. There is no going back.

Tu regere imperio populos, Romane, memento.

For my part, I delight in observing the imitation of our free institutions, and even our habits and manners in Colonies, at a distance of 3,000 or 4,000 miles from the Palace of Westminster. . . .

It is hardly necessary to say, that when the majority in any of our dependencies declare by their representatives that they wish to separate from us, no attempt should be made to detain them. The faults committed by George

Grenville, Charles Townshend, and Lord North can never be repeated.

Of course this remark does not apply to places like Gibraltar and Malta. . . .

The Minister who tries to weaken the attachment of our North American Provinces to Great Britain, will be sure to rouse the grievous indignation of the people of England, and will be punished, if not by impeachment, at all events by eternal infamy.

Earl Russell, *Speeches and Despatches* (1870). pp. 153–4.

PART IX

OFFICIAL OPINION: CIVIL SERVANTS OF THE COLONIAL OFFICE

50: SIR JAMES STEPHEN. Letter dictated to Lady Stephen for Mr. Cunningham

Cambridge, 20 March 1850

Stephen (1789–1859) served in the legal department of the Colonial Office from 1813 and was Permanent Under-Secretary from 1836 to 1847. He drafted the Act of Emancipation in 1833, breaking the Sabbath to do so: a prominent member of the Clapham Sect, he considered his position in the Colonial Office an opportunity to do something for the negroes. He was under constant attack from the Colonial Reformers as "Mr. Over-Secretary Stephen" and "Mr. Mother-Country" (as the latter he is depicted in Buller's *Responsible Government for Colonies*); he has been justified by recent research (see P. Knaplund: *James Stephen and the British Colonial System, 1813-1847* (Madison, 1953).

On retirement he became Regius Professor of Modern History at Cambridge and was Professor at the East India College, Haileybury, 1855–7.

My husband says that he thinks no wise or reasonable man would ever affirm broadly and generally that a mother country ought at some time or other to part with her colonies. On such a subject it seems to him to be the duty of a statesman to act on broad principles, not on peremptory rules.

Applying the question to this country, he thinks that England ought never to give up a single colony. He thinks that the course taken with Canada, on which he bestowed many years' labour, is the only right course. It was that of cheerfully relaxing, one after another, the bonds of authority, as soon as the colony itself clearly desired that relaxation—so substituting a federal for a

THE CONCEPT OF EMPIRE

colonial relation, the change being real, not nominal—
no national pride wounded, or national greatness
diminished, or national duty abandoned. It remains for
the Canadians to cut the last cable which anchors them
to us. But it is for them, not for us, to take that step, and
to assume the consequent responsibility.

The same system is in progress with the Australian
colonies. The rest are unfit for it—detached islands with
heterogeneous populations—wretched burdens to this
country, which in an evil hour we assumed, but which
we have no right to lay down again.

We emancipate our grown-up sons, but keep our un-
married daughters, and our children who may chance to
be rickety, in domestic bonds. The analogy is a very close
one.

Further, (I need not tell you that I am writing from
dictation,) I am bidden to say that you should look at a
very late report of a committee of Privy Council on the
Australian Constitutions,[1] of which report my husband
is the author, and at a book by G. C. Lewis on Colonial
Dependencies. The first will show you what we are
actually doing. The second is an exposition of the principles on which we ought to act. . . .

    Printed in C. E. Stephen, *The First Sir James Stephen* (1906),
pp. 143–4.

51 : SIR JAMES STEPHEN. Speech to the Meeting of
the National Association for the Promotion of Social
Science

Liverpool, 13 October 1858

IN the first place, I venture to say—though Sir George
Lewis scouts it as so much rhetorical nonsense—that the

  [1] 1849 [ed.].

glory of being the metropolis of these magnificent dependencies is a real and a substantial advantage to Great Britain and Ireland, although I confess that I am unable to define the nature or to express the amount of that advantage in any authentical or statistical terms. But of the most precious treasures of a great nation, how many are there which cannot be spanned by the theodolite or weighed by the steelyard, or measured by avoirdupoise? and, of such treasures, is there any more precious than the title which such a nation may have established to the esteem and gratitude of mankind at large by the wise, magnanimous, and beneficent use of her powers? And when were such national powers ever employed more wisely, or magnanimously, or beneficially, than when we converted the American and Australian wildernesses into the abodes of populous commonwealths, the inheritors of our christianity and civilisation, and impressed with the very image and superscription of our ancient constitutional monarchy?

This is indeed a glory which the world at large will never celebrate or recognise; but what then? True glory is not dependent on external suffrages. It can exist and flourish without them; nay, it can so exist in the highest conceivable, or rather in the highest inconceivable degree; for we are bidden to ascribe to the King of Kings Himself not the kingdom and the power only, but the glory also; the glory, that is, of reigning over that boundless kingdom, and of using that almighty power, for the welfare of all who are subject to His dominions —the glory of bestowing blessings upon them, not the glory of receiving benedictions from them.

Not only are we to expect no applause from other states for our colonisation of the world, but so long as we "hold that princely heritage in fee" we must expect to be regarded by our neighbours with every distrust, jealousy and ill-will. In reference to them we must always be drifting towards the state of isolation so much abhorred of diplomatists; and in the time of need we shall too often find our alliances with them but so many treacherous quicksands. With our colonies it is not so. They are bound to us by alliances which they will hold sacred and inviolable as long as we ourselves continue to be true and faithful to them. . . .

They are compacts of which nature herself is the guarantee, and which will therefore remain dear and venerable to the contracting parties, even after many provocations and many contests; for these are after all family quarrels which, if more bitter than any other, are also more readily and effectually reconciled.

The tacit alliances between ourselves and our colonies may be said to be either domestic, or foreign, or religious, or commercial. By domestic alliances I mean their and our joint assent to the principle that they and we are all one people, so that no one of us is merely a member of a single realm or province, but that each one of it is also a member of a mighty empire, to the public trusts and honours and emoluments of every part of which we are all equally entitled to aspire on equal terms. By our foreign alliances with our colonies, I mean their and our adoption of all the relations, whether of peace or war, into which our Sovereign may enter with any other potentate, so that each component part of the Queen's dominions has always the same friends, the same allies, and the same enemies. By our religious alliances with our colonies—I mean their concurrence with us in allowing every one to worship according to the law of his own conscience without incurring on that account any pain or penalty, or civil disability, or political disqualification.

And by commercial alliance I mean the guarantee to be found both in the imperial and in all the colonial statute books, that within their respective jurisdictions every person in the Queen's allegiance shall enjoy an absolute freedom of buying and selling what and where and when and how he likes, unobstructed by any partial law or favour of others, and unburdened by any duties excepting only such as may be imposed with a real and an exclusive view to the interests of the public revenue. Such are the four main articles of the great federal compact between the fifty united states of the British empire.

But all these articles are not intended for all times. It is evidently possible, I think it is probable, that the day will come when our Canadian and our native dependencies will calmly and deliberately insist on being dependencies no longer, but on being as independent in form and in name as they are already in truth and in reality. And when that demand shall be so made, is there a man among us who would discharge, I do not say a single cannon, but so much as a single lucifer match, to resist it? May the union be perpetual; but if it shall ever cease to be spontaneous and cordial it will also cease to be valuable. Our colonies have evidently the power, if they shall ever find the will, to dissolve the federal compact with us, so far as it is either domestic or foreign. But so far as it is religious and commercial, neither they nor we can entirely dissolve it. To a great extent it must, in these respects, remain indissoluble. To this hour we maintain a tacit, yet a binding alliance, religious and commercial, with the United States. The third generation of American citizens are still, I believe, looking with some yearnings of the heart, and with some filial pride, to the land of their and our ancestry. That they are

looking to it with much commercial complacency is not a matter of doubtful belief, but of certain knowledge.
Printed as a pamphlet, pp. 3–4.

52 : HERMAN MERIVALE. *Lectures on Colonization and Colonies*

1861

Merivale was Drummond Professor of Political Economy at Oxford from 1837 to 1842. There he delivered between 1839 and 1841 the lectures from which these extracts are taken. They were reprinted with additions in appendices (also represented here) in 1861 after he had served from 1847 to 1859 as Permanent Under-Secretary at the Colonial Office. He then became head of the India Office from 1859 until his death in 1874.

THE mere effort of directing the mind to travel abroad to those new regions of romance and expectation, where all is life, and hope, and active energy, affords a relief to the spirits, which again feel wearied and fettered when it is called back to fix its attention at home. This yearning after the distant and the unseen is a common propensity of our nature; and how much is the force of that "secret impulse" cherished and strengthened, in the minds of us Englishmen, by all the associations in the midst of which we are educated! Masters of every sea, and colonists of every shore, there is scarcely a nook which our industry has not rendered accessible, scarcely a region to which the eye can wander in the map, in which we have not some object of national interest—some factory for our trade, some settlement of our citizens. It is a sort of instinctive feeling to us all, that the destiny of our name and nation is not here, in this narrow island which we occupy; that the spirit of England is volatile, not fixed; that it lives in our language, our commerce, our industry, all those channels of intercommunication by which we embrace and connect the vast multitude of states, both civilised and uncivilised, throughout the world. No circumstance, in my view, affords at once such a proof of our vocation to this great end, and such an augury of our success in the pursuit of it, as the peculiar and (in a certain sense of the word) unselfish interest with which schemes of colonization are regarded by almost all classes of society; the sanguine hopes we are apt to entertain of their success, the sacrifices we are willing to make for their promotion, even with little or no regard to the manner in which they may affect our economical prosperity at home.

Surely, few things are more important to the welfare of an infant nation than to be impressed with a sense of its own permanent existence—its own nationality, so to speak—by the evidence of institutions rooted as it were in the soil, and protected by the same safeguard with which the constitution fences the property of individuals and the sovereignty of the monarch. The situation of a modern colonist is very different from that which imagination rather than history suggests, when we carry our minds back to the foundation of states and empires. He comes from an old country, his habits regulated by its usages, his mind full of its institutions. Perhaps he is strongly attached to those institutions: perhaps he is discontented with them. But, in either case, his strongest impressions, his most vehement emotions, are connected with them. He lives mentally in the past and future rather than the present, in the society which he has left, and that of which he dreams as a distant possibility, rather than that which he contributes to create. He regards the immediate social prospects of the new community, as such, at first with comparative indifference;

it is the home of his industry, not of his thoughts: he cares little about its development from within; but all his old party feelings are excited in furthering or in opposing the transplantation of laws and establishments from the mother country. And these feelings are inherited by his descendants for many generations; their strength diminishes very gradually. There is something almost grotesque in the institution of Orange Lodges in Upper Canada, and Pitt Club dinners in Australia. . . .

The consequence of this is, a tendency in new colonial communities to allow those institutions which are of domestic origin to grow up carelessly and at random; to frame laws merely for actual emergencies; to fill up the foundations with rubbish, and let future generations care for the finished building. There are some who believe such improvised and practical institutions to be the best of all, or rather the only useful ones. But those who contemplate national establishments not merely with a view to their immediate adaptation for use, but as contributing most essentially, among other causes, to form the mind and temper of the people itself, cannot but think that it is well to commence the building with some reference to a preconceived idea, not inflexible indeed, but still independent, and to give pledges, as it were, to the future, binding the people to revere and guard the durable elements of moral greatness. Nothing could tend more decidedly towards imparting the requisite fixity and self-existence to colonial societies, than to place on a permanent footing endowments for education, both for popular schools and colleges. And, the same would be true in a still higher degree of a national church establishment, if that establishment could really comprehend the mass of the community.

May we not conceive England as retaining the seat of

the chief executive authority, the prescriptive reverence of her station, the superiority belonging to her vast accumulated wealth, and as the commercial metropolis of the world; and united, by these ties only, with a hundred nations,—not unconnected, like those which yielded to the spear of the Roman, but her own children, owning one faith and one language? May we not figure to ourselves, scattered thick as stars over the surface of this earth, communities of citizens owning the name of Britons, bound by allegiance to a British sovereign, and uniting heart and hand in maintaining the supremacy of Britain on every shore which her unconquered flag can reach? These may be extravagant views; but, if rightly understood, they have this advantage,—that the pursuit of them cannot lead the mind to wander in an unprofitable track. They are altogether inconsistent with the notions which have at different times led this country so fatally astray, in the defence of valueless rights or imaginary advantages; they are altogether inconsistent with the idea of a subjection enforced by bayonets—of a subjection bought through the means of a constant and galling expenditure, or by the still more injurious method of conceding commercial monopolies. Every step which could be taken towards the construction o.· maintenance of a union thus cemented would be a step favourable to the individual well-being and prosperity of every member. Every experiment in this direction would be serviceable alike to the colony affected by it, whether the ultimate destiny of that colony were an equitable connexion, or a bloodless separation.

The following passages were added among the Appendices of 1861.

No colonial minister can venture to oppose, with

deliberate steadiness, the supporters of any prevalent and popular doctrine. If he recalls troops from distant colonial possessions, and maintains the principle that their inhabitants must provide for their own internal peace and security against natives, he will no doubt find strong assistance from those who believe that the colonists should be taught to rely on themselves, and still stronger from the prevailing desire for economy in national expenditure. But, on the other hand, he has to encounter all the interests connected with the particular colony in question: and he has, in addition, to reckon on opposition from that body so long and justly powerful in British assemblies, who constitute themselves the protectors of inferior races, and regard with apprehension any measure which tends to withdraw them from the exercise of that protection. And, besides all this, there are real or supposed dangers in every such change of moment, which it requires great political courage to confront. An extermination of natives—a massacre of settlers—these are the terrors ever present to the mind of the executive at home, which render it loth to part, until the very last moment, with that security which has hitherto been enjoyed at the easy cost of military expenditure. And besides this, there is always looming in the distance the phantom of colonial disaffection. There is the fear lest the colonists should lose the wish to remain longer connected with a country which refuses to spend money on them. That the fear is unphilosophical all statesmen will admit, and that colonial attachment will not be retained by this kind of tribute, if it were worth retaining at such cost. But though prepared to recognize colonial independence as the natural ultimate result of modern colonial policy, none of them wish to see the revolution commence in their own day.

The consequence of these opposing political tendencies is a vacillation of purpose greatly to be regretted. The same series of events continually recurs in colonies thus circumstanced. In every period of tranquillity, some preparation is made for weaning colonists from their reliance on Imperial arms. Troops are gradually withdrawn. But the colonists—pretty well assured of what is coming—make very slight effort to create a defensive force. Then comes a rebellion, or a border war. Troops are hurried back from England, and the danger is at length averted at an expense greatly exceeding what would have occurred if they had remained in the colony. Then the old process of withdrawal begins again. The colonists are again threatened with being left to themselves, and again exhorted to military preparation—threats which they have learnt to estimate at their just value, and exhortations which have no power to stir them from their inertness produced both by habit and by calculation. For there is a principle in their resistance. The same community which will cheerfully contribute, with a generosity far outstripping its apparent means, to any object of public munificence in which Old England is interested, will hold out as long as it can against any invitation to take on itself its own charges, hitherto defrayed by the mother country. And thus the course of affairs goes on, period after period, in the same vicious circle. The principle of military protection from home, openly avowed and consistently acted on, would have cost far less money than the opposite principle maintained in theory, and perpetually departed from in practice.

Similar inconsistency has attended our dealings with the civil government of colonies thus circumstanced. Nothing can be more reasonable than that, where the mother country protects, at her own expense, the settlers from the natives, she should retain in her own hand, to a very considerable extent, their domestic administration. Unless she does so, she is liable to be dragged on all occasions into conflicts which the measures of the colonists themselves have provoked, and then to find the employment of her warlike resources impeded by want of harmony between the civil and military authorities. But these very obvious maxims have been disregarded. We have given the class of colonies of which I speak free institutions as a kind of bribe to take care of themselves. The colonists have taken the bribe, but show no disposition whatever to take on their necks the yoke of the supposed condition. . . .

There should be no hesitation in acting on the broad principle that the natives must, for their own protection, be placed in a situation of acknowledged inferiority, and consequently of tutelage. This is the old Spanish system, . . . the only one which has success to appeal to in its favour. It has been in later years too much the fashion to rely on phrases; to imagine that by proclaiming that all fellow-subjects of whatever race are equal in the eye of the law, we really make them so. There cannot be a greater error, nor one more calculated to inflict evil on those classes whom it is intended to benefit. The Caffre or the Maori may be rendered equal in legal rights with the settler, but he is not really equal in the power of enjoying or enforcing those rights, nor can he become so until civilization has rendered him equal in knowledge and in mental power. But a state of fictitious equality is far worse for him than one of acknowledged inferiority, with its correlative protection. If we intend to deal with the aborigines of countries of which we have taken possession as equals, then we must exclude settlers from contact with them. We must adopt what in these lectures has been called the policy of insulation—that of the United States—and leave them, in their allotted reserves, subject to their own laws and usages, so far as our established morality may allow of these prevailing. There we may entrust them to the good offices of the missionary, and the " protector," so far as these can reach. But, if we adopt the opposite policy, that of " amalgamation," then we shall assuredly find that they can only meet with the whites in the same field of hopeful industry on the footing of inferiors, and that, if such subordinate position is not recognized by law, and compensated by legal protection, it will be enforced, at a heavy disadvantage to them, by the prevailing sentiment of the conquering race.

Lectures on Colonization and Colonies (1861 ed.), pp. 137–8, 597–9, 634–5, 519–23.

53: SIR HENRY TAYLOR. Memorandum to the Duke of Newcastle, Secretary of State for the Colonies

26 February 1864

Taylor was a leading figure in the Colonial Office. He refused to succeed Stephen as Permanent Under-Secretary in 1847 and was allowed, from 1859 until his retirement in 1872, to live in Bournemouth because of ill health and have the despatches sent to him there. A minor poet, he also wrote *The Statesman* (1836), a study of the relations between the civil service and the Government.

As to our American possessions, I have long held and often expressed the opinion that they are a sort of *damnosa haereditas*; and when your Grace and the Prince of Wales were employing yourselves so successfully in conciliating the colonists, I thought that you were drawing closer ties which might better be slackened if there were any chance of their slipping away altogether. I think that a policy which has regard to a not very far-off future should prepare facilities and propensities for separation; and I therefore agree entirely in Sir Charles Elliot's preference of a local and indigenous military force. So long as there shall be a single imperial battalion in the provinces, the whole imperial army and exchequer, and the honour of the crown, will be committed to its support under difficulties; and circumstances may arise in which a large proportion of the imperial army and treasure will not be more than enough. This is what I fear. As to the current expenses of garrisons during peace, it is comparatively unimportant as a mere matter of finance what portion of them shall be borne by the provinces and this country respectively; but viewed as a part of a system and an implied pledge, the future contingencies involved seem to me most formidable. In my estimation the worst consequence of the late dispute with the United States has been that of involving this country and its North American provinces in closer relations and a common cause.

• I should desire to throw the current military expenditure upon the colonists, as tending, by connecting self-protection with self-government, to detach the colonies and promote their independence and segregation at an earlier day, and thereby to withdraw this country in time from great contingent dangers. If there be any motives which should plead for a prolonged connection, it appears to me that they are of a cosmopolitan and philanthropic nature, and not such as grow out of the interests of this country, though there are no doubt some minor English interests which are the better for the connection. There are national obligations also to be regarded, and some self-sacrifice is required of this country for a time. All that I would advocate is a preparatory policy, loosening obligations, and treating the repudiation by the colonists of legislative and executive dependence as naturally carrying with it some modification of the absolute right to be protected. As to *prestige*, I think it belongs to real power, and not to a merely apparent dominion by which real power is impaired. With regard to the Cape, which has been hitherto the extreme case of military expenditure for the protection of a colony, I think the question should be regarded as purely philanthropic—a question whether this country thinks it her duty to save and civilise barbarous tribes, whatever be the cost, or is prepared to let loose upon them the barbarous passions of civilised men. If the former, warfare must be conducted at the Cape by British troops under British control and at the cost of the British treasury. If the latter, it is essential to this country's good name that irresponsibility should be established by separation.

Printed in Sir H. Taylor's *Autobiography* (1885), II, pp. 234-6.

54: SIR FREDERIC ROGERS. Letter to Sir Henry
Taylor

1865

Rogers had been a fellow of Oriel College, Oxford and a member of the staff of *The Times*; he served in the Colonial Office from 1846 and was Permanent Under-Secretary from 1860 to 1871. On retirement he was promoted to the peerage as first Baron Blachford—this might be the real gravamen of the anti-Imperialist charge against Gladstone for Rogers was apt to voice separatist views (cf. No. 75).

I GO very far with you in the desire to shake off all responsibly governed colonies; and as to North America, I think if we abandon one we had better abandon all. I should wholly abhor being left with a pitiful remanet on my hands—say Prince Edward Island or Newfoundland. I also go with you in hating the talk about *prestige*. But I think our present relation to Canada involves an understanding that we are not to let other people take them from us unless they like to go. And I am inclined to think that allowing them to be taken from us for fear of consequences to ourselves in the way of war and taxation, would be one of those ungenerous chicken-hearted proceedings which somehow or other bring their own punishment in the long run, and indicate the declining spirit of a nation. There is something beyond philosophy, or at least my philosophy, in such doings. I cannot justify Bruce for giving battle on disadvantageous ground rather than abandon a woman in labour; yet I not only honour him for it, but feel that, if he had not been the man to do that, he would not have been the man to win all that he did win. So of Canada: nothing can be more provoking than to be obliged (if we are obliged) to fight the United States in the place and manner which are most disadvantageous to ourselves, for a colony which is no good to us and has no real care for us. Yet somehow I would not wish England to refrain from doing so; for England would not be great, courageous, successful England if she did. I am not sure that this is inconsistent with your letters. Indeed, I understand you as wishing, not that we should repudiate the obligation, but that we should let it wear out, and help it, as occasion may offer, to do so.

Ibid., pp. 241–2.

Part X

SEPARATIST OPINION: THE GOLDWIN SMITH PERIOD

55: GOLDWIN SMITH. *The Empire*

1863

The book from which these extracts are taken appeared first as letters to the *Daily News* in 1862–3. Goldwin Smith was then Regius Professor of Modern History at Oxford, a Chair he held from 1858 to 1866. Family distress led him to emigrate: to take a Chair at Cornell as Professor of English and Constitutional History (1868–1881) and to settle down in that most loyal city of Toronto. Here he continued until his death in 1910—"the last survivor of the Manchester School", he called himself—to proclaim his anti-Imperialist views and to tell the Canadians that their country was artificial and that their future lay in the United States.

THERE is but one way to make Canada impregnable, and that is to fence her round with the majesty of an independent nation. To invade and conquer an independent nation, without provocation, is an act from which, in the present state of opinion, even the Americans would recoil. The manifest unwillingness of the Canadians to be annexed was a greater tower of strength on the late occasion than our arms or theirs.

To protect dependent Colonies we not only burden our overtaxed people with gratuitous taxation, but scatter our forces, naval as well as military, over the globe, leaving the heart of England open to a sudden blow. What do we gain in return? What is the use of appointing Governors of Colonies, except to the circle of men who make Governing Colonies their profession? The time was when the universal prevalence of commercial monopoly made it well worth our while to hold Colonies in dependence for the sake of commanding their trade. But that time is gone. Trade is everywhere free, or becoming free; and this expensive and perilous connexion has entirely survived its sole legitimate cause. It is time that we should recognise the change that has come over the world.

We have, in fact, long felt that the Colonies did nothing for us. We now are very naturally beginning to grumble at being put to the expense of doing anything for them. If they are to do nothing for us, and we are to do nothing for them, where is the use of continuing the connexion?

We vaguely dream of making institutions for the colonies after the model of our own. The history of our own institutions ought to teach us that constitutions are not made, but grow; and that, to be strong and respected, they must be developed by a nation itself out of the elements of its own character and circumstances, not imposed on it, however benevolently, from without. We vaguely dream—some at least, vaguely dream—of propagating constitutional monarchy and aristocracy over our colonial empire. A glance at the history of constitutional monarchy and aristocracy ought to shew us that they are the modified offspring of feudalism, native to the feudal soil, and as incapable of being transplanted to a land of small estates and social equality as the trees of the tropics are of being transplanted to Canadian snows.

We are keeping the Colonies in a perpetual state of political infancy, and preventing the gristle of their frames from being matured and hardened into bone. Not only so—not only do we retard their political development, but we actually give it a wrong bias, and that in a direction which perhaps is not generally suspected. We are making them extravagantly democratic. Their nominal subjection to the British Crown masks the want of a conservative element in their institutions, and makes them feel free to plunge with impunity into all the excesses of universal suffrage. In case they ultimately part from us violently (as, if emancipation is too long delayed, they must) this fatal bias will be aggravated. America was flung into her wild democracy partly by the force with which she parted from monarchy and aristocracy at her revolution.

In the same manner we are overlaying the religion of the Colonies with a feeble Anglicanism, the creature of historical accidents in this country, and incapable of permanently forming the spiritual life of a new nation.

Our presence in Canada artificially preserves from absorption the French Canadian element, an antediluvian relic of old French society with its torpor and bigotry, utterly without value for the purposes of modern civilisation.

That connexion with the Colonies, which is really a part of our greatness—the connexion of blood, sympathy, and ideas—will not be affected by political separation. And when our Colonies are nations, something in the nature of a great Anglo-Saxon federation may, in substance if not in form, spontaneously arise out of affinity and mutual affection.

Is it possible to believe that any unity of design, or indeed any design at all, has run through this the supposed political training of the infant Colonies by the Central Office which we and they in imagination identify with England? Can any act of the Central Office be shewn to have been beneficial to the political character of the Colonies, saving those by which, under the auspices of wise and generous Colonial Ministers, it has parted of late years with a great part of its power?

To ask these questions is not to disparage English statesmanship. When we consider what the political education of a nation is—how natural yet how complex —how evidently it depends, like that of a man, on self-exertion, on self-control, on self-applied experience, on the instinctive adaptation of institutions to circumstances,— and how little any one can comprehend the circumstances but those who actually feel their pressure,—we shall be inclined greatly to doubt whether this process can be successfully carried on or guided from without, and not only from without but from the distance of the whole globe, not by a single man whose actions might at least be uniform, but by a succession of men, at the rate of thirteen in twenty years, each bringing to the task notions, a temper, party connexions, and a party bias of his own. We shall be inclined to cry that we must " let that alone for ever." Is there anything in the experience of the world recorded by history that at all approaches to such an undertaking, or hold out the slightest hope of its success?

In ancient times Empire was Empire. The Roman extorted from his dependencies both military force and revenue. Spain extorted revenue. We are too moral to extort either force or revenue from our dependencies even if we had the power. While we monopolised their trade in a general reign of monopoly, they brought us a real advantage, though of a narrow and selfish kind. Now they bring us no advantage at all. But the system has been established, many prejudices and some interests are bound up with it, and reasons must be found or invented for maintaining it. The reasons found or invented are, as might be expected, various and discordant enough. Now it is the amount of the Colonial trade; now it is the security of the Colonial trade; now it is the preference of our people for the Colonies as places of emigration. When facts overturn all these arguments, it is glory, national spirit, *prestige*. I give an agent an immense sum of money to invest for me. He tells me that he has bought me an estate. I ask to see the estate: he tells me that the money is laid out not in an estate but in houses. I ask to see the houses: he tells me that it is laid out not in houses but in railway shares. I ask for my scrip: he tells me that it is not laid out in railway shares but invested in the Funds. I ask for the transfer receipt; and he tells me that it is not invested in the Funds but in something much better and nobler, in *prestige*. I look in the French dictionary for *prestige*, and find that it is " an illusion, a juggling trick, an imposture."

I am no more against Colonies than I am against the solar system. I am against dependencies, when nations are fit to be independent. If Canada were made an independent nation she would still be a Colony of England, and England would still be her Mother Country in the full sense in which those names have been given to the most famous examples of Colonization in history. Our race and language, our laws and liberties, will be hers. Our God will be her God. Our great writers, the ministers of our moral empire, will still sway her mind; and when she turns from reclaiming the wilderness—her first duty—to intellectual pursuits, her great writers will sway the mind of England in their turn. . . .

What is proposed is, not that Canada shall cease to be a Colony of England, but that she shall cease to be a dependency: that she shall elect her own chief magistrate, coin her own money, decide her own causes finally in her own law-courts, and have the power of making peace and war.

Is there any reason why, after the separation of the Governments, natives of Canada should not still be allowed, on coming to reside within the pale of English law, to become British citizens, to acquire all kinds of property, and to exercise, if otherwise duly qualified, all political rights? Is there any reason why wealthy and aristocratic Canadians should not still look to this country for the honours and rewards of life, if their own country, unhappily for her and for them, fails to win the allegiance of their hearts? Is this any reason why Canada should not keep the old flag, with such difference as the Heralds' College may require? There would, let me say once more, be no " casting off " in such an emancipation, except the casting off of the child, who, grown to manhood, leaves his father's house to win wealth and honours of his own.

When people talk of the dependencies as the very soul of England, they forget that the oak flourished broad and deep before these parasites began to cling round its trunk and feed upon its life.

India . . . stands on a footing of its own, apart from the other dependencies of our Empire. There we have not only placed ourselves in a position from which it is hard to retire, but taken upon us duties which we are bound for the present to perform. If we were to leave India we should leave it to anarchy. There is no power, Hindoo or Mahometan, to which we could make over our trust. We have destroyed or degraded all the native Governments; and we alone stand in their room. We are wedged in the oak which we have rent. . . .

It is safer to put it thus than to say that we have a "mission" to keep India. Mission is a large word. All sorts of men and nations have missions, and some of their missions are of a very objectionable kind. Spain had a mission, undertaken in a most religious spirit, and sanctioned by the highest religious authority, to send bucaneering expeditions into the New World, and fill it with misery and blood. Prince Louis Bonaparte had a mission to strangle French liberty in its sleep. France herself has a mission which keeps all her neighbours under arms. "A mission," historically speaking, is little more than another name for a tendency to rapine. Providence no doubt puts conquered territories into the conqueror's hands; and Providence puts the stolen purse into the pocket of the thief.

"Responsibility" is another word of the same kind. It is perhaps more frequently used than "mission" to defend the retention of what you have got in those special cases where the retention is very unprofitable to the nation at large, but profitable or agreeable to a class. In these cases, the class feels that, on whichever side the balance of political and economical advantage may be, it has "responsibilities" of a higher kind which it is not at liberty to resign.

So far as the investment of capital is concerned, our dominion gives no special advantage to its possessors. A capitalist of any country in Europe may invest in Indian railroads as freely as an Englishman; and the downfall of the British dominion, if it ruined either, would ruin both alike.

It will be admitted at once that we draw no military force from India. The employment of a few Sepoys in Egypt or in China is but a nominal exception to this rule.

16   223

It may be said, however, that India, though it furnishes no military force to this country, pays, unlike our other dependencies, for its own military defence. This is apparently, but it is not really, the case. The Cape was occupied, and is held by us, merely as a post on the road to India; and the expenses of that station, which have been enormous, must therefore be set down to the account of our Indian Empire. Other English ships may touch at the Cape, but these ships might safely be left to the course of nature and the interest of the Cape Colonists. It is our anxiety for the safety of the route to India which compels us to keep the place in our own hands. The same may be said of Mauritius. But, moreover, our great force in the Mediterranean and our military stations there, are maintained partly on account of the necessity, or the alleged necessity, of overawing the powers which command the overland route. And, besides all this, our general policy is influenced, and we are frequently entangled in quarrels, and sometimes in wars, by causes in which our alarm for the safety of the Indian Empire has its share. The late war with Russia arose, not perhaps in a great degree, but still in some degree, from this source. As to the general envy and hatred of the world, which attend vast territorial aggrandizement, they are by most people, in reasoning about these matters, set down as a source of strength, though to others they may appear to be rather a source of weakness.

The principle of Colonial Emancipation does not apply to India, because it is a conquered country, not a Colony; and to throw up the government without making any provision for the preservation of order when we are gone, would be to do a great wrong to the people in addition to those which have been already done. But the course of affairs, if it continues as it is at present, seems likely in this case also to enforce a change in the relation between England and her dependency.

The Empire (1863), pp. 2–6, 48–9, 93–4, 123–4, 125–6, 129, 257–8, 270–1, 292–3.

56: RICHARD COBDEN. Letter to Colonel Cole

20 March 1865

THE most interesting debate of the session hitherto has been on Canadian affairs. This is a subject of increasing interest, and the projected confederation of the British North American colonies will bring it into great prominence this session. It seems to be generally accepted here as a desirable change, though I fail to discover any immediate interest which the British public have in the matter. There is no proposal to relieve us from the expense and risk of pretending to defend those colonies from the United States—a task which, by the way, everybody admits to be beyond our power. Then I cannot see what substantial interest the British people have in the connexion to compensate them for guaranteeing three or four millions of North Americans living in Canada, &c., against another community of Americans living in their neighbourhood. We are told indeed of the ' loyalty ' of the Canadians; but this is an ironical term to apply to people who neither pay our taxes nor obey our laws, nor hold themselves liable to fight our battles, who would repudiate our right to the sovereignty over an acre of their territory, and who claim the right of imposing their own customs duties, even to the exclusion of our manufactures. We are two peoples to all intents and purposes, and it is a perilous delusion to both parties to attempt to

225

keep up a sham connexion and dependence which will snap asunder if it should ever be put to the strain of stern reality. It is all very well for our Cockney newspapers to talk of defending Canada at all hazards. It would be just as possible for the United States to sustain Yorkshire in a war with England, as for us to enable Canada to contend against the United States. It is simply an impossibility. Nor must we forget that the only serious danger of a quarrel between those two neighbours arises from the connexion of Canada with this country. In my opinion it is for the interest of both that we should as speedily as possible sever the political thread by which we are as communities connected, and leave the individuals on both sides to cultivate the relations of commerce and friendly intercourse as with other nations. I have felt an interest in this confederation scheme, because I thought it was a step in the direction of an amicable separation. I am afraid from the last telegrams there may be some difficulty, either in your province or in Lower Canada, in carrying out the project. Whatever may be the wish of the colonies will meet with the concurrence of our Government and Parliament. We have recognized their right to control their own fate, even to the point of asserting their independence whenever they think fit, and which we know to be only a question of time. All this makes our present responsible position towards them truly one-sided and ridiculous. There seems to be something like a dead-lock in the political machinery of the Canadas, which has driven their leading statesmen into the measure of confederation. I suspect that there has been some demoralization and corruption in that quarter, and that it is in part an effort to purify the political system by letting in new blood. There is also, I think, an inherent weakness in the parody of our old English constitution, which is performed on the miniature scenes of the colonial capitals, with their speeches from the throne, votes of confidence, appeals to the country, changes of ministry, &c., and all about such trumpery issues that the game at last becomes ridiculous in the eyes of both spectators and actors.

Morley, *Life of Cobden* (1881 ed.), Vol. II, pp. 470–1.

57: ROBERT LOWE. Speech on Canadian Defence

House of Commons, 23 March 1865

Lowe (1811–92), later first Viscount Sherbrooke, had been in Australia from 1842 to 1850 where he was a member of the New South Wales legislative council. His experiences there made him distrustful of democracy, leading him to oppose his government's reform proposals in 1866.

WE ought, in my opinion, to tell Canada that we will defend her with all our strength; that we consider her interests bound up in ours, and that we will fight for her to the last, so long as she belongs to us; but that we see no chance of successfully defending her on her own ground. If she chooses British connection she must take it subject to this condition, that she will have to defend her own soil in case of invasion; that we will make diversions elsewhere, and defend her in what we think the most efficient way, and that if our arms are crowned with success, she shall be the first object of our consideration in making peace. We should also represent to her that it is perfectly open to her to establish herself as an independent Republic, and that if she thinks that will make her position safer and more tenable, we do not desire to drag her into any danger. It is our duty, too, to represent to her that, if after well-weighed consideration, she thinks it more to her interest to join the great American Republic itself ("No, No!")—it is the duty of Canada to deliberate for her own interests and her own happiness, and it is our duty to put before her the real relation of things, not as seen through the illusion of dignity and glory, and things of that sort, but as they really are; and to assure her that, whatever course she may take, she shall have in us a friend, a protector, and an ally up to the time of her departure. But I cannot think it is the best attitude for those who, with me, think that we cannot defend Canada in Canada to encourage her to believe that we will resist an invasion which we cannot resist—to stir her up, relying on our support, to incur dangers from which we cannot deliver her. It appears to me that there is mutual deception. We expect Canada to defend herself, and Canada expects us to defend her.

Hansard, Third Series, Vol. CLXXVIII, cs. 153–4.

58: BENJAMIN DISRAELI. Letter to Lord Derby

Hughenden Manor, 30 September 1866

Disraeli's change of opinion on Imperial affairs from separatism in the fifties and sixties to a positive outlook in 1872 (No. 67) is a mark of the renewed Imperialism in England around 1870. Here he echoes the policy of recalling the garrisons—the dominant view of the period—and of withdrawal from West Africa that had been recommended by a Select Committee of the House of Commons the previous year.

WE must seriously consider our Canadian position, which is most illegitimate. An army maintained in a country which does not permit us even to govern it! What an anomaly!

It can never be our pretence, or our policy, to defend the Canadian frontier against the U.S. If the colonists

228

can't, as a general rule, defend themselves against the Fenians, they can do nothing. They ought to be, and must be, strong enough for that. Power and influence we should exercise in Asia; consequently in Eastern Europe, consequently also in Western Europe; but what is the use of these colonial deadweights which *we do not govern*?

I don't regret what we did the other day about Canada, because the circumstances were very peculiar. A successful raid of the Fenians was not off the cards, which would have upset your untried Ministry, and might have produced an insurrection in Ireland; and it was not fair to the Canadians, when, at the last, they were making some attempts at self-defence, to allow them to be crushed in the bud of their patriotism. But the moment the American elections are over, we should withdraw the great body of our troops, and foster a complete development of self-government.

Leave the Canadians to defend themselves; recall the African squadron; give up the settlements on the west coast of Africa; and we shall make a saving which will, at the same time, enable us to build ships and have a good Budget.

What is more, we shall have accomplished something definite, tangible, for the good of the country. In these days, more than ever, the people look to results. What we have done about Canada is perfectly defensible, if it is not looked upon as a permanent increase of our Canadian establishments.

Buckle, *Life of Disraeli*, Vol. IV, pp. 476–7.

59: JOHN BRIGHT. Speech on Canadian Confederation

House of Commons, 28 February 1867

THE CONCEPT OF EMPIRE

THERE are persons in this country, and there are some also in the North American provinces, who are ill-natured enough to say that not a little of the loyalty that is said to prevail in Canada has its price. I think it is natural and reasonable to hope that there is in that country a very strong attachment to this country. But if they are to be constantly applying to us for guarantees for railways, and for grants for fortresses, and for works of defence, then I think it would be far better for them and for us—cheaper for us and less demoralizing for them —that they should become an independent State, and maintain their own fortresses, fight their own cause, and build up their own future without relying upon us. And when we know, as everybody knows, that the population of Canada is in a much better position as regards the comforts of home, than is the great bulk of the population of this country, I say the time has come when it ought to be clearly understood that the taxes of England are no longer to go across the ocean to defray expenses of any kind within the Confederation which is about to be formed. . . .

For my share, I want the population of these provinces to do that which they believe to be best for their own interests—to remain with this country if they like it, in the most friendly manner, or to become independent States if they wish it. If they should prefer to unite them-selves with the United States, I should not complain even of that. But whatever be their course, there is no man in this House or in those provinces who has a more sincere wish for their greatness and their welfare than I have who have taken the liberty thus to criticise this Bill.

Speeches on Questions of Public Policy by John Bright (ed. Thorold Rogers, 1868), I, pp. 161–3.

60: SIR CHARLES WENTWORTH DILKE
Greater Britain

1868

This book appeared after Dilke's tour round the world in 1866–7. It is emblematic of the change of popular opinion. Dilke's views on Canada echo those of Goldwin Smith; with regard to Australia he considers separation inevitable. He then comes to take a more positive view, one that was fully set out in his *Problems of Greater Britain* (1890). In the development of his views he had a deep effect on his friend, Joseph Chamberlain.

THE position of Canada is in many ways anomalous: of the two chief sections of our race—that in Britain and that in America—the latter is again split in twain, and one division governed from across the Atlantic. For such government there is no pretext, except the wishes of the governed, who gain by the connexion men for their defence, and the opportunity of gratifying their spite for their neighbours at our expense. Those who ask why a connexion so one-sided, so opposed to the best interests of our race, should be suffered to continue, are answered, now that the argument of " prestige " is given up, that the Canadians are loyal, and that they hate the Americans, to whom, were it not for us, they must inevitably fall. That we should spend blood and treasure in protecting them against the consequences of their hate. The world should have passed the time when local dislikes can be suffered to affect our policy towards the other sections of our race; but even were it otherwise, it is hard to see how twelve thousand British troops, or a royal standard hoisted at Ottawa, can protect a frontier of two thousand miles in length from a nation of five and thirty millions. Canada, perhaps, can

231

defend herself, but we most certainly cannot defend her: we provoke much more than we assist.

As for Canadian "loyalty," it appears to consist merely of hatred towards America, for while we were fighting China and conquering the rulers of Japan, that we might spread free trade, our loyal colonists of Canada set upon our goods protective duties of 20 per cent which they have now in some degree removed, only that they may get into their hands the smuggling trade carried on in breach of the laws of our ally, their neighbour. We might, at least, fairly insist that the connexion should cease unless Canada will entirely remove her duties.

At bottom, it would seem as though no one gained by the retention of our hold on Canada. Were she independent, her borders would never again be wasted by Fenian hordes, and she would escape the terrible danger of being the battle-field in which European quarrels are fought out. Canada once republican, the Monroe doctrine would be satisfied, and its most violent partisans would cease to advocate the adoption of other than moral means to merge her territories in the Union. An independent Canada would not long delay the railway across the continent to Puget Sound, which a British bureau calls impossible. England would be relieved from the fear of a certain defeat by America in the event of war—a fear always harmful, even when war seems most unlikely;—relieved, too, from the cost of such panics as those of 1861 and 1866.

Did Canada stand alone, no offence that she could give America would be likely to unite all sections of that country in an attempt to conquer her; while, on the other hand, such an attempt would be resisted to the death by an armed and brave people, four millions strong. As it is,

SEPARATIST OPINION: GOLDWIN SMITH PERIOD

any offence towards America committed by our agents, at any place or time, or arising out of the continual changes of policy and of ministry in Great Britain, united to the standing offence of maintaining the monarchical principle in North America, will bring upon unhappy Canada the whole American nation, indignant in some cause, just, or seeming just, and to be met by a people deceived into putting their trust in a few regiments of British troops, sufficient at the most to hold Quebec, and to be backed by reinforcements which could never come in time, did public opinion in Great Britain so much as permit their sailing.

On the other hand, in all history there is nothing stranger than the narrowness of mind that has led us to see in Canada a piece of England, and in America a hostile country. There are more sons of British subjects in America than in Canada, by far; and the American looks upon the old country with a pride that cannot be shared by a man who looks to her to pay her soldiers.

The independence of Canada would put an immediate end to much of the American jealousy of Great Britain—a consideration which of itself should outweigh any claim to protection which the Canadians can have on us. The position which we have to set before us in our external dealings is, that we are no more fellow-countrymen of the Canadians than of the Americans of the North or West.

The case of the flies is plain enough. The Maori and the English fly live on the same food, and require about the same amount of warmth and moisture: the one which is best fitted to the common conditions will gain the day, and drive out the other. The English fly has had

233

to contend not only against other English flies, but against every fly of temperate climates: we have traded with every land, and brought the flies of every clime to England. The English fly is the best possible fly of the whole world, and will naturally beat down and exterminate, or else starve out, the merely provincial Maori fly. . . .

Natural selection is being conducted by nature in New Zealand on a grander scale than any we have contemplated, for the object of it here is man. In America, in Australia, the white man shoots or poisons his red or black fellow, and exterminates him through the workings of superior knowledge; but in New Zealand it is peacefully, and without extraordinary advantages, that the Pakéha beats his Maori brother.

When a Briton takes a survey of the colonies, he finds much matter for surprise in the one-sided nature of the partnership which exists between the mother and the daughter lands. No reason presents itself to him why our artisans and merchants should be taxed in aid of populations far more wealthy than our own, who have not, as we have, millions of paupers to support. We at present tax our humblest classes, we weaken our defences, we scatter our troops and fleets, and lay ourselves open to panics such as those of 1853 and 1859, in order to protect against imaginary dangers the Australian gold-digger and the Canadian farmer. There is something ludicrous in the idea of taxing St. Giles's for the support of Melbourne, and making Dorsetshire agricultural labourers pay the cost of defending New Zealand colonists in Maori wars. . . .

As for our so-called defence of the colonies, in wartime we defend ourselves: we defend the colonies only during peace. In war-time they are ever left to shift for themselves, and they would undoubtedly be better fit to do so were they in the habit of maintaining their military establishments in time of peace. The present system weakens us and them—us, by taxes and by the withdrawal of our men and ships; the colonies, by preventing the development of that self-reliance which is requisite to form a nation's greatness. The successful encountering of difficulties is the marking feature of the national character of the English, and we can hardly expect a nation which has never encountered any, or which has been content to see them met by others, ever to become great. In short, as matters now stand, the colonies are a source of military weakness to us, and our " protection " of them is a source of danger to the colonists. No doubt there are still among us men who would have wished to have seen America continue in union with England, on the principle on which the Russian conscripts are chained each to an old man—to keep her from going too fast—and who now consider it our duty to defend our colonies at whatever cost, on account of the "prestige " which attaches to the somewhat precarious tenure of these great lands. With such men it is impossible for colonial reformers to argue: the standpoints are wholly different. To those, however, who admit the injustice of the present system to the taxpayers of the mother-country, but who fear that her merchants would suffer by its disturbance, inasmuch as, in their belief, action on our part would lead to a disruption of the tie, we may plead that, even should separation be the result, we should be none the worse off for its occurrence. The retention of colonies at almost any cost has been defended—so far as it has been supported by argument at all—on the ground that the connexion conduces to trade, to which argument it is sufficient to answer that no one has ever succeeded in showing what effect upon trade the connexion can have, and that as excellent examples to the contrary we have the fact that our trade with the Ionian Islands has greatly increased since their annexation to the kingdom of Greece, and a much more striking fact than even this —namely, that while the trade with England of the Canadian Confederation is only four-elevenths of its total external trade, or little more than one-third, the English trade of the United States was in 1860 (before the war) nearly two-thirds of its total external trade, in 1861 more than two-thirds, and in 1866 (first year after the war) again four-sevenths of its total trade. Common institutions, common freedom, and common tongue have evidently far more to do with trade than union has; and for purposes of commerce and civilisation, America is a truer colony of Britain than is Canada. . . .

The trade argument being met, and it being remembered that our colonies are no more an outlet for our surplus population than they would be if the Great Mogul ruled over them, as is seen by the fact that of every twenty people who leave the United Kingdom, one goes to Canada, two to Australia, and sixteen to the United States, we come to the " argument " which consists in the word " prestige." When examined, this cry seems to mean that, in the opinion of the utterer, extent of empire is power—a doctrine under which Brazil ought to be nineteen and a half times, and China twenty-six times as powerful as France. Perhaps the best answer to the doctrine is a simple contradiction: those who have read history with most care well know that at all times extent of empire has been weakness. England's real empire was small enough in 1650, yet it is rather doubtful whether her " prestige " ever reached the height it did while the Cromwellian admirals swept the seas. The idea conveyed by the words " mother of free nations " is every bit as good as that contained in the cry " prestige," and the argument that, as the colonists are British subjects, we have no right to cast them adrift so long as they wish to continue citizens, is evidently no answer to those who merely urge that the colonists should pay their own policeman.

It may, perhaps, be contended that the possession of " colonies " tends to preserve us from the curse of small island countries, the dwarfing of mind which would otherwise make us Guernsey a little magnified. If this be true, it is a powerful argument in favour of continuance in the present system. It is a question, however, whether our real preservation from the insularity we deprecate is not to be found in the possession of true colonies—of plantations such as America, in short— rather than in that of mere dependencies. That which raises us above the provincialism of citizenship of little England is our citizenship of the greater Saxondom which includes all that is best and wisest in the world. . . .

After all, the strongest of the arguments in favour of separation is the somewhat paradoxical one that it would bring us a step nearer to the virtual confederation of the English race.

England in the East is not the England that we know. Flousy Britannia, with her anchor and ship, becomes a mysterious Oriental despotism, ruling a sixth of the human race, nominally for the natives' own good, and certainly for no one else's, by laws and in a manner opposed to every tradition and every prejudice of the whole of the various tribes of which this vast population is composed—scheming, annexing, out-manœuvring

Russia, and sometimes, it is be feared, out-lying Persia
herself. . . .

Although despotic, our government of India is not
bad; indeed, the hardest thing that can be said of it is
that it is too good. We do our duty by the natives man-
fully, but they care little about that, and we are continually hurting their prejudices and offending them in
small things, to which they attach more importance than
they do to great. To concilitate the Hindoos, we should
spend 10,000*l*. a year in support of native literature to
please the learned, and 10,000*l*. on fireworks to delight
the wealthy and the low-caste people. Instead of this,
we worry them with municipal institutions and benevolent institutions that they cannot and will not understand. . . .

We are levelling all ranks in India; we are raising the
humblest men, if they will pass certain examinations, to
posts which we refuse to the most exalted of nobles unless
they can pass higher. A clever son of a bheestie, or
sweeper, if he will learn English, not only may, but must
rise to be a railway baboo, or deputy-collector of customs; whereas for Hindoo rajahs or Mohamedan nobles
of Delhi creation, there is no chance of anything but
gradual decline of fortune. Even our Star of India is
democratic in its working: we refuse it to men of the
highest descent, to confer it on self-made viziers of native
States, or others who were shrewd enough to take our
side during the rebellion. All this is very modern, and
full of " progress," no doubt; but it is progress towards
imperialism, or equality of conditions under paternal
despotism.

Not only does the democratic character of our rule set
the old families against us, but it leads also to the failure
of our attempt to call around us a middle class, an

educated thinking body of natives with something to lose, who, seeing that we are ruling India for her own good, would support us heart and soul, and form the best of bucklers for our dominion. As it is, the attempt has long been made in name, but, as a matter of fact, we have humbled the upper class, and failed to raise a middle-class to take its place. We have crushed the prince without setting up the trader in his stead. . . .

On the whole, however, it may be admitted, that our Indian government is the best example of a well-administered despotism, on a large scale, existing in the world. Its one great fault is over-centralization; for, although our rule in India must needs be despotic, no reason can be shown why its despotism should be minute.

The greatest of the many changes in progress in the East is that India is being made—that a country is being created under that name where none has yet existed; and it is our railroads, our annexations, and above all our centralising policy, that are doing the work. There is reason to fear that this change will be hastened by the extension of our new codes to the former " non-regula-tion provinces," and by government from at home, where India is looked upon as one nation, instead of from Cal-cutta, where it is known to be still composed of fifty; but so rapid is the change, that already the Calcutta people are as mistaken in attempting to laugh down our phrase " the people of India," as we were during the mutiny when we believed that there was an " India " writhing in our clutches. Whether the India which is being thus rapidly built up by our own hands will be friendly to us, or the reverse, depends upon ourselves. The two prin-ciples upon which our administration of the country might be based have long since been weighed against each other by the English people, who, rejecting the

THE CONCEPT OF EMPIRE

principle of a holding of India for the acquisition of prestige and trade, have decided that we are to govern India in the interest of the people of Hindostan. We are now called on to deliberate once more, but this time upon the method by which our principle is to be worked out. That our administration is already perfect can hardly be contended so long as no officer not very high in our Indian service dares to call a native a " friend." The first of all our cares must be the social treatment of the people; for while by the Queen's proclamation the natives are our fellow-subjects, they are in practice not yet treated as our fellow men.

Whether, indeed, dependencies pay or do not pay their actual cost, their retention stands on a wholly different footing to that of colonies. Were we to leave Australia or the Cape, we should continue to be the chief customers of those countries: were we to leave India or Ceylon, they would have no customers at all; for, falling into anarchy, they would cease at once to export their goods to us and to consume our manufactures. When a British Governor of New Zealand wrote that of every Maori who fell in war with us it might be said that, " from his ignorance, a man had been destroyed whom a few months' enlighten-ment would have rendered a valuable consumer of British manufactured goods," he only set forth with grotesque simplicity considerations which weigh with us all; but while the advance of trade may continue to be our chief excuse, it need not be our sole excuse for our Eastern dealings—even for use towards ourselves. With-out repeating that which I have said with respect to India, we may especially bear in mind that, although the theory has suffered from exaggeration, our dependencies still form a nursery of statesmen and of warriors, and that we should irresistibly fall into national sluggishness of thought, were it not for the world-wide interests given us by the necessity of governing and educating the inhabitants of so vast an empire as our own.

Sir C. W. Dilke, *Greater Britain* (1868), I, pp. 77–80, 391–2, II, pp. 148, 152–7, 374–5, 380–1, 388–9, 394–5.

PART XI

RENEWED IMPERIALISM

61 : JAMES ANTHONY FROUDE. Article in
Fraser's Magazine

January 1870

Froude proclaimed himself an Imperialist in his Rectorial address at St. Andrew's in 1869. He went on an unofficial fact-finding tour for Carnarvon in South Africa in 1874, and was sent to represent the home Government at an abortive conference on federation there in 1875. He came to sympathise with the Boers, urging separation in their particular case. His more typical attitude to Empire is seen in these articles (also No. 65) and in his book *Oceana* (1886) (No. 79), written after a world tour.

PATRIOTISM is no longer recognized as the supreme virtue which once it was believed to be. 'Prejudice in favour of England,' that proud belief in England which made men ready to sacrifice themselves and all belonging to them in the interests of their country, is obsolete and out of fashion. . . .

Other nations, once less powerful or not more powerful than ourselves, are growing in strength and numbers, and we too must grow if we intend to remain on a level with them. Here at home we have no room to grow except by the expansion of towns which are already overgrown, which we know not certainly that we can expand. If we succeed it can only be under conditions unfavourable and probably destructive to the physical constitution of our people, and our greatness will be held by a tenure which in the nature of things must become more and more precarious.

Is there then no alternative? Once absolutely our own,

and still easily within our reach, are our eastern and western colonies, containing all and more than all that we require. We want land on which to plant English families where they may thrive and multiply without ceasing to be Englishmen. The land lies ready to our hand. The colonies contain virgin soil sufficient to employ and feed five times as many people as are now crowded into Great Britain and Ireland. Nothing is needed but arms to cultivate it ; while here, among ourselves, are millions of able-bodied men unwillingly idle, clamouring for work, with their families starving on their hands. What more simple than to bring the men and the land together? Everything which we could most desire exactly meeting what is most required is thrust into our hands, and this particular moment is chosen to tell the colonies that we do not want them and they may go. The land, we are told impatiently, is no longer ours. A few years ago it was ours, but to save the Colonial Office trouble we made it over to the local governments, and now we have no more rights over it than we have over the prairies of Texas. If it were so, the more shame to the politicians who let drop so precious an inheritance. But the colonies, it seems, set more value than we do on the prosperity of the empire. They care little for the profit or pleasure of individual capitalists. They see their way more clearly perhaps because their judgment is not embarrassed by considerations of the Chancellor of the Exchequer's budget. Conscious that their relations with us cannot continue on their present footing, their ambition is to draw closer to us, to be absorbed in a united empire. From them we have no difficulty to fear, for in consenting they have everything to gain. They are proud of being English subjects. Every able-bodied workman who lands on their shores is so much added to their wealth as well as ours. If we do not attempt to thrust paupers and criminals on them, but send labourers and their families adequately provided, they will absorb our people by millions, while in desiring to remain attached to England they are consulting England's real interests as entirely as their own. Each husband and wife as they establish themselves will be a fresh root for the old tree, struck into a new soil. . . .

Let it be once established that an Englishman emigrating to Canada, or the Cape, or Australia, or New Zealand, did not forfeit his nationality, that he was still on English soil as much as if he were in Devonshire or Yorkshire, and would remain an Englishman while the English empire lasted; and if we spent a quarter of the sums which were sunk in the morasses at Balaclava in sending out and establishing two millions of our people in those colonies, it would contribute more to the essential strength of the country than all the wars in which we have been entangled from Agincourt to Waterloo. No further subsidies would be needed to feed the stream. Once settled they would multiply and draw their relations after them, and at great stations round the globe there would grow up, under conditions the most favourable which the human constitution can desire, fresh nations of Englishmen. So strongly placed, and with numbers growing in geometrical proportion, they would be at once feeding-places of our population, and self-supporting imperial garrisons themselves unconquerable. With our roots thus struck so deeply into the earth, it is hard to see what dangers, internal or external, we should have cause to fear, or what impediments could then check the indefinite and magnificent expansion of the English Empire.

Printed in J. A. Froude, *Short Studies on Great Subjects* (Second Series), pp. 155, 171–3, 174–5.

62: WILLIAM EDWARD FORSTER. Speech at Bradford
17 January 1870

Forster (1818–86) had been Under-Secretary at the Colonial Office, 1865–6, developing then an interest in the Colonies. On the fall of Gladstone's government in 1874 he was freed to fulfil his " long-cherished wish " of visiting the United States which he entered by way of Quebec and Ontario. In 1880 he would have preferred to have become Secretary for the Colonies rather than that for Ireland. He was elected Chairman of the Imperial Federation League at its formation in 1884 (No. 73).

IT is too late now—it would require an evening of itself —to descant upon that question, to me more important than almost any other, the colonial question; but I cannot sit down without just stating that, although I disagree with very much that has been said by representatives of the colonies lately, yet I rejoice that the question has been brought forward as it is. I rejoice that it has been received as it is, because it makes it clear to me that neither in England nor in the colonies do we intend that the English Empire shall be broken up. It may be a dream, but I still believe in its fulfilment, I believe that the time will come when, by some means or another, statesmen will be able to weld a bond together which will unite the English-speaking people in our colonies at present—unite them with the mother country in one great confederation. I believe also in the fulfilment of this other dream, that, whatever may be the passing disagreement, the time will come, and come quickly, when there will be no discord between us and our kinsmen in the United States. I may not live to see it; but there are many here who will live to see it—such firm and lasting friendship among all English-speaking people that that firm bond of friendship will bring such blessings of peace to these peoples, that it will be such a lesson of the advantages of concord to the rest of the world, that the other nations of civilization will, for very shame's sake, learn war no longer.

From a corrected account in a letter from Forster, in *The Times*, 21 January 1870.

63: Debate in the House of Lords

14 February 1870

Carnarvon, Conservative Colonial Secretary 1866–7 and 1874–8, in initiating this debate, voices the popular feeling stirred up by the Government's recall of the Imperial garrisons. Granville, Gladstone's Colonial Secretary, replies.

EARL OF CARNARVON: My lords, schemes have been put forward for what may be called a Confederation of the Empire. There has been a consciousness that this great Empire is Imperial in name, and local in effect and in power; and there has accordingly been a desire to tighten the bonds which at present seem to have a tendency to relax. Confederation, it has been said, might be accomplished either by giving the Colonies representation in the British Parliament or by some such agency as the Supreme Court of the United States. I do not, however, think it worth while to go into that question. I have often weighed the arguments for and against it, and though I would gladly accept such a Confederation if I thought it possible, I am afraid it is really impossible. . . .

It is as if a father, rightly or wrongly, had parted with his estate to his children, and in later years, on re-consideration, was desirous of repossessing himself of his power. But he would find that it had really gone, and that he could only appeal to the natural affection of his children. That I believe to be our present position towards our Colonies. But does it follow that no improvement in our present relations is possible, and that we must drift on carelessly, reckless whither we are going? Certainly not; and I am confident that if on the part of English statesmen there exists—as I believe there does on the part of colonial statesmen—a desire to find a remedy, and to knit up the different portions of the Empire once more into closer bonds with one another, a way can be found, and more or less effectually, the task can be accomplished. The problem is to secure and preserve on the one hand the self-government which you have given to the different Colonies, and on the other hand to add to it a more real connection than that which now exists. It may be hard, but I do not believe it in any sense impossible. There are several influences, at all events, which may greatly tend to facilitate such a result. In the first place, a greater sympathy, a greater heartiness of expression, a greater affection, a more sincere pride in this great Empire, are all circumstances which would tend to promote the object in view.

Now, there can be no doubt that in our colonial Empire, which has been the gradual growth of time and circumstances, the powers exercised by the Imperial Government on the one hand, and the colonial authorities on the other, have not been clearly marked out. It would be well if Her Majesty's Government would consider the practicability of defining some of these powers. Time, no doubt, was when without much difficulty we might have had one great commercial system. That has passed by. Time was also when we might have had one financial system. I do not think it is too late even now to have one common coinage in Her Majesty's Empire. Moreover, I can conceive many cases in which the law might, with advantage to England, and still greater to the Colonies, be made common and uniform throughout every part of the Empire. These are questions at which, of course, I can only hint, but which deserve the attention of the Government, and on which they might safely invite the co-operation of our great Colonies. Above all they ought to consider what should be the principles upon which the military defence of the Empire should be placed. They should bear in mind that the military organization of the Empire might be a great source of strength, and, that, at all events, it is the one great tie which still holds the Colonies to England.

I wish, indeed, it were possible that an Englishman and a Colonist, when they went to their respective countries, should feel that they were members of the same great Empire, that they should know no difference whatever except in sky and climate, and that in all other respects the Englishman should feel himself a citizen in Canada, and the Canadian should feel himself no stranger in England. It is impossible not sometimes to indulge in the belief—though circumstances at this moment are adverse—that such a great Confederation might even yet be achieved—a Confederation of which England might be the centre, and of which all the members would be bound to her by a tie which might go on for uncounted generations. What fatal policy is it then which tempts us deliberately and with our eyes open to throw all this to the winds—to abandon these sources of possible—and if possible then of incalculable—strength, and to allow this country to subside into the position of a second Holland?

EARL GRANVILLE: The noble Earl . . . suggested the drawing of a dispatch to define in black and white the exact relations of the mother Country to the self-governing Colonies. I may be wrong, but I have great doubts whether such a proceeding would not have the effect rather of dissolving than of cementing the union. Would it not at once excite the greatest possible jealousy among the Colonies, and give rise to the greatest suspicion that we intended to take back from the Colonies some portion of that perfect freedom which has been granted to them? I do not agree with the noble Earl that the great bond between the Colonies and this country is the military protection afforded to the former; for I am of opinion that the ties which bind us together are loyalty to the Crown, goodwill between the Colonies and the mother Country, and a reciprocity of mutual advantages. When this state of things shall cease to exist, the idea of compelling by force any great and self-governing Colony to remain connected with this country is an idea which no statesman would entertain; though no statesman should take too seriously any lightly expressed wish on the part of a Colony for separation from this country.

Hansard, Third Series, Vol. CXCIX, cs. 196, 198–9, 200–1, 216.

64: W. E. GLADSTONE. Speech in the House of Commons

26 April 1870

IF you look back to the history of the colonial connection between European Powers and trans-Atlantic possessions you find that it is the nature of those possessions to grow, and so to grow as to alter essentially, in obedience to laws stronger than the will of man, the conditions of their

relations to the countries with which they were originally
connected, until they arrive at that stage of their progress
in which separation from the mother country inevitably
takes place. It is impossible, however, to look back with
satisfaction to the mode in which that separation has
occurred. In every instance it has been brought about by
war and bloodshed, involving an inheritance of pain,
hatred, and shame; whereas in reason there ought to be
nothing to preclude the hope, when the growth of a
colonial possession is such as to make separation from the
mother country a natural and beneficial result, that that
separation, so far from being effected by violence and
bloodshed, might be the result of a peaceable and
friendly transaction. Surely it is a great object to place,
if possible, our colonial policy on such a footing, not for
the purpose of bringing about a separation, but of providing a guarantee that, if separation should occur, it
should be in a friendly way. That is the sense, the principle, and the secret of our policy with regard to colonial
reform. But it is not an easy matter to escape from the
false position in which we were involved 30 or 40
years ago, when not only was there much wrong, but
when, we may say, looking back with the light of the
experience we have since gained, there was nothing right
in the relations of our Colonies with the mother country.
We have had experience of the policy of restraint
attempted to be applied by European countries to their
colonial possessions; and we have not only that experience in former generations to guide us, but we have also
had most serious warnings addressed to ourselves,
especially in the case of the great Colony of Canada.
Therefore, it is an honourable chapter in the history of
our own times that there has been a great and almost
continuous effort among our statesmen, without distinc-

tion of party, to work out a policy such as to avoid the peril and disgrace, which, whenever the period should arrive, would attach to separation effected by violence and bloodshed. This is done to the present hour, and it is not, as supposed, the introduction of a new policy, but the successive application of principles now established and recognized by persons of authority of every shade of politics, and received, it may be said, with universal assent. That is the case as regards the policy we have endeavoured humbly to pursue; and it does not, in my opinion, tend to weaken the relations between the mother country and the Colonies, but, on the contrary, while securing the greatest likelihood of a perfectly peaceable separation, whenever separation may arrive, gives the best chance of an indefinitely long continuance of a free and voluntary connection. That is the footing on which we, like our predecessors, have endeavoured to found our colonial policy. Freedom and voluntaryism form the character of the connection, and our policy is not to be regarded as a surreptitious or clandestine means of working out the foregone purpose of casting off the Colonies, but as the truest and best, if not the only means, of fulfilling our obligations to them. . . .

We never said that for the sake of economical results the obligation of any duty was to be made light of. With respect to colonial defence, though the pecuniary burden entailed was the chief evil we had to contend with, still I thought that the greatest evil done by that system was done to the Colonies themselves. We did not teach our Colonies to rely upon themselves; but we taught them to rely that, come what would, they would be defended by a power thousands of miles away. It is impossible to establish a free community unless you have along with the enjoyment of the privileges of freedom a fair distribution of the burdens which they entailed. Unless men are taught to rely upon themselves they can never be truly worthy of the name of freemen.

Hansard, Third Series, Vol. CC, cs. 1900–3.

65: J. A. FROUDE. Article in *Fraser's Magazine*

August 1870

ENGLAND, itself, is committed for good or evil to be a great manufacturing country. Let her manufactures cease, and her political greatness is at an end. It is not equally necessary that they should be extended beyond their present limit. It is not equally necessary that the stability of the Empire should exclusively depend on them. Providence or our father's energy has brought splendid territories under the British flag, where fresh communities may spring up dependent on less precarious terms. The millions to be hereafter added to our numbers may be occupied in the cultivation of land, whilst our efforts at home may be turned, for the future, rather to improving the quality of what we produce than multiplying the quantity of it, and to bringing under control the dirt, and ignorance, and disease, and crime which are making our great towns into nurseries of barbarism. The employers might allay their alarms. The initial loss, if loss there was, would compensate itself in the goodwill of the employed, and in the improved work in which that goodwill would show itself. The surest road to the development of trade, it has been proved to demonstration, lies in the development of the colonies. . . .

The terms on which the colonies are to remain attached to us may be left to settle themselves. There is no occasion for present change, if it be understood that we have no desire to part with them, and if colonists are admitted freely to such honours and privileges as the State confers on distinguished subjects. Healthy confederations must grow, and cannot be made. The only stable bond of union is mutual goodwill.

Printed in *Short Studies on Great Subjects,* Second Series, pp. 318–9.

66: ALFRED, LORD TENNYSON. *Idylls of the King*
TO THE QUEEN
Lines added in 1872

AND that true North[1], whereof we lately heard
A strain to shame us 'keep you to yourselves;
So loyal is too costly! friends—your love
Is but a burthen: loose the bond, and go.'
Is this the tone of empire? here the faith
That made us rulers? this, indeed, her voice
And meaning, whom the roar of Hougoumont
Left mightiest of all peoples under heaven?
What shock has fool'd her since, that she should speak
So feebly? wealthier—wealthier—hour by hour!
The voice of Britain, or a sinking land,
Some third-rate isle half-lost among her seas?
There rang her voice, when the full city peal'd
Thee and thy Prince! The loyal to their crown
Are loyal to their own far sons, who love
Our ocean-empire with her boundless homes
For ever-broadening England, and her throne
In our vast Orient, and one isle, one isle,
That knows not her own greatness: if she knows
And dreads it we are fall'n.

[1] Canada.

67: BENJAMIN DISRAELI. Speech at the Crystal
Palace
24 June 1872

IF you look to the history of this country since the advent
of Liberalism—forty years ago—you will find that there
has been no effort so continuous, so subtle, supported by
so much energy, and carried on with so much ability and
acumen, as the attempts of Liberalism to effect the disintegration of the Empire of England. And, gentlemen,
of all its efforts, this is the one which has been the
nearest to success. Statesmen of the highest character,
writers of the most distinguished ability, the most
organised and efficient means, have been employed in
this endeavour. It has been proved to all of us that we
have lost money by our Colonies. It has been shown with
precise, with mathematical demonstration, that there
never was a jewel in the Crown of England that was so
truly costly as the possession of India. How often has it
been suggested that we should at once emancipate ourselves from this incubus! Well, that result was nearly
accomplished. When those subtle views were adopted by
the country under the plausible plea of granting self-
government to the Colonies, I confess that I myself
thought that the tie was broken. Not that I for one
object to self-government; I cannot conceive how our
distant Colonies can have their affairs administered
except by self-government.

But self-government, in my opinion, when it was conceded, ought to have been conceded as part of a great
policy of Imperial consolidation. It ought to have been
accompanied by an Imperial tariff, by securities for the
people of England for the enjoyment of the unappro-
priated lands which belonged to the Sovereign as their
trustee, and by a military code which should have pre-

cisely defined the means and the responsibilities by which the Colonies should be defended, and by which, if necessary, this country should call for aid from the Colonies themselves. It ought, further, to have been accompanied by the institution of some representative council in the metropolis, which would have brought the Colonies into constant and continuous relations with the Home Government. All this, however, was omitted because those who advised that policy—and I believe their convictions were sincere—looked upon the Colonies of England, looked even upon our connection with India, as a burden upon this country; viewing everything in a financial aspect, and totally passing by those moral and political considerations which make nations great, and by the influence of which alone men are distinguished from animals.

Well, what has been the result of this attempt during the reign of Liberalism for the disintegration of the Empire? It has entirely failed. But how has it failed? Through the sympathy of the Colonies for the Mother Country. They have decided that the Empire shall not be destroyed; and in my opinion no Minister in this country will do his duty who neglects any opportunity of reconstructing as much as possible our Colonial Empire, and of responding to those distant sympathies which may become the source of incalculable strength and happiness to this land.

The issue is not a mean one. It is whether you will be content to be a comfortable England, modelled and moulded upon Continental principles and meeting in due course an inevitable fate, or whether you will be a great country, an Imperial country, a country where your sons, when they rise, rise to paramount positions, and obtain not merely the esteem of their countrymen, but command the respect of the world.

Buckle, *Life of Disraeli*, Vol. V, pp. 194–5, 196.

68: W. E. FORSTER. Address to the Philosophical Institution of Edinburgh

5 November 1875

JUDGING from what I have heard, or read, and what little I have myself seen, I should say that an Englishman, or a Scotchman, or an Irishman, and their children, remain English, Scotch, or Irish, wherever they be; or, if there be a change, it is that the distinct characteristics of the inhabitants of the three kingdoms tend to be lost in their common similarity. In the province of Quebec, we are continually reminded that Frenchmen can be loyal subjects to the British Queen, and strong supporters of the British connection; but in Toronto or Kingston, or other towns and villages of Upper Canada, I had to look out for the St. Lawrence, or the lakes, or the forest, to feel that I was not at home. Even in the States the difference is so completely on the surface, and so quickly disappears, that it soon requires an actual effort of the mind to remember that the farmers of the West, or the citizens of Boston, are not as English as ourselves.

The fact is, English-speaking men and women look at life and its problems, especially the problems of Government, with the same eyes everywhere. Slavery distorted the vision of many for a time, but now there is more difference between the German and the British monarchies, and between the French and the American Republics, than there is between the British monarchy and the American Republic. Doubtless society in the new communities is, and probably for some time will be, more democratic than with us. Men start more equally than in the old country, and it will take time before it will be found out that one man runs faster than another. But are not the tendencies at home also democratic? We cannot send over to Australia a ready-made aristocracy. But we, too, have our democracy, and already we have found it convenient that Australia tries democratic experiments which help us to solve the problems with which we know we must deal. If any one thinks it is either probable or desirable that any Anglo-Saxon community should develop political ideas opposed to those of our forefathers—for instance, the Latin idea of an emperor, or elected despot,—it would be quite consistent for such a person to desire that our Colonial Empire should be dissolved, in the hope that emperors should be chosen by the new nations. But believing, as I do, that on the whole Representative Government is the best form of government, that by which orderly pro-gress is best secured, I, for my part, rejoice in the con-viction that a common preference for this form of government is one of the strongest ties which bind together all who speak our language.

Yet many millions of our race prefer a Republic to a Monarchy. Yes, but remember these facts: first, that we so treated their fathers that we almost forced them to be Republicans; secondly, that many of them now acknowledge that at least it is a moot question whether, as regards the real meaning of the word, and its true significance, our Limited Monarchy is not a more com-plete Republic than their own; and lastly, that the great majority of the colonists in America, Australia, and Africa are as loyal to our Monarchy as we are ourselves. Not merely because they honour and respect our Queen; not merely because of their personal feeling towards the

Royal Lady under whose rule they have grown from
childhood to lusty youth; but because they are as proud
as we are of the traditions of our history, and as convinced as we are of the actual advantages of an hereditary executive. In fact, it seems to me to be not one of
the least reasons for preserving our connection with the
Colonies, that what may be termed the local tendencies,
very generally the result of local selfishness, will both
with them and with us be in measure checked, and
counteracted, and overbalanced by great Imperial
interests—Imperial because they are great.

And now, if any of you have followed me thus far in
the line of thought which I have taken, he will, I think,
be ready with the question—If you think this future
association possible, if you see no insuperable physical
or moral bar to prevent it, in what way do you expect it
to be formed? What kind of federation do you propose?
My reply is, I am ready with no proposition. I believe
any precise proposition would be premature; and for this
reason, that as yet no change in our relations is necessary.
As Mr. Arthur Mills stated . . . " The present principle
of our colonial policy is to ripen these communities to
the earliest possible maturity," [1] and when they have
obtained this maturity, it will be for us and for them to
consider what, under the circumstances then existing,
will be the best bond of union. All that is required now
is to imbue them and ourselves with the desire that the
union should last, with the determination that the
Empire shall not be broken up—to replace the idea of
eventual independence, which means disunion, by that
of association on equal terms, which means union. If
this be done, we need not fear that at the fitting time
this last idea will realise itself.

[1] Arthur Mills, *Outlines of Colonial Constitutions*, 1856.

We may, however, try to define what must be the
necessary conditions of such union. I have not time to
do more than mention my definition. You must test it for
yourselves. It seems to me that in order that our Empire
should continue, all its different self-governing communities must agree in maintaining allegiance to one
monarch;—in maintaining a common nationality, so
that each subject may find that he has the political rights
and privileges of other subjects wheresoever he may go
in the Realm; and, lastly, must agree not only in maintaining a mutual alliance in all relations with foreign
powers, but in apportioning among themselves the
obligations imposed by such alliance. I have seen it proposed that there should be an attempt to escape the third
of these conditions. It has been suggested that a colony
might, if it pleased, be considered neutral in any war in
which we might be engaged; especially this has been
urged for Canada. I cannot suppose that any one who
supports this view can either contemplate or desire the
continuance of the Imperial connection. The very
essence of such continuance is a common patriotism;—
the feeling throughout all the different communities that,
notwithstanding the seas that roll between them, they
are yet one nation; and that all their inhabitants are
fellow-countrymen. But patriots cannot stipulate that
they will not fight for their country, or arrange to desert
their fellow-countrymen when in danger; nor would any
foreign belligerent be bound by any such attempt to wage
war on the principle of limited liability. There might,
however, be this qualification of this condition. It might
be understood that any member of the Federation, either
the mother country, or any one of its children, should
have an acknowledged right to withdraw from the
mutual alliance on giving reasonable notice. I do not

look forward to such an understanding; still less should I propose it. But even if this proviso were attached to my third condition of union, I do not think that the union would be dissolved; because I do not believe that fear of war would induce this notice of withdrawal, or rather of desertion, to be given. I may be told that I merely ground this belief on sentimental hopes. But the sentiments of courage, of honour, of fidelity, have long been facts in British—yes, and also in Irish—history. And why should the children have less of these sentiments than their fathers?

W. E. Forster, *Our Colonial Empire* (1875), pp. 22–5.

69: JOHN BRIGHT. Speech on India

Manchester, 11 December 1877

I BELIEVE that it is our duty not only to govern India well now for our own sakes and to satisfy our own conscience, but so to arrange its government and so to administer it that we should look forward to the time—which may be distant, but may not be so remote—when India will have to take up her own government, and administer it in her own fashion. I say he is no statesman—he is no man actuated with a high moral sense with regard to our great and terrible moral responsibility, who is not willing thus to look ahead, and thus to prepare for circumstances which may come sooner than we think, and sooner than any of us hope for, but which must come at some not very distant date. By doing this, I think we should be endeavouring to make amends for the original crime upon which much of our power in India is founded, and for the many mistakes which have been made by men whose intentions have been good. I think it is our duty, if we can, to approach this great question in this spirit,

THE CONCEPT OF EMPIRE

and to try rightly to discharge the task committed to us, as the Government and rulers of the countless and helpless millions of that country. If we seek thus to deal with those millions, and men in after ages condemn our fathers for the policy which for the time bound India to England, they may award praise to us and to those who come after us for that we have striven to give them that good government and that freedom which He who is supreme over all lands and all peoples will in His own good time make the possession of all His children.

Public Addresses by John Bright (ed. Thorold Rogers, 1879), p. 448.

70: W. E. GLADSTONE. *England's Mission*

Article in *The Nineteenth Century,* September 1878

THE sentiment of empire may be called innate in every Briton. If there are exceptions, they are like those of men born blind or lame among us. It is part of our patrimony: born with our birth, dying only with our death; incorporating itself in the first elements of our knowledge, and interwoven with all our habits of mental action upon public affairs. It is a portion of our national stock, which has never been deficient, but which has more than once run to rank excess, and brought us to mischief accordingly, mischief that for a time we have weakly thought was ruin. In its normal action, it made for us the American colonies, the grandest monument ever erected by a people of modern times, and second only to the Greek colonisation in the whole history of the world. In its domineering excess, always under the name of British interests and British honour, it lost them by obstinacy and pride. Lord Chatham who forbade us to tax, Mr. Burke who forbade us to legislate for them, would have saved them. But they had to argue for a limitation of English power; and to meet the reproach of the political wiseacres, who first blustered on our greatness, and then, when they reaped as they had sown, whined over our calamities. Undoubtedly the peace of 1782–3, with its adjuncts in exasperated feeling, was a terrible dismemberment. But England was England still: and one of the damning signs of the politics of the school is their total blindness to the fact, that the central strength of England lies in England. Their eye travels with satisfaction over the wide space upon the map covered by the huge ice-bound deserts of North America or the unpenetrated wastes of Australasia, but rests with mortification on the narrow bounds of latitude and longitude marked by nature for the United Kingdom. They are the materialists of politics: their faith is in acres and in leagues, in sounding titles and long lists of territories. They forget that the entire fabric of the British Empire was reared and consolidated by the energies of a people, which was (though it is not now) insignificant in numbers, when compared with the leading States of the Continent; and that if by some vast convulsion our transmarine possessions could be all submerged, the very same energies of that very same people would either discover other inhabited or inhabitable spaces of the globe on which to repeat its work, or would without them in other modes assert its undiminished greatness. Of all the opinions disparaging to England, there is not one which can lower her like that which teaches that the source of strength for this almost measureless body lies in its extremities, and not in the heart which has so long propelled the blood through all its regions, and in the brain which has bound and binds them into one.

In the sphere of personal life, most men are misled through the medium of the dominant faculty of their nature. It is round that dominant faculty that folly and flattery are wont to buzz. They play upon vainglory by exaggerating and commending what it does, and by piquing it on what it sees cause to forbear from doing. It is so with nations. For all of them the supreme want really is, to be warned against the indulgence of the dominant passion. The dominant passion of France was military glory. Twice, in this century, it has towered beyond what is allowed to man; and twice has paid the tremendous forfeit of opening to the foe the proudest capital in the world. The dominant passion of England is extended empire. It has heretofore been kept in check by the integrity and sagacity of her statesmen, who have not shrunk from teaching her the lessons of self-denial and self-restraint. But a new race has arisen; and the most essential or the noblest among all the duties of government, the exercise of moral control over ambition and cupidity, have been left to the intermittent and feeble handling of those who do not govern.

Between the two parties in this controversy there is a perfect agreement that England has a mighty mission in the world; but there is a discord as fundamental upon the question what that mission is.

I. With the one party, her first care is held to be the care of her own children within her own shores, the redress of wrongs, the supply of needs, the improvement of laws and institutions. Against this homespun doctrine, the present Government appears to set up territorial aggrandisement, large establishments, and the accumulation of a multitude of fictitious interests abroad, as if our real interests were not enough; and since the available store of national time and attention is a fixed quantity, there ensues that comparative remissness in domestic affairs, which is too conclusively shown by the beggarly returns of our legislation, the aggravation of our burdens, and the fast-growing arrears of business.

II. With the one party, the great duty and honour and charge of our transmarine Colonial Empire is, to rear up free congenital communities. They receive a minority of our emigrants, of whom the larger number go to the United States of America; but, in receiving this minority, they enlarge for our outgoing population the field of choice, and by keeping them within the Empire diminish the shock and severance of change. Commercially our colonies unhappily embrace to a great extent, like the United States, the principles of Protectionism, and they are quietly suffered to carry them even into caricature by enforcing them against the parent country; but they have not within themselves the same scope and variety of production which allow those principles to receive in the United States such large effect; and from many causes, none of them involving coercion or command, the capitative addition made by their population to our commerce is larger than in the case of any foreign country. It is felt at the same time that Great Britain has, against the merely material advantages of these possessions, greatly enlarged her military responsibilities in time of war. Energetic efforts, indeed, have been necessary to relieve the mother country from military charge for the colonies in ordinary years of peace; and these have been largely, but not as yet uniformly, successful. Still, whatever be in these respects the just balance of the account, it is felt that the colonial relation involves far higher elements of consideration; that the founding of these free, growing, and vigorous communities has been a specific part of the work providentially assigned

267

to Britain. The day has gone by, when she would dream of compelling them by force to remain in political connection with her. But, on the other hand, she would never suffer them to be torn away from her; and would no more grudge the cost of defending them against such a consummation, than the father of a family grudges the expense of the food necessary to maintain his children.

> Put the world's whole strength
> Into one giant arm, it shall not force
> This lineal honour from us.[1]

There is then probably little difference among us as to the practical propositions, which bear upon our colonial relations with British North America and the magnificent Australasian group; relations, that may now be stated, on one side at least, to have reached a normal condition.

But here also the frame of mind is different, with which, from the two sides respectively, our colonies are regarded. It is the administrative connection, and the shadow of political subordination, which chiefly give them value in the sight of the party, who at home as well as abroad are striving to cajole or drive us into Imperialism. With their opponents, it is the welfare of these communities which forms the great object of interest and desire; and if the day should ever come, when in their own view that welfare would be best promoted by their administrative emancipation, then and then only the Liberal mind of England would at once say, 'Let them flourish to the uttermost; and, if their highest welfare requires their severance, we prefer their amicable independence to their constrained subordina-

---

[1] Shakespeare's *Henry IV*, Pt. II. Act IV, Sc. 5 (author's note).

tion.' The substance of the relationship lies, not in dis-
patches from Downing Street, but in the mutual
affection, and the moral and social sympathies, which
can only flourish between adult communities when they
are on both sides free.

The vainglorious boast, which Ministers, aware that
there could be no reply, have inserted in the speech of
her Majesty on the prorogation of Parliament, as to aid
which the Colonies would have given in a war that might
have been, can only excite ridicule. No man of sense
believes that the Colonies are likely to become, in a
serious manner, parties to any great European war.
Handfuls of men or even of money may be supplied by
individual zeal; but it is hardly to be desired, for their
own sake or ours, that they should become real parties to
contests, over the inception, conduct, and conclusion of
which they can exercise no effective control. Ostentatious
proclamation to the world of the military aid they are to
give us is much more likely to check, than to develop, any
disposition of that kind; and savours strongly of an age
of imposture. Here again the material view has eclipsed
every other. What we want from the Colonies is something better than ' food for powder.' To give birth and
existence to these States, which are to form so large a
portion of the New World, is a noble feature in the
work and mission of this nation, as it was of old in the
mission of Greece. Nor are the economical results of
this splendid parentage to be despised. But to suppose
that these territories, severed greatly from one another,
and uniformly from us, by thousands upon thousands of
miles of dissociating ocean, can ever be to the mother
country like continuous territories, is a superstition
equally gross and mischievous, and, by setting up
imaginary sources of strength, tends only to enhance that

neglect of domestic interests, which has already become so serious an evil.

Moreover, the prospective multiplication of possessions oversea is, to say the least, far from desirable. It is difficult to regard without anxiety the formidable extension, which has been given to our boundaries at the Cape. During the last forty years, those possessions have cost us probably from twenty to thirty millions sterling in wars and military establishments; and an annexation like that of the Transvaal will entail the heaviest responsibility on the Government, should it be found that our sovereignty has been imposed by force on an unwilling population. We do not want Bosnian submissions. Especially is it inexpedient to acquire possessions which, like Cyprus, never can become truly British, because they have acquired indelibly an ethnical character of their own. In them we remain as masters and as foreigners, and the connection at its best has not the ennobling features which, in cases like America and Australasia, give a high moral purpose to the subsisting relation, and compensate for the serious responsibilities which in given contingencies it may entail.

Nineteenth Century, IV, September 1878, pp. 569–573.

PART XII

THE 1880's: IMPERIAL FEDERATION

71: JOHN ROBERT SEELEY. *The Expansion of England*

1883

Seeley was Professor of Modern History at Cambridge from 1869 to 1894. This book is a reprint of lectures delivered in 1881–2. It is said that it was on Seeley's account that Joseph Chamberlain, on whom the influence of this book was profound, sent his son Austen to Cambridge. Seeley supported the formation and work of the Imperial Federation League and was made a K.C.M.G. in 1884.

I REMARKED before that Greater Britain is an extension of the English State and not merely of the English nationality. But it is an equally striking characteristic of Greater Britain that nevertheless it *is* an extension of the English nationality. When a nationality is extended without any extension of the State, as in the case of the Greek colonies, there may be an increase of moral and intellectual influence, but there is no increase of political power. On the other hand when the State advances beyond the limits of the nationality, its power becomes precarious and artificial. This is the condition of most Empires; it is the condition for example of our own empire in India. The English State is powerful there, but the English nation is but an imperceptible drop in the ocean of an Asiatic population. And when a nation extends itself into other territories the chances are that it will there meet with other nationalities which it cannot destroy or completely drive out, even if it succeeds in conquering them. When this happens, it has a great and

permanent difficulty to contend with. The subject or
rival nationalities cannot be perfectly assimilated, and
remain as a permanent cause of weakness and danger.
It has been the fortune of England in extending itself to
evade on the whole this danger. For it has occupied parts
of the globe which were so empty that they offered an
unbounded scope for new settlement. There was land
for every emigrant who chose to come, and the native
races were not in a condition sufficiently advanced to
withstand even the peaceful competition, much less the
power, of the immigrants.

This statement is true on the whole. The English
Empire is on the whole free from that weakness which
has brought down most empires, the weakness of being
a mere mechanical forced union of alien nationalities.
It is sometimes described as an essentially feeble union
which could not bear the slightest shock, with what
reason I may examine later, but it has the fundamental
strength which most empires and some commonwealths
want.

There can be no dispute about the value of organised
States in the less crowded parts of the globe. But why
should these be our own colonies? There is nothing to
prevent the emigrant from settling in a colony belonging
to some different European State or in an independent
State. Why need we trouble ourselves therefore to keep
up colonies of our own?

This is a strange question, which would never be
asked in England but for an exceptional circumstance.
Most people like to live among their own countrymen,
under the laws, religion and institutions they are accustomed to. They place themselves moreover most really
and practically at a disadvantage by going to live among

people who speak a different language. As a matter of fact, we do not find that, the course of emigration being free, any large number of Englishmen yearly settle in those New World States which are really foreign, that is, in the South American Republics or in Brazil or in Mexico. There would be no question at all about the value of colonies, and we should all as a matter of course consider that only by means of colonies was it possible to bring the wealth of the New World within the reach of our population, if it were not for the existence of the United States. But the United States are to us almost as good as a colony; our people can emigrate thither without sacrificing their language or chief institutions or habits. And the Union is so large and prosperous and fills our view so much, that we forget how very exceptional its relation to us is, and also that if it is to us almost as good as a colony, this is only because it was constructed out of English colonies. In estimating the value of colonies in the abstract, we shall only confuse ourselves by recollecting this unique case; we ought to put the United States entirely out of view.

Considered in the abstract then, colonies are neither more nor less than a great augmentation of the national estate. They are lands for the landless, prosperity and wealth for those in straitened circumstances. This is a very simple view, and yet it is much overlooked, as if somehow it were too simple to be understood. History offers many examples of nations cramped for want of room; it records in many cases how they swarmed irresistibly across their frontiers and spread like a deluge over neighbouring countries, where sometimes they found lands and wealth. Now we may be very sure that never any nation was half so much cramped for want of room in the olden time as our own nation is now.

If the United States and Russia hold together for another half century, they will at the end of that time completely dwarf such old European States as France and Germany, and depress them into a second class. They will do the same to England, if at the end of that time England still thinks of herself as simply a European State, as the old United Kingdom of Great Britain and Ireland, such as Pitt left her. It would indeed be a poor remedy, if we should try to face these vast states of the new type by an artificial union of settlements and islands scattered over the whole globe, inhabited by different nationalities, and connected by no tie except the accident that they happen all alike to acknowledge the Queen's authority. But I have pointed out that what we call our Empire is no such artificial fabric, that it is not properly, if we exclude India from consideration, an Empire at all, that it is a vast English nation, only a nation so widely dispersed that before the age of steam and electricity its strong natural bonds of race and religion seemed practically dissolved by distance. As soon then as distance is abolished by science, as soon as it is proved by the examples of the United States and Russia that political union over vast areas has begun to be possible, so soon Greater Britain starts up, not only a reality, but a robust reality. It will belong to the stronger class of political unions. If it will not be stronger than the United States, we may say with confidence that it will be far stronger than the great conglomeration of Slavs, Germans, Turcomans and Armenians, of Greek Christians, Catholics, Protestants, Mussulmans and Buddhists, which we call Russia.

A time may conceivably come when it may be practicable to leave India to herself, but for the present it is necessary to govern her as if we were to govern her for ever. Why so? Not mainly on our own account. Some tell us that our honour requires us to maintain the acquisition which our fathers made with their blood, and which is the great military trophy of the nation. To my mind there is something monstrous in all such notions of honour; they belong to that primitive and utterly obsolete class of notions, of which I have spoken before, which rest upon a confusion between the ideas of government and property. Nothing is to be considered for a moment but the well-being of India and England, and of the two countries India, as being by much the more nearly interested, by much the larger, and by much the poorer, is to be considered before England. But on these very principles, and especially on account of the interest of India, it is impossible for the present to think of abandoning the task we have undertaken there. We might do so if our own interest alone were considered. Not that it would be easy, now that such a vast trade has grown up and such vast sums of English money, particularly in these latest years, have been invested in the country. But it would be possible. On the other hand if we consider the interest of India, it appears wholly impossible. Much may be plausibly alleged against the system under which we govern India. It may be doubted whether it is altogether suited to the people, whether it is not needlessly expensive, and so forth. We may feel a reasonable anxiety as to what will come in the end of this unparalleled experiment. But I think it would be a very extreme view to deny that our Government is better than any other which has existed in India since the Mussulman conquest. If it should ultimately fail more than any one imagines, we could never leave the country in a state half so deplorable as that in which we found it.

A very moderately good Government is incomparably better than none. The sudden withdrawal even of an oppressive Government is a dangerous experiment. Some countries, no doubt, there are, which might pass through such a trial without falling into anarchy. Thinly peopled countries, or countries whose inhabitants had been long accustomed to much freedom of action, might be trusted to devise for themselves very speedily as much government as might be necessary. But what a mockery to lay down such propositions with India in view! When we began to take possession of the country, it was already in a state of wild anarchy such as Europe has perhaps never known. What government it had was pretty invariably despotic, and was generally in the hands of military adventurers, depending on a soldiery composed of bandits whose whole vocation was plunder. . . .

India . . . is of all countries that which is least capable of evolving out of itself a stable Government. And it is to be feared that our rule may have diminished what little power of this sort it may have originally possessed. For our supremacy has necessarily depressed those classes which had anything of the talent or habit of government. The old royal races, the noble classes, and in particular the Mussulmans who formed the bulk of the official class under the Great Moguls, have suffered most and benefited least from our rule. This decay is the staple topic of lamentation among those who take a dark view of our Empire; but is it not an additional reason why the Empire should continue? Then think of the immense magnitude of the country; think too that we have undermined all fixed moral and religious ideas in the intellectual classes by introducing the science of the West into the midst of Brahminical traditions. When you have made all these reflexions, you will see that to withdraw our Government from a country which is dependent on it, and which we have made incapable of depending upon anything else, would be the most inexcusable of all conceivable crimes and might possibly cause the most stupendous of all conceivable calamities.

If India does begin to breathe as a single national whole—and our own rule is perhaps doing more than ever was done by former Governments to make this possible—then no such explosion of despair, even if there were cause for it, would be needed. For in that case the feeling would soon gain the native army, and on the native army ultimately we depend. We could subdue the mutiny of 1857, formidable as it was, because it spread through only a part of the army, because the people did not actively sympathise with it, and because it was possible to find native Indian races who would fight on our side. But the moment a mutiny is but threatened, which shall be no mere mutiny, but the expression of a universal feeling of nationality, at that moment all hope is at an end, as all desire ought to be at an end, of preserving our Empire. For we are not really conquerors of India, and we cannot rule her as conquerors; if we undertook to do so, it is not necessary to inquire whether we could succeed, for we should assuredly be ruined financially by the mere attempt.

The dominion of Rome over the western races was the empire of civilisation over barbarism. Among Gauls and Iberians Rome stood as a beacon-light; they acknowledged its brightness, and felt grateful for the illumination they received from it. The dominion of England in India is rather the empire of the modern world over the medieval. The light we bring is not less real, but it is probably less attractive and received with less gratitude. It is not a glorious light shining in darkness, but a somewhat cold daylight introduced into the midst of a warm gorgeous twilight.

This Empire held at arm's length, paying no tribute to us, yet costing nothing except through the burden it imposes on our foreign policy, and neither modifying nor perceptibly influencing our busy domestic politics; this Empire nevertheless held firmly and with a grasp which does not slacken but visibly tightens; the union of England and India, ill-assorted and unnatural as it might seem to be, nevertheless growing closer and closer with great rapidity under the influence of the modern conditions of the world, which seem favourable to vast political unions; all this makes up the strangest, most curious, and perhaps most instructive chapter of English history. It has been made the subject of much empty boasting, while those who have looked deeper have often been disposed to regard the whole enterprise with despondency, as a kind of romantic adventure which can lead to nothing permanent. But, as time passes, it rather appears that we are in the hands of a Providence which is greater than all statesmanship, that this fabric so blindly piled up has a chance of becoming a part of the permanent edifice of civilisation, and that the Indian achievement of England as it is the strangest, may after all turn out to be the greatest, of all her achievements.

We have been led to take a much more sober view of the Empire than would satisfy the bombastic school. At the outset we are not much impressed with its vast extent, because we know no reason in the nature of things why a state should be any the better for being large, and because throughout the greater part of history very large states have usually been states of a low type. Nor again can we imagine why it should be our duty to maintain our Empire for an indefinite time simply out of respect for the heroism of those who won it for us, or because the abandonment of it might seem to betray a want of spirit. All political unions exist for the good of their members, and should be just as large, and no larger, as they can be without ceasing to be beneficial. It would seem to us insane that if the connexion with the colonies or with India hampered both parties, if it did harm rather than good, England should resolve to maintain it to her own detriment and to that of her dependencies.

The Expansion of England (1888 ed.) pp. 45–6, 58–9, 75–6, 193–6, 234, 244, 261–2, 294.

72: ARCHIBALD PHILIP PRIMROSE, EARL OF ROSEBERY. Australian Speeches

Rosebery had resigned from his Under-Secretaryship at the Home Office because of Gladstone's inaction over Scottish matters. He then toured the world, making these speeches in Australia. It was this tour that turned him into an advocate of the Empire which he henceforth preached in season and out of season. So outspoken did he become that of his speech on 11 October 1888 (No. 80) the *Spectator* commented that he "thought only of opinion in the Colonies". In the Liberal division over the Empire he became the acknowledged leader of the Liberal Imperialists and was Prime Minister, 1894–5.

Sydney, 10 December 1883

I WILL ask you only to remember one thing in your dealings with the old country, as I wish statesmen in the old country to remember it in their dealings with you. It is that neither you nor they should reason too much from precedent or from history. It has made its own history; it is creating its own precedent, it is steering its path into the future, where no chart and no compass can guide it. Least of all can she forecast her own relations with her own Empire, and God forbid that you or I, or any of us, or any of them in the old country, should attempt to do it at this time. Let us do the best we can, and work for the best. She can only blindly work, trying to do her best for these her children—for her greatest children as for her least children—and in that attempt I pray she may be successful. Her relations with her colonies cannot any longer be defined. People talk of the Roman colonies, of the Greek colonies, of the military colonies, and of the American colonies. We have nothing to do with those colonies. They have interesting records, but they furnish no guidance now for the British Empire. We have out-lived that time of minority and instruction. Her relations with her colonies are, it seems to me, of a complicated and of an intricate nature. They are connected by a golden thread of affection and of descent. They are cemented, Gentlemen, more closely than anything by the fact that there are few of us in England who have not got relations or kinsfolk working among you here. When they talk of cutting us adrift from you, or cutting you adrift from us, people do not seem to remember that that is the case, and that we do not care deliberately to cut ourselves off from our own blood and our own flesh. But as regards your relations with the mother-country, I would sum them up in a single sentence, by saying that, in the strict sense of the word, she does not attempt to guide, she does not pretend to control, but she does regard her giant offspring with a pride which it would be the merest affectation to conceal.

Adelaide, 18 January 1884

I SAY that these are no longer colonies in the ordinary
sense of the term, but I claim that this is a nation—a
nation not in aspiration or in the future, but in performance and fact. I claim that this country has established
to be a nation, and that its nationality is now and will be
henceforward recognised by the world. Sir, that is a great
position to take, and I think the facts I have stated sub-
stantiate it. But there is a further question, and it is this:
Does this fact of your being a nation, and I think you feel
yourselves to be a nation, imply separation from the
Empire? God forbid! There is no need for any nation,
however great, leaving the Empire, because the Empire
is a commonwealth of nations. . . .

It seems to me that hand in hand they may yet follow
up a career of usefulness to mankind—led by those
common and eternal principles of justice which alone
can exalt and sustain a nation, and which we proudly
boast and humbly hope have long guided and directed
the British Empire; which have been the pillar of cloud
by day and the pillar of fire by night that have guided
us to so many achievements and through so many
troubles. I believe that every day we remain united we
shall be less anxious to part. I believe that every day we
remain united it will be considered more desirable that
we should continue so, not merely for our own selfish
interests, but for the interest of humanity at large:
because it is on the British race, whether in Great Britain,
or the United States, or the Colonies, or wherever it may
be, that rest the highest hopes of those who try to pene-
trate the dark future, or who seek to raise and better the
patient masses of mankind. Each year the power and
the prerogative of that race appear to me to increase;
each year it seems to fill more and more of the world. I

283

believe that the connection of the British Empire will remain, for the reason that it is desirable for civilisation that it should continue to exist. I confess I think that each day that we live we shall be more and more unwilling to see this ancient Empire of ours—raised with so much toil, colonised with so much energy, cemented with the blood and sweat of so many generations—pass away like a camp struck noiselessly in the night, or split into isolated and sterile communities, jealous among themselves, disturbed by suburban disputes and parochial rivalries, dwindling possibly, like the Italian States of the middle ages, into political insignificance, or degenerating into idle and polite nonentity. And, sir, let me remind this assemblage of the fact—that empires, and especially great empires, when they crumble at all, are apt to crumble exceedingly small.

Crewe, *Lord Rosebery* (1931), Vol. I, pp. 182–3, 185–7.

73: IMPERIAL FEDERATION. Report of the Conference held at the Westminster Palace Hotel

29 July 1884

The Rt. Hon. W. E. FORSTER in the chair: It is quite true that there have been some gentlemen, and there may still be a few gentlemen—but I believe they are becoming fewer every day—who try to persuade themselves we should be better off at home if we were left to ourselves, and who look forward with pleasure—perhaps I should hardly say with pleasure, but without pain—to Australians and Canadians and South Africans ceasing to be our fellow-countrymen. Well, to my mind that prospect is unbearable, and I believe it is to yours also. It means, in my opinion, the weakening of England, the increased probability of war among Christian nations, and—I do not think the words too strong—the throwing back of the progress of civilisation.

It is sometimes said that England would be richer if she could get rid of her colonial responsibilities. Well, I believe that, as a rule, the material interests of a nation are not best served by making their promotion the sole, or even the chief, aim. The result is national degradation, and with it the loss of power, and even the faculty of making money. But, putting aside this somewhat abstract consideration, there is no fact more proved by practical experience than that the trade does follow the flag. Therefore, we may well believe that, if the flag be lowered, trade will suffer. So much for the English view of the matter, which I have endeavoured to express in a very few words.

There are influential colonists present who can—and I doubt not will—tell us that the prospect of separation is as hateful in the Colonies as it is here—that, in their opinion, it means danger to the Colonies themselves, and an arrest of their growth; and I believe they will also tell you that there is no colonial feeling stronger than the longing that there should be such treatment of her Colonies by England as will make separation improbable, or even impossible. We Englishmen, both at home and in the Colonies, have a different future in our mind's eye in this matter than we had a generation ago, or even than we had nine or ten years ago, when I remember trying to impress what were then thought to be rather fantastic views upon the public. But you see the reason why that is the case. The inventions of science have overcome the great difficulties of time and space which were thought to make separation almost a necessity, and we feel now that we can look forward, not to the isolated

independence of England's children, but to their being
united to one another, and with the mother-country, in
permanent family union. I feel certain that, to the public
generally, as well as to you, that prospect is as pleasant
as the prospect of separation is painful. In private
affairs—and I think it is the same in public affairs—
plans or hopes for the future greatly modify action in the
present; and therefore we naturally are now asking ourselves what can be done to avoid the calamity of separation and insure the fulfilment of this beneficent idea of
union. We are met here to-day to answer this question.
We want to see how we can make this desire for union a
fact, and how we can realise this grand idea of unity. I
believe we must not stand by looking on. We must not
suppose that present ties are in themselves strong enough
to bear straining; they require to be pulled and knit
together. Difficulties may arise—intercolonial difficulties, and difficulties, perhaps, between England and her
Colonies—which might lead to separation if we do not
take care to prevent them.

In the words of the resolution which will be submitted to you—simply submitted for discussion—it must
be clear that the relations of our Colonies with the
mother-country must ultimately end either in disintegration or in some form of Federation. We have given our
Colonies—those of our own race—full self-government.
We should have been acting with the greatest possible
folly and injustice if we had not done so; but this self-
government must end in one or other of two ways—
isolated independence, or some form of general union
which is expressed in the common term Federation.
What will be the actual form of this Federation is not,
to my mind, the question to-day. The word does not
necessarily imply a Federal Parliament. It may, for

instance, be fulfilled by a council of representatives of the different Colonies. In fact, all that is implied is that there should be some combination together of the Colonies with the mother-country which would bind them so that separation would be felt to be a most improbable result. I think myself that they are the real foes of union—or at any rate the disbelievers or sceptics of its possibility—who would ask us to-day what should be the form of Federation, or demand at this moment a written Federal Constitution.

As the population and power of the Colonies increase, both absolutely and relatively to the power and population of England, it will every day become more and more clear that the ultimate terms of Federation must in some manner or another be framed on the principles of perfect equality. That will appear more and more clear as time goes on. In the meantime, what is wanted is this—that those who have power and influence in England or in the Colonies should be possessed by the Federal idea, that they should seize every opportunity of working together in good fellowship and sympathy and mutual self-respect; that they should strive to co-operate in common defence, and that they should take counsel together in all Imperial matters, and especially as regards each colony in any relations with any foreign Government.

Rt. Hon. W. H. SMITH: I have no claim whatever to appear at a Federal meeting like this, for my connection with the Colonies is exceedingly slight. It consists only of that connection, which, I believe, almost all Englishmen have—a connection of interest, a connection of investment, and therefore I can only speak from the point of view of an Englishman desirous of seeing the interests of his country and the interests of the Colonies, which are identified with England, promoted and advanced. But, gentlemen, I can quite understand why I have been selected to take part in this meeting. It is in order to show that politicians of this country of all orders, degrees, and parties have one common aim and purpose, and that is the security, the development, the advancement, and the prosperity of the Empire, that we regard our Colonial friends, our cousins, and our neighbours as Englishmen in the full and true intent of the word, and that they are entitled and should obtain as complete a place in the management and in the control of the affairs of the Empire as we Englishmen claim in our own little island. In saying this I do not wish to go an atom further than my friend, Mr. Forster, has gone. We are not here to discuss the details of any scheme of Federation. We are not here to prepare a scheme which shall be put forward for the acceptance of Great Britain or the Colonies. We are here to insist upon the principle to which your Chairman has given expression in the fullest and strongest terms—the principle of unity—a unity of sympathy, of common interest, of a common purpose, and of a common object.

Imperial Federation: Report of the Conference held 29 July 1884, at the Wesminster Palace Hotel (1884), pp. 26–28, 29–30.

74: EARL OF ROSEBERY. Speech to the Seventeenth Trades Union Congress

11 September 1884

WHY is it that this question is a matter of real and vital interest to you? Do these emigrants belong to the upper classes, or mainly to the middle class? No, they are almost entirely belonging to the working classes. (" Hear,

hear," and cheers.) It is you who send forth these thousands to these distant countries. They are your brothers, your children, your kinsfolk, your friends, and what I have to ask you to-day is this—Do you wish that these kinsfolk and these friends of yours shall remain permanently associated with the fortunes of the empire, or whether they shall wander away to nations, however akin, who are not under the dominion of the British Crown? Shall they remain in your country or leave it? If they go to India they are in Great Britain; if they go to Canada they are in Great Britain; if they go to Australia they are in Great Britain; if they go to the United States they go to institutions highly to be commended, in many respects far in advance of ours, to be associated with a people to whom we are akin and whom we love, but who are not our people and which are not our institutions. What I want to know is this—Will you be severed from these emigrants whom you send out by a bond of nationality for all time to come? That is the point where this question touches the Trades Union Congress. And though it is known to you all here that emigrants who go forth are sent out by you, and are blood of your blood and bone of your bone, people say that this is not a man's question. I can say—it may seem paradoxical, but it is absolutely true—that this question is more important than the franchise question which is now agitating the country. . . .

I know that a great many working men, both here and in the colonies, take an even larger view of this question than I have indicated. They hope, not so much for a bond of the British Empire, as for the league of English-speaking people all over the world. I quite admit the sublimity of that conception; but we are practical men —we have to deal with what is nearest hand and likely to be achieved. I do not believe that the league of English-speaking people is likely to be achieved in our time; but what I want to point out is, whether it comes in our time or not, I do not suppose that Great Britain, when she enters that federation or league, will be more considered if she came at the head of a great empire than if she came with only the two islands to which the Nihilising section of colonists would wish to reduce us. I wish, in conclusion, to sum up what I have ventured to urge. In the first place, I have taken it for granted that the continuance of the British Empire is a matter of great interest both to ourselves and the friends of freedom throughout the world. In the second place, I venture to affirm that the bond which binds this Empire together must either become stronger or weaker, and it cannot continue to exist in its somewhat indefinite position. In the third place, I venture to assert that it is desirable that union should become stronger. In the fourth place, I wish to lay down that this question concerns principally those classes who have peopled the Empire. In the fifth place, you, as representatives at any rate of a large portion of that class, should place this question on your programme, and take it into serious consideration. Sixthly, it must become a matter of principle and creed with the working classes, both here and in the colonies, before it becomes a question of practical politics. I want this Congress, therefore, to give this matter their constant and their serious consideration. It is only by constant meditation and discussion that a question, however vital, soaks into the great mass of the people. Nothing can be done, indeed, in this matter without the impulse that comes from the popular will both here and in the colonies. I would ask you then to give this impulse and to prove yourselves by embracing this vast and elevating question not merely Britons, keenly watching and canvassing every question that arises within these islands, not merely representatives discussing sectional subjects, but bright participators of the Empire, which, either at home, or in India, or in the colonies, offers a variety of guarantee and opportunities to her workers, the working men of all classes, which can be offered by no other country in the world. (*Loud cheers.*)

Printed in the Official Report of the Seventeenth Trades Union Congress.

75: JOSEPH CHAMBERLAIN. Speech on Egypt and the German Colonial challenge

Birmingham, 5 January 1885

In the days of his Radical origin Chamberlain had boasted of being " parochially minded ". The change from anti-Imperialism in the seventies was gradual: in the responsibilities of office in the Gladstone government (1880–5), in his visits to North America (1887–8) and Egypt (1889). This speech both marks a stage in that development and points to the dissensions on Imperial policy in the government. The break with the Liberals which occurred over Ireland in 1886 freed Chamberlain to develop his new Imperialism in alliance with the Conservatives in whose government he was Colonial Secretary, 1895–1903 (Nos. 85 *seq.*). Chamberlain's ideas may be further studied in W. L. Strauss, *Joseph Chamberlain and the Theory of Imperialism.*

WE are in Egypt at this time in pursuance of an unselfish object. Our task has proved of greater magnitude than we had anticipated. It is one, indeed, of almost unexampled difficulty. We have met with hostility and opposition in quarters where we had reason to hope for assistance and co-operation. But we will not be driven from our intentions. We will not yield one jot either to the perfidious

291

suggestion of dubious friends abroad or to the interested clamour of financial greed at home, and we will not destroy the independence which we are solemnly pledged to Europe and to Parliament to respect. I hope and believe that in this course we shall have your approval and that you will know how to distinguish between a policy of justice and a policy of weakness. It is not the bravest man who blusters most, and the universal bully, at a time of pinch, is very likely to be found a universal coward. . . .

If we are to be thrown into an agony of apprehension every time any other nation shows signs of restlessness, our power of effective intervention will be lessened when there is real occasion to put it forth. It would be humiliating, indeed, if England, the mistress of half the world, were to be driven to imitate the conduct of an angry scold and indulge in a fit of hysterical passion because Germany had snapped up some unconsidered trifle of territory which we have hitherto not thought it worth while to acquire. If it be necessary, as I think it may be, to review our foreign and colonial policy in the light of recent events, let us face the altered circumstances of the problem in the spirit of full grown men, and not with the pettish outcry of frightened children. I regret the action, however natural it may seem on some grounds, which the German Government has thought it necessary to take [in New Guinea] . . . .

It does not need a prophet to predict that in the course of the next half-century the Australian colonies will have attained such a position that no Power will be strong enough to ignore them, and that they will have a supreme authority in the Pacific seas; and, for my part, I cannot look with any confidence on any settlement which may be made in those regions in defiance of their united opposition.

Meanwhile we are not unmindful of our obligations. If foreign nations are determined to pursue distant colonial enterprises we have no right to prevent them. We cannot anticipate them in every case by proclaiming a universal protectorate in every unoccupied portion of the globe's surface which English enterprise has hitherto neglected. But our fellow subjects may rest assured that their liberties, their rights, and their interests are as dear to us as our own ; and if ever they are seriously menaced, the whole power of the country will be exerted for their defence, and the English democracy will stand shoulder to shoulder throughout the world to maintain the honour and the integrity of the Empire.

The Times, 6 January 1885.

76: FREDERIC ROGERS, BARON BLACHFORD.
Article in *The Pall Mall Gazette*
19 January 1885

I am bound to avow myself one of that apparently small minority who look upon Federation as an unattainable phantom, on grounds which I ought at least generally to indicate. Even in the matter of foreign policy, about which alone the question could arise, I cannot conceive the possibility of our having continued to conduct the Government of the United States of America and the United Kingdom of Great Britain by one sovereign authority, localised either in London or in Washington, or with one foot in one place and one in the other. And what would, in any contingency, have become impossible by this time in the case of the United States, must, as it appears to me, become impossible, as time goes on, in the case of all great and distant Anglo-Saxon colonies. If so, the question is not whether the useful and interesting tie which at present connects us can last for ever—or

even for very long—but whether that transitional relation will be longest and most beneficially preserved by
tightening or relaxing it. Hitherto we have proceeded on
the principle of relaxation, and by so doing we are
admitted, I believe, to have gained more in mutual
contentment than we have lost in authority. I admit,
however, that the question has changed its aspect.
Formerly it was found that we endangered the connexion
by claiming to interfere with the local affairs of the
colonists. The doubt now is whether we shall not
endanger it and ourselves by allowing them to interfere
with our Imperial policy. My own strong impression is
that we shall. The notion of a great Anglo-Saxon
alliance, not formed with a specific object, as to arrest
the supremacy of some overgrown power or immoral
principle, but on a general understanding (as I conclude)
that all shall join in furthering the wishes and interests of
each, seems to me likely, if, *per impossibile,* it should last
long enough, to degenerate into a successful or unsuccess-
ful contrivance for bullying the rest of the world. To
contend for such an alliance on the ground that Anglo-
Saxons—the great exterminators of aborigines in the
temperate zone—would, when confederated, set a new
and exceptional example of justice and humanity, seems
to me a somewhat transcendental expectation.

Printed in *Letters of Lord Blachford* (ed. Marindin, 1896), pp.
425–6.

77: W. E. FORSTER. Article in *The Nineteenth Century*

March 1885

The news of Gordon's death at Khartoum in January 1885
shocked the British Empire. Offers of help were made from many
Colonies but most were rejected by the War Office.

IT is to me most painful to differ from Mr. Bright, but I expected his opposition, because in one respect he is the most conservative of our statesmen. There is no man with any mental power approaching to his to whose mind a new idea has such difficulty of access.

But what did Mr. Bright say on the 29th of January at Birmingham?—'The idea,' he said, 'in my opinion is ludicrous that the British Empire—that is, the United Kingdom with all its colonies—should form one country, one interest, one undivided interest for the purposes of defence.' 'They' (that is the Federation League who proclaim these ludicrous notions) 'must be blind to the lessons of history.'

Yes, but history teaches many lessons now-a-days, and they follow so fast one upon another that it is not always easy to learn them. It may be well for us all, Mr. Bright included, to study this last lesson of history. The Governments of the Dominion of Canada, of New South Wales, of Victoria, of Queensland, of South Australia, have declared that the United Kingdom, with all its colonies, do form one country for the purposes of defence. They have made this declaration on behalf of their people by the offer to give, not only their money but their men, for the defence of the Flag in a war of more than usual danger and privation, and their people have supported their Government in these offers with patriotic enthusiasm.

The union of the mother-country with her children is, thanks to this patriotism, more close and more intimate than it was a month ago.

But is there more probability of its being permanent?

The advocates of disunion, or perhaps it would be more fair to call them the believers in necessary disintegration, will tell us that this colonial enthusiasm is a

THE CONCEPT OF EMPIRE

temporary caprice, or at best but a passing feeling, on which no reliance can be placed. I am content to ask those who hold this view to learn the lessons which history will teach them; but may I venture to say one word to the friends of Union? Some of them may perhaps think that this action of the colonies affords an opportunity of securing the permanent unity of the Empire by the immediate elaboration and definition of a scheme of Federation. I would rather venture to say that this colonial action would seem to show that the time has not yet come for such definition, and for this reason, that no scheme which could now be devised, and no system which could now be defined, would adequately express the feelings in men's minds.

The idea of the permanent unity of the realm, the duty of preserving this union, the blessings which its preservation will confer, the danger and loss and disaster which will follow from disunion, are thoughts which possess the minds of Englishmen both here and over the seas. These thoughts are expressing themselves in deeds; let this expression continue; at present it helps our cause far more effectually than any possible scheme.

The Nineteenth Century, XVII (March 1885), pp. 552–3.

78: EARL OF ROSEBERY. Letter to Sir Henry Ponsonby

Foreign Office, 13 April 1886

The holding of the India and Colonial Exhibition, to which Rosebery is referring in this letter to the Queen's private secretary, and the first Colonial Conference (1887) were the two tangible successes of the influence of the Imperial Federation League.

MANY thanks for your note, which is, I suppose, conclusive. But it is a thousand pities. The symbol that unites this vast empire is a crown and not a bonnet. These colonists and Hindoos who have come from every part of the world to see their sovereign open this exhibition regard her as their Sovereign. They will never have another opportunity as long as they live of saying 'We saw our Queen come as Queen and Empress to perform her part as head of this Empire, wearing the Sign which unites us all; by which she is Queen of New South Wales and the Cape of Good Hope, Queen of Newfoundland, Queen of New Zealand, Empress of India, etc., etc.' To have seen their crowned Queen will impress their imagination; and they will go to their various homes feeling that they realise the monarchy under which they live as an institution and not a person. To see the Queen in morning dress will gratify their personal loyalty, and interest them profoundly, but it will not impress them with the fact that they have seen the ancient and permanent symbol as distinguished from the personality of the monarch.

You must remember that to nine-tenths of these colonists a Queen without a crown is hardly a Queen at all, and that, if the Queen on this historical occasion appears before them as the lady president of a republic might, you lose the opportunity of a political inspiration and a cohesive memory. Alas—however—we cannot struggle with the inevitable.

Crewe, *Lord Rosebery*, Vol. I, pp. 264–5.

79: J. A. FROUDE. Oceana
1886

'IMPOSSIBILITY' is a word of politicians who are without the wish or without the capacity to comprehend new conditions. An 'empire' of Oceana there cannot be. The English race do not like to be parts of an empire.

But a ' commonwealth ' of Oceana held together by common blood, common interest, and a common pride in the great position which unity can secure—such a commonwealth as this may grow of itself if politicians can be induced to leave it alone.

It has become doubtful even to the political economist whether England can trust entirely to free trade and competition to keep the place which she has hitherto held. Other nations press us with their rivalries. Expenses increase, manufactures languish or cease to profit. Revenue, once so expansive, becomes stationary. ' Business ' may, probably will, blaze up again, but the growth of it can no longer be regarded as constant, while population increases and hungry stomachs multiply, requiring the three meals a day whatever the condition of the markets. Hence those among us who have disbelieved all along that a great nation can venture its whole fortunes safely on the power of underselling its neighbours in calicoes and iron-work no longer address a public opinion entirely cold. It begins to be admitted that were Canada and South Africa and Australia and New Zealand members of one body with us, with a free flow of our population into them, we might sit secure against shifts and changes. In the multiplying number of our own fellow-citizens animated by a common spirit, we should have purchasers for our goods from whom we should fear no rivalry; we should turn in upon them the tide of our emigrants which now flows away, while the emigrants themselves would thrive under their own fig tree, and rear children with stout limbs and colour in their cheeks, and a chance before them of a human existence. Oceana would then rest on sure foundations; and her navy—the hand of her strength and the symbol of her unity—

would ride securely in self-supporting stations in the four quarters of the globe.

Happy, it is often said, the country which has no history. Growing nations may pass their childhood in obscurity and amusement, but the neutral condition cannot last for ever. They must emerge out of it in some way, or they might as well never have existed. The rising Australians are 'promising young men.' If they mean to be more, they must either be independent, or must be citizens of Oceana. . . .

If those colonies remain attached to the mother-country, a great and prosperous destiny seems, in human probability, assured to them. If fate and official want of wisdom divide us asunder, these colonies will also, I suppose, form eventually a great nation, or several nations, but they will have to pass through the fire of affliction. Trials await them of many kinds, as certain as the disorders of childhood, some made by fate, some by human wilfulness. Nations cannot mature, any more than each individual of us, without having their school lessons drilled into them by painful processes. ἐν πάθει μαθεῖν is the law of human progress, from the growth of the schoolboy to the growth of the largest community. The Australians, being of English blood, will probably pass successfully through their various apprenticeships. It is possible, on the other hand, that they may repeat the experience of the Spanish colonies in America, and have a long period before them of war and revolution. Human nature is very uniform, and the Spaniards in the sixteenth century were as advanced a race as we. They had degenerated before their colonies were cast adrift, and British communities may hope reasonably for a better future than befel any

Spanish settlement which achieved its independence. But dangers of some kind there must be, and the Australian colonists will not expose themselves unnecessarily to the accidents inseparable from isolation. Their nationality at present is English, and if they leave us it will be by the action of Great Britain herself, not by any action of their own. To the question what political measures should be taken to preserve the union, they would answer generally, no measures at all save in a better organisation of the navy. Let well alone. The ties which hold us together are daily strengthening of themselves. The trade of England with the colonies grows far more rapidly than with any other parts of the world. Intercourse is increasing. Melbourne and Sydney are as easy of access now as New York was fifty years ago. Steam and telegraph have made an end of distance. The English in the colonies and the English at home will not fall out if the officials in Downing Street do not set them by the ears. If the officials persist, there will be the remedy of the unwilling duellists who turned their pistols on the seconds that had made the quarrel.

In the present state of public feeling, the danger is rather from premature experiments on the part of those who are anxious to see the union assume a more defined form.

Another project has been suggested, I know not whether I need mention it. A new Parliament, a Federal Parliament, composed of representatives for all parts of the empire, is to sit side by side with the existing Parliament and relieve it of the charge of foreign and colonial policy. The ministry will have to be chosen from this new Parliament. On it will fall the decision of all questions of peace or war. Therefore it will have the overruling voice in the taxation which its acts may make necessary. The House of Commons is now omnipotent. No man, or body of men, has been known yet to relinquish voluntarily powers of which he was in present possession. Who is to persuade the House of Commons to abdicate half its functions, and construct a superior authority which would reduce it to the level of a municipal board? What force short of revolution and soldiers' bayonets could bring them to it? Of all the amateur propositions hitherto brought forward, this of a Federal Parliament is the most chimerical and absurd.

Is there then nothing which can be done? Must we drift on at the mercy of man or the mercy of circumstances, drift as we always do drift when we abandon the helm on the lee shore of disintegration? Everything may be done which it is fit and right to do if we know our bearings, if we know the ocean currents, and the capabilities of the ship which carries us. But we must look at the facts as they are, not as in our imaginative enthusiasm, or equally imaginary alarms, we may wish or fear them to be. What, then, are the facts, and what is our object? We say that we desire the colonies to be united to the empire. They are united already, united by the bond of nature. The inhabitants of Victoria and New South Wales are as completely subjects of the Queen of Great Britain as any of ourselves; they are as proud of their sovereign, they are as heartily loyal, they as little dream of throwing off their allegiance. Nay, perhaps they have more part in David than those who are nearer to the throne. Their attachment is enhanced by the emotional enchantment of distance. Well then, let this identity be recognised in all communications which are exchanged with them. They complain of the coldness of tone and almost estrangement with which they have been hitherto addressed: and the complaint is not without reason. When they make impetuous demands upon us, when they require us, as in the case of New Guinea, to challenge one of the Great Powers of Europe on account of injuries which to us seem visionary, we may be right and wise in declining; but we might so decline as to show them that we understand their feelings, respect their ambition, regard even their impatience as a sign that they are zealous for the greatness of Oceana. Kind words cost nothing, and kind words would be precious to these far-off relations of ours, for they would show that the heart of England was with them.

J. A. Froude, *Oceana* (1886), pp. 12, 13–4, 194, 214–5, 220–2.

80: EARL OF ROSEBERY. Speech to the Leeds Chamber of Commerce

11 October 1888

THERE was at one time in this country a very great demand, founded on the belief that our Colonies were not trading with us as well as they do now, to be free from the responsibility of a Colonial Empire. I think that demand has to a great extent ceased; but the people of this country will, in a not too distant time, have to make up their minds what footing they wish the Colonies to occupy with respect to them, or whether they desire their Colonies to leave them altogether. It is, I believe, absolutely impossible for you to maintain in the long run your present loose and indefinite relations to your Colonies, and retain those Colonies as parts of the Empire. That is a question as to which Chambers of Commerce ought to be able to make up their minds very definitely, because, in the first place, it is a commercial question. I do not believe, if our Colonies left us in that amicable spirit in which they tell us they might leave us—I do not believe that if they left us in however amicable a spirit—you would find them as good customers as they are now.

We have an opportunity of comparing our relations between a Colony that has left us and the Colonies that remain with us. When I speak of a Colony that has left us, I mean, of course, the United States. The United States have taken from us during the last ten years an average of £24,350,000 of home produce. Their population is nearly 60,000,000, and therefore they have taken of our home produce at the rate of about eight shillings a head. Now Canada, which, as you know, is coterminous with the United States, and which remains to us, has taken on an average £7,300,000 during the last ten years. Take the population at 5,000,000, and that gives nearly thirty shillings a head, or nearly three and a half times what the United States take from us. You may say that the United States have a more hostile tariff against us than Canada has. But if you think for a moment you will remember that if Canada were to leave us she would be pretty certain to adopt the tariff of the United States, and we should not be nationally benefited by that proceeding.

But let us take one other great Colony abroad. Let us take the case of Australia. Australia takes from us on an average £24,500,000—or about the same as the whole of the United States, though its population is only 3,250,000—or at the rate of £7 a head, being more than seventeen times more than the United States with its population of 60,000,000.

I do not see that you can obtain the great boon of a peaceful Empire, encircling the globe with a bond of commercial unity and peace, without some sacrifice on your part. No great benefit, no such benefit as that, can be obtained without a sacrifice. You will have, I think, to admit the Colonies to a much larger share in your affairs than you do at present. You will have to give them a right to prompt the voice of England when it speaks abroad to a much greater extent than you do at present. You must be prepared for demands, sometimes unreasonable, such as spoiled children sometimes make. You must be prepared, in some respects, to diminish your insular freedom of action on behalf of your great offspring abroad. But to my mind the sacrifice is worth it. The cause which we call Imperial Federation, for want of a better name, is worthy not merely of the attention of Chambers of Commerce, but of the devotion of the individual minds of the people of this country. For my part, if you will forgive me this little bit of egotism, I can say from the bottom of my heart that it is the dominant passion of my public life. Ever since I traversed those vast regions which own the sway of the British Crown outside these islands, I have felt that there was a cause which merited all the enthusiasm and energy that man could give to it. It is a cause for which any man might be content to live; it is a cause for which, if needs be, anyone might be content to die.

Printed in S. H. Jeyes, *Lord Rosebery* (London, 1906), pp. 98–101.

81: GOLDWIN SMITH. *Canada and the Canadian Question*

1891

THERE is a Federation which is feasible, and, to those who do not measure grandeur by physical force or extension, at least as grand as that of which the Imperialist dreams. It is the moral federation of the whole English-speaking race throughout the world, including all those millions of men speaking the English language in the United States, and parted from the rest only a century ago by a wretched quarrel, whom Imperial Federation would leave out of its pale. Nothing is needed to bring this about but the voluntary retirement of England as a political power from a shadowy dominion in a sphere which is not hers. . . .

Unless all present appearances on the political horizon are delusive, the time is at hand when the upheaval of the labour world, and the social problems which are coming into view, will give the politicians more serious and substantial matter for thought than the airy fabric of Imperial Federation.

Goldwin Smith, *Canada and the Canadian Question* (1891), pp. 265–6.

Part XIII

"THE CHAMBERLAIN ERA"

82: SIR WILLIAM HARCOURT. Letter to Lord Rosebery

Malwood, 27 September 1892

Harcourt, who was Chancellor of the Exchequer 1886 and 1892–5, was a leader of the Little Englander group in the Liberal Party. After he had opposed action in Uganda in the House of Commons while in opposition, he had to find the finance for the successive steps by which, under Rosebery's impetus, the government moved towards the proclamation of a Protectorate in 1894.

WHAT seems to be at issue is a whole policy. Are we to attempt to create another India in Africa? The next goal on which the annexationists are bent is fully revealed in the communication of Major Wingate of April 24 (Mem. on the effect on Egypt of the withdrawal from Uganda), a most significant document. It is my conviction that we have already as much Empire as the nation can carry. If you give the heart too much work to do by extending the limbs and the frame beyond measure you enfeeble its action, and it succumbs. It is said, "We have India and Canada and Australia, why not Africa?" That is like a landowner who, having secured many great estates which he can with difficulty manage, thinks it an argument for buying more and mortaging those which he has for the purchases. That can only end in bankruptcy. I am amused at the people who call themselves Imperialists. I always remember the first pages in Gibbon on the "moderation of Augustus," in which he shows how for the first two centuries of the greatest and wisest Empire that ever existed the cardinal principle was the non-

309

extension of the Empire, and whenever it was departed from they came to grief.

A. G. Gardiner, *Life of Sir William Harcourt* (1923), II, pp. 196-7.

83 : EARL OF ROSEBERY. Speech at the Anniversary Banquet of the Royal Colonial Institute

1 March 1893

SINCE 1868[1] the Empire has been growing by leaps and bounds. That is, perhaps, not a process which everybody witnesses with unmixed satisfaction. It is not always viewed with unmixed satisfaction in circles outside these islands. There are two schools who view with some apprehension the growth of our Empire. The first is composed of those nations who, coming somewhat late into the field, find that Great Britain has some of the best plots already marked out. To those nations I will say that they must remember that our colonies were taken—to use a well-known expression—at prairie value, and that we have made them what they are. We may claim that whatever lands other nations may have touched and rejected and we have cultivated and improved are fairly parts of our Empire, which we may claim to possess by an indisputable title. But there is another ground on which the extension of our Empire is greatly attacked, and the attack comes from a quarter nearer home. It is said that our Empire is already large enough and does not need extension. That would be true enough if the world were elastic, but, unfortunately, it is not elastic, and we are engaged at the present moment in the language of mining in " pegging out claims for the future." We have to consider not what we want now, but what we shall want in the future. We have to consider

[1] Year of the foundation of the Royal Colonial Institute (ed.).

what countries must be developed either by ourselves or some other nation, and we have to remember that it is part of our responsibility and heritage to take care that the world, as far as it can be moulded by us, shall receive the Anglo-Saxon and not another character.... We have to look forward beyond the chatter of platforms and the passions of party to the future of the race of which we are at present the trustees, and we should in my opinion grossly fail in the task that has been laid upon us did we shrink from responsibilities and decline to take our share in a partition of the world which we have not forced on, but which has been forced upon us.

The Times, 2 March 1893.

84: ROBERT ARTHUR TALBOT GASCOYNE-CECIL, MARQUESS OF SALISBURY. Speech in the House of Lords

14 February 1895

Salisbury was Prime Minister of the Conservative Governments of 1885, 1886–92, and 1895–1902; with the exception of two short periods, he was his own Foreign Secretary. He thus conducted the negotiations with rival powers in the division of Africa, supervised the expansion of the Chartered Companies and the beginnings of the Protectorates before they were handed over to the Colonial Office.

I KNOW that when the Treasury lays its hand on any matter concerning the future development of the British Empire, the chances of an Imperial policy are small; and I am bound to add that I do not think, whatever the natural tendencies of the Treasury may be, they are likely to be diminished or corrected under the guidance of which they at present have the advantage. I think Her Majesty's Government are dealing lightly and cavalierly with a very grave matter. It is a question in which time is all important, and time is being allowed to run through our fingers. The noble Earl [Kimberley] treated the matter as if it was purely a question of administration. Of course the question of administration interests us very much, and we hope that great advantage may be conferred upon the natives by the introduction of English Government, and the enforcement of the peace which accompanies English rule; but the administration of the country is not the sole or the main object that should interest us. It is our business in all these new countries to make smooth the paths for British commerce, British enterprise, the application of British capital, at a time when other paths, other outlets for the commercial energies of our race are being gradually closed by the commercial principles which are gaining more and more adhesion. Everywhere we see the advance of commerce checked by the enormous growth which the doctrines of Protection are obtaining. . . .

The moral of that consideration is that it is the duty of the Government to spare no opportunity of opening fresh outlets for the energy of British commerce and enterprise, and I confess that not wholly, but in a great measure, this great undertaking of England with respect to Uganda has been taken, to my mind, and, I believe, to the mind of vast numbers in this country, for the reason that it is a country of enormous fertility, and it has what many countries of fertility have not—a large, increasing population, or, at least, a population that will increase under the favourable conditions of peace, and a population of very fair intelligence. It is a matter of vital importance that British commerce should have free access to that country, free access to the whole of the upper valley of the Nile. But what is going on? Can we afford to sit with our hands before us and say that when

312

the Treasury can be pacified, that when Sir William Harcourt's Imperial instincts receive an additional reinforcement we can undertake this matter, which we are now calmly putting upon the shelf, and can complete the railway, on the commencement of which we counted many, many months ago? We have no such respite given us. We have no such liberty of delay. There are four, if not five, Powers that are steadily advancing towards the upper waters of the Nile. There will be a competition—I will use no stronger word—for the advantages which predominance in that region will confer. . . .

You must open the path. It is for you to make the communication. It is for you to enable our people to get there. It is for you to enable capital to be invested and commerce to be extended. I therefore should look upon it as a deep disgrace to the present generation, if, with the opportunities we have, we were by sheer delay and carelessness, by sheer anxiety to avoid or make the financial difficulty of the moment, or by undue respect paid to a philosophy which in this country is now wholly antiquated and outworn—we were to allow the opportunity of a splendid empire for our grandchildren to slip from our grasp.

Hansard, Fourth Series, Vol. XXX, cs. 698–701.

85 : JOSEPH CHAMBERLAIN. Speech at Walsall

15 July 1895

WHATEVER the cause of bad trade may be, we have to look for remedies. I am not going to make wild promises that I cannot fulfil, or to give pledges that I know must be broken, but I say that to my mind the cause of bad trade, of want of employment, is clear. It is the continual growth of our population at the same time that our trade and industry does not grow in proportion, and if we want our trade and industry to grow we must find new markets for it. Old markets are getting exhausted, some of them are being closed to us by hostile tariffs, and unless we can find new countries which will be free to take our goods you may be quite satisfied that lack of employment will continue to be one of the greatest of social evils, and it is because I believe this that I have accepted the office which I have the honour to hold. It is because I desire to see whether there may not be room for still further developing our resources in these new countries and for opening up British markets. What is the state of the case? Great Britain, the little centre of a vaster Empire than the world has ever seen, owns great possessions in every part of the globe, and many of those possessions are still almost unexplored, entirely un-developed. What would a great landlord do in a similar case with a great estate? We know perfectly well, if he had the money, he would expend some of it, at any rate, in improving the property, in making communications, in making outlets for the products of his land, and that, it seems to me, is what a wealthy country ought to do with regard to these territories which it is called upon to control and to govern. That is why I am an advocate of the extension of the Empire. That is why I distrust, and always have distrusted, the late Government, because in their ranks were men who notoriously were "Little England" men, who took every opportunity of carping at and criticizing those brave Englishmen who have made for us homes across the sea, men who are opposed to any extension of the responsibilities and obligations of Empire, men who are unworthy sons of the ancestors who have made this country what it is.

The Times, 16 July 1895.

86: JOSEPH CHAMBERLAIN. Speech at the
Imperial Institute

11 November 1895

MY career as Secretary of State for the Colonies is yet to
be made; but I will say this, that no one has ever been
wafted into office with more favourable gales. It is to me
an encouragement and a great delight to find that in the
colonies and in the mother country there is some confidence, at all events, in my desire to bring them closer
together. I will venture to claim two qualifications for
the great office which I hold, and which, to my mind,
without making invidious distinctions, is one of the most
important that can be held by any Englishman. These
qualifications are that, in the first place, I believe in the
British Empire and, in the second place, I believe in the
British race. I believe that the British race is the greatest
of governing races that the world has ever seen. I say
that not merely as an empty boast, but as proved and
evidenced by the success which we have had in adminis-
tering the vast dominions which are connected with
these small islands. I think a man who holds my office is
bound to be sanguine, is bound to be confident, and I
have both those qualifications. I wish sometimes that
the English people were not so apt to indulge in self-
criticism, which, although it does no harm at home, is
sometimes misinterpreted abroad. We are all prepared
to admire the great Englishmen of the past. We speak
of the men who made our Empire, and we speak of them
as heroes as great as any that have lived in the pages of
history; but when we come to our own time we doubt
and hesitate, and we seem to lose the confidence which I
think becomes a great nation such as ours; and yet, if we
look even to such comparatively small matters as the

expeditions in which Englishmen have recently been engaged, the administrations which Englishmen have recently controlled, I see no reason to doubt that the old British spirit still lives in the Englishmen of to-day. When I think of the incidents of such a campaign as that of Chitral, when I think of the way in which in numerous provinces in India—and I might speak from my own experience of the administration in Egypt—of the way in which a number of young Englishmen, picked as it were haphazard from the mass of our population, having beforehand no special claims to our confidence, have nevertheless controlled great affairs, and with responsibility placed upon their shoulders have shown a power, a courage, a resolution, and an intelligence, which have carried them through extraordinary difficulties—I say that he is indeed a craven and a poor-spirited creature who despairs of the future of the British race.

Foreign and Colonial Speeches (1897), pp. 88–90.

87: JOSEPH CHAMBERLAIN. Speech at the
Canada Club Dinner

London, 25 March 1896

WHAT is the greatest of our common obligations? It is Imperial defence. What is the greatest of our common interests? It is Imperial trade. And those two are very closely connected. It is very difficult to see how you can pretend to deal with the great question of Imperial defence without having first dealt with the question of Imperial trade. Imperial defence is largely a matter of ways and means, and ways and means are dependent upon the fiscal and other commercial arrangements you may make; and, therefore, the conclusion to which I

arrive is this—that if the people of this country and
the people of the colonies mean what they have been
saying, and if they intend to approach this question of
Imperial unity in a practical spirit, they must approach
it on its commercial side.

We have a great example before us in the creation of
the German Empire. How was that brought about? You
all recollect that, in the first instance, it commenced with
the union of two of the States which now form that great
empire in a commercial Zollverein. . . . It developed
until it became a bond of unity and the foundation of
the German Empire.

We have another reason why we should approach this
subject from its commercial side; and that is, that in
regard to this the colonies, to whose feelings we must
pay the utmost deference, who must, in fact, in one sense
at any rate, take the initiative in any movement, have
clearly pointed, by their action, to commercial union as
the point upon which, as they consider, the whole subject is most ripe.

Ibid., pp. 166–7.

88: JOSEPH CHAMBERLAIN. Speech at the Royal
Colonial Institute Dinner

31 March 1897

As regards the self-governing colonies we no longer talk
of them as dependencies. The sense of possession has
given place to the sentiment of kinship. We think and
speak of them as part of ourselves, as part of the British
Empire, united to us, although they may be dispersed
throughout the world, by ties of kindred, of religion, of
history, and of language, and joined to us by the seas
that formerly seemed to divide us.

But the British Empire is not confined to the self-governing colonies and the United Kingdom. It includes a much greater area, a much more numerous population in tropical climes, where no considerable European settlement is possible, and where the native population must always vastly outnumber the white inhabitants; and in these cases also the same change has come over the Imperial idea. Here also the sense of possession has given place to a different sentiment—the sense of obligation. We feel now that our rule over these territories can only be justified if we can show that it adds to the happiness and prosperity of the people, and I maintain that our rule does, and has, brought security and peace and comparative prosperity to countries that never knew these blessings before.

In carrying out this work of civilisation we are fulfilling what I believe to be our national mission, and we are finding scope for the exercise of those faculties and qualities which have made of us a great governing race. I do not say that our success has been perfect in every case, I do not say that all our methods have been beyond reproach; but I do say that in almost every instance in which the rule of the Queen has been established and the great *Pax Britannica* has been enforced, there has come with it greater security to life and property, and a material improvement in the condition of the bulk of the population. No doubt, in the first instance, when these conquests have been made, there has been bloodshed, there has been loss of life among the native populations, loss of still more precious lives among those who have been sent out to bring these countries into some kind of disciplined order, but it must be remembered that that is the condition of the mission we have to fulfil. There are, of course, among us—there always are among

318

us, I think—a very small minority of men who are ready to be the advocates of the most detestable tyrants, provided their skin is black—men who sympathise with the sorrows of Prempeh and Lobengula, and who denounce as murderers those of their countrymen who have gone forth at the command of the Queen, and who have redeemed districts as large as Europe from the barbarism and the superstition in which they had been steeped for centuries. . . .

You cannot have omelettes without breaking eggs; you cannot destroy the practices of barbarism, of slavery, of superstition, which for centuries have desolated the interior of Africa, without the use of force; but if you will fairly contrast the gain to humanity with the price which we are bound to pay for it, I think you may well rejoice in the result of such expeditions as those which have recently been conducted with such signal success in Nyasaland, Ashanti, Benin, and Nupé—expeditions which may have, and indeed have, cost valuable lives, but as to which we may rest assured that for one life lost a hundred will be gained, and the cause of civilisation and the prosperity of the people will in the long run be eminently advanced. But no doubt such a state of things, such a mission as I have described, involves heavy responsibility. In the wide dominions of the Queen the doors of the temple of Janus are never closed, and it is a gigantic task that we have undertaken when we have determined to wield the sceptre of empire. Great is the task, great is the responsibility, but great is the honour; and I am convinced that the conscience and the spirit of the country will rise to the height of its obligations, and that we shall have the strength to fulfil the mission which our history and our national character have imposed upon us.

THE CONCEPT OF EMPIRE

In regard to the self-governing colonies our task is much lighter. We have undertaken, it is true, to protect them with all the strength at our command against foreign aggression, although I hope that the need for our intervention may never arise. But there remains what then will be our chief duty—that is, to give effect to that sentiment of kinship to which I have referred and which I believe is deep in the heart of every Briton. We want to promote a closer and a firmer union between all members of the great British race, and in this respect we have in recent years made great progress—so great that I think sometimes some of our friends are apt to be a little hasty, and to expect even a miracle to be accomplished. I would like to ask them to remember that time and patience are essential elements in the development of all great ideas. Let us, gentlemen, keep our ideal always before us. For my own part, I believe in the practical possibility of a federation of the British race, but I know that it will come, if it does come, not by pressure, not by anything in the nature of dictation from this country, but it will come as the realisation of a universal desire, as the expression of the dearest wish of our colonial fellow-subjects themselves.

That such a result would be desirable, would be in the interest of all our colonies as well as of ourselves, I do not believe any sensible man will doubt. It seems to me that the tendency of the time is to throw all power into the hands of the greater empires, and the minor kingdoms—those which are non-progressive—seem to be destined to fall into a secondary and subordinate place. But, if Great Britain remains united, no empire in the world can ever surpass it in area, in population, in wealth, or in the diversity of its resources.

Mr. Chamberlain's Speeches (ed. Boyd, 1914), Vol. II, pp. 2–5.

89: MARQUESS OF SALISBURY. Reply to the toast,
"The Legislatures of the Empire," at the Banquet to
the Colonial Prime Ministers

Imperial Institute, 18 June 1897

I AM not underrating the importance or the dignity of
younger Assemblies who are associated in this toast. I
can remember considerable misgivings when they were
set up, and I am bound as a Tory to confess that I was
not entirely free from those misgivings. But I am also
bound to confess that they were entirely without foundation and mistaken; and without going into particular
allusions which might be painful, I think that the dignity
and character with which the deliberations of our
colonial Assemblies are conducted have nothing to learn
from the proceedings of Parliaments even in the most
ancient cities of this continent. Sir, I will not detain you
longer, but I will remind you that this toast really does
include within itself all the aspirations and hopes with
which we have associated ourselves together this evening.
We are representing here the growing Empire of Great
Britain. We do not know precisely what future is before
us. We are aware that we are the instruments of a great
experiment. There has been many emigrations, many
colonies, before our time. The relation between mother
country and dependency has often been set up, but those
empires have never lasted, for either the colonies have
been swept away by some superior force, or the mother
country, by unjust and imprudent government, has
driven the colonies to sever the bond which bound them.
The fact has been that such empires have never lasted.
We are undertaking the great experiment of trying to
sustain such an empire entirely upon the basis of mutual
goodwill, sympathy, and affection. There is talk of fiscal

union, there is talk of military union. Both of them to a certain extent may be good things. Perhaps we may not be able to carry them as far as some of us think, but in any case they will not be the basis on which our Empire will rest. Our Empire will rest on the great growth of sympathy, common thought, and feeling between those who are in the main the children of a common race, and who have a common history to look back upon and a common future to look forward to. It is the triumph of a moral idea in the construction of a great political organization which is the object and the effort in which we have all joined, and of which our meeting together is the symbol and the seal; but the success of this effort will depend upon the conduct of these various Legislatures, great and small, because with them at last the government must lie. It depends upon their character and their self-restraint, whether this experiment shall succeed.

The Times, 19 June 1897.

90: SIR MICHAEL HICKS-BEACH. Speech on Imperial Defence

30 June 1897

Hicks-Beach, a life-long Conservative, had been chief Secretary for Ireland 1874–8 and 1886–7. He succeeded Carnarvon at the Colonial Office in 1878 and was at first offered the same post in the Salisbury government of 1885–6. Instead he held in that and in the government of 1895–1902 the position of Chancellor of the Exchequer. In this last Cabinet there were frequent clashes with Chamberlain over "Treasury control" of Colonial policy, leading to his offer to resign in 1899. He opposed Chamberlain's tariff reform ideas, describing himself as "a thorough-going free-trader".

OUR Colonies are great and growing nationalities. The

other day Canada was spoken of with just pride by its Premier as a nation. That is true. Canada is a nation. Canada has a commercial Marine second to very few in the world; but what does Canada pay for her Navy? How many sailors does Canada send to the Imperial Navy? How many thousands a year does Canada contribute to the cost of the Imperial Navy? When they come to business, this is a question which will have to be very carefully discussed between her Majesty's Government and the Premiers of our great self-governing Colonies.

Now, I admit with pride and pleasure that these great communities are nations; and if they are nations they ought to bear national responsibilities. I do not for a moment believe that they are unwilling to bear those responsibilities. I give them every credit for the efforts which they have made in the past, and for the effort which was voluntarily made by the Cape Colony the other day to bear a share in those great responsibilities. I do not think for a moment that, conscious of their power as great nationalities, they would wish to shirk those responsibilities on the ground on which formerly they might fairly have claimed exemption when struggling and poor communities. No, not at all. It is a matter on which her Majesty's Government and the Government of the Colonies ought to take council together speedily, and I hope and trust that it may be settled by some satisfactory conclusion.

But, as Chancellor of the Exchequer, I am bound to put before you the fact that forty millions of people in the United Kingdom pay twenty-two millions a year for the cost of our common Navy; while ten millions of people of the same race in our Colonies pay but a few thousands a year and find but a very few men. That cannot and ought not to be a permanent settlement of the relations between the great self-governing Colonies and the United Kingdom.

Printed in Imperial Federation (Defence) Committee pamphlet (1897): *The Colonies and the Navy*, p. 20.

91: JOHN MORLEY. Speech on the Annexation of the Sudan

House of Commons, 24 February 1899

Morley (1838–1923) maintained his Radicalism untinged by the Imperialism of his earlier friend Chamberlain. His protests were constant against wars in South Africa and intervention in Egypt. The Boer war led him to retire temporarily from politics—to write the *Life of Gladstone*. As Secretary for India (1905–10) in the Liberal Government he assisted in the restoration of self-government in South Africa and sponsored the Indian Councils Act of 1909 (the 'Morley-Minto Reforms'), which he saw only as a means of learning Indian opinions, for he rejected any theory of India as a nation that should be compared to Canada or Ireland.

I WOULD like to point out three distinct differences between India and this new Empire that you propose to set up at the Equator. You have not a strong natural frontier as India has. I do not quite know whether we shall be told what the Government reckons their frontier to be, but I will undertake to say it is not a strong natural frontier such as India possesses. You have not, in the second place, a comparatively civilised and settled population, but you have vast hordes of savages; and, thirdly, your dominions would be coterminous at point after point with Powers who may or may not be your friends. You will have the most difficult of tasks in keeping the peace on your boundaries and frontiers, and everybody who gives the slightest consideration to it will perceive that the conditions under which the Government of India subsists and carries on its beneficent work are not

324

one of them realised in the case of the new India you
are going to set up at the Equator. . . .

Our experience in Uganda and the experience of the
King of the Belgians in the Congo State show that all
these anticipations that you will have quiet in your ring
fence in civilising and humanising these wretched
savages is a dream of the most fatuous kind. I am going to quote from the Chancellor of the Exchequer[1] a
passage as to which I am in profound accord with him—

> " I think we shall be wiser if we attempt rather to develop what
> we have already acquired than to attempt to add still further to the
> extent of our Empire. Every extension of our Empire means an
> extension of our Army and possibly of our Navy. Our Navy may
> be increased indefinitely, subject to the supply of seamen, but
> our Army is not capable under our present system of indefinite
> extension. Therefore, we are endeavouring, as far as we can, to
> utilise our subject races. That is an excellent and successful
> policy, but it is not a policy which is capable of indefinite expan-
> sion, because it will be a bad day for this country if we trust for
> the maintenance of our Empire and our power to foreign mercen-
> aries rather than to our own troops."

That was a speech delivered a day or two before this
new annexation, and I quote the Chancellor of the Exchequer not in any way to annoy him, but because he
says better and with more authority than I have exactly
what I think. I wonder what we are doing in Uganda?
Are those British troops? They are our own troops in one
sense, but are they not exactly the kind of troops the
right honourable Gentleman meant when he spoke of
"foreign mercenaries"? I consider that will be, indeed, a
bad day, as the Chancellor of the Exchequer said. Even
those who know less history than the Chancellor of the
Exchequer does are aware that if there is one lesson that
history teaches more constantly and more impressively

[1] Sir Michael Hicks-Beach (ed.).

than another it is that when an empire or kingdom relies, not upon its own people, but on bands of foreign mercenaries, its decline and fall may not be rapid, but it is sure. There is one other remark I should like to make touching a similar point, and I do not think it is unworthy the attention of such a practical body as the House of Commons is. Is it good to extend these areas of your dominion which are only capable of being governed by despotic rulers? I cannot think that it is good. It cannot be good for the ruler; it cannot be good for national character; it cannot be good for the maxims and principles of free government. When you annex this great new territory you must recognise the fact that you cannot set up a Parliament in the Soudan. You must govern it by a ruler practically despotic, though, I hope, with pretty firm and stiff instructions and supervision from this country. But however all this may be, by the step that you have taken, depending as it does upon despotic rule, calling as it does for enormous expenditure, involving as it does the use of troops which are not British, you are unconsciously—and history will mark us as having done it—transforming the faces and conditions of your Empire.

Hansard, Fourth Series, Vol. LXVII, cs. 466–8.

92: EARL OF ROSEBERY. Rectorial Address at Glasgow University

16 November 1900

How marvellous it all is! Built not by saints and angels, but the work of men's hands; cemented with men's honest blood and with a world of tears, welded by the best brains of centuries past; not without the taint and reproach incidental to all human work, but constructed on the whole with pure and splendid purpose. Human, and yet not wholly human, for the most heedless and the most cynical must see the finger of the Divine. Growing as trees grow, while others slept; fed by the faults of others as well as by the character of our fathers; reaching with the ripple of a resistless tide over tracts and islands and continents, until our little Britain woke up to find herself the foster-mother of nations and the source of united empires. Do we not hail in this less the energy and fortune of a race than the supreme direction of the Almighty? Shall we not, while we adore the blessing, acknowledge the responsibility? And while we see, far away in the rich horizons, growing generations fulfilling the promise, do we not own with resolution mingled with awe the honourable duty incumbent on ourselves? Shall we then falter or fail? The answer is not doubtful. We will rather pray that strength may be given us, adequate and abundant, to shrink from no sacrifice in the fulfilment of our mission; that we may be true to the high tradition of our forefathers; and that we may transmit their bequest to our children, aye, and please God, to their remote descendants, enriched and undefiled, this blessed and splendid dominion.

Printed as *Questions of Empire* (1900), p. 37.

93: **JOSEPH CHAMBERLAIN.** Speech at Birmingham

16 May 1902

THE position of this country is not one without anxiety to statesmen and careful observers. The political jealousy of which I have spoken, the commercial rivalry more serious than anything we have yet had, the pressure of hostile tariffs, the pressure of bounties, the pressure of subsidies, it is all becoming more weighty and more apparent. What is the object of this system adopted by countries which, at all events, are very prosperous themselves—countries like Germany and other large Continental States? What is the object of this policy of bounties and subsidies? It is admitted; there is no secret about it; the intention is to shut out this country, as far as possible, from all profitable trade with those foreign States and, at the same time, to enable those foreign States to undersell us in British markets. That is the policy; and we see that it is assuming a great development, that old ideas of trade and free competition have changed. We are face to face with great combinations, with enormous trusts, having behind them gigantic wealth. Even the industries and commerce which we thought to be peculiarly our own, even those are in danger. It is quite impossible that these new methods of competition can be met by adherence to old and antiquated methods which were perfectly right at the time at which they were developed. At the present moment, the Empire is being attacked on all sides and, in our isolation, we must look to ourselves. We must draw closer our internal relations, the ties of sentiment, the ties of sympathy, yes, and the ties of interest. If by adherence to economic pedantry, to old shibboleths, we are to lose opportunities of closer union which are offered us by our colonies, if we are to put aside occasions now within our grasp, if we do not take every chance in our power to keep British trade in British hands, I am certain that we shall deserve the disasters which will infallibly come upon us.

Printed in J. Amery, *Life of Joseph Chamberlain,* Vol. IV, p. 405

94: JOSEPH CHAMBERLAIN. Speech opening the
Colonial Conference

30 June 1902

OUR paramount object is to strengthen the bonds which
unite us, and there are only three principal avenues
by which we can approach this object. They are:
Through our political relations in the first place;
secondly, by some kind of commercial union. In the
third place, by considering the questions which arise out
of Imperial defence. These three great questions were
considered at the last Conference, and, I think, it is clear
that they must form the principal subject of our deliberations on this occasion, and, indeed, of those of any
future conferences which may afterwards be held. . . .

I may be considered, perhaps, to be a dreamer, or too
enthusiastic, but I do not hesitate to say that, in my
opinion, the political federation of the Empire is within
the limits of possibility. I recognise, as fully as anyone
can do, the difficulties which would attend such a great
change in our constitutional system. . . . But . . . I hold
that, as we must put no limits to science, as the progress
which has already been made is only an indication of the
progress which may be made in the future . . . we have
no right to put, by our action, any limit to the Imperial
patriotism of the future; and it is my opinion that, as
time goes on, there will be a continually growing sense
of the common interests which unite us, and also
perhaps, which is equally important, of the common
dangers which threaten us. . . .

I would venture to refer to an expression in an eloquent
speech of my right honourable friend, the Premier of the
Dominion of Canada. . . . "If you want our aid call us
to your Councils." Gentlemen, we do want your aid.

We do require your assistance in the administration of the vast Empire which is yours as well as ours. The weary Titan staggers under the too vast orb of its fate. We have borne the burden for many years. We think it is time that our children should assist us to support it, and whenever you make the request to us, be very sure that we shall hasten gladly to call you to our Councils. If you are prepared at any time to take any share, any proportionate share, in the burdens of the Empire, we are prepared to meet you with any proposal for giving to you a corresponding voice in the policy of the Empire. . . . I have always felt myself that the most practical form, in which we could achieve our object, would be the establishment . . . of a real Council of the Empire to which all questions of Imperial interest might be referred; and, if it were desired to proceed gradually, as probably would be our course, . . . the Council might in the first instance be merely an advisory council. . . . But, although that would be a preliminary step, it is clear that the object would not be completely secured until there had been conferred upon such a Council executive functions, and perhaps also legislative powers; and it is for you to say, gentlemen, whether you think the time has come when any progress whatever can be made in this direction.

If we chose . . . the Empire might be self-sustaining; it is so wide, its products are so various; its climates so different that there is absolutely nothing which is necessary to our existence, hardly anything which is desirable as a luxury which cannot be produced within the boundaries of the Empire itself.

[But] . . . the Empire at the present time, and especially the United Kingdom which is the great market of the world—derives the greatest part of its necessaries from foreign countries, and exports the largest part of its available . . . produce also to foreign countries.

Now, I confess, that, to my mind, that is not a satisfactory state of things and I hope you will agree with me that everything, which can possibly tend to increase the interchange of products between the different parts of the Empire, is deserving of our cordial encouragement.

We feel confident—we think that it is a matter which demands no evidence or proof that . . . it would enormously increase our inter-Imperial trade; that it would hasten the development of our Colonies; that it would fill up the spare places in your lands with an active, intelligent and industrious, and above all a British population; that it would make the mother country entirely independent of foreign food and raw material.

We, in the United Kingdom, for centuries past have been holding our house like a strong man armed against all our enemies. We have felt, throughout all the period, the burdens as well as the privileges and advantages of empire. We see now that all other nations are also arming to the teeth. I want you to consider for a moment what is the present position of the smaller nations with whom, in population, you may more closely compare yourselves. What is the position of such nations in Europe as Greece, the Balkan States, or Holland, or the South American Republics? Why, gentlemen, they are absolutely independent nations, accordingly, they have to bear burdens for their military or naval defences, or for both, as the case may be, to which yours bear no proportion whatever. I point out to you, therefore, that, in the clash of nations, you have hitherto derived great

advantages, even from a purely material standpoint, .
from being a part of a great Empire. But the privileges,
which we enjoy, involve corresponding obligations. The
responsibilities must be reciprocal and must be shared in
common, and I do not think that any empire may be said
to be on a sure foundation which is not based upon a
recognised community of sacrifices.

Printed in J. Amery, *Life of Joseph Chamberlain*, Vol. IV,
pp. 420–1, 436–7, 425.

95 : JOHN ATKINSON HOBSON. *Imperialism: a Study*
1902

The importance of this work has been referred to in the intro-
duction. Hobson's work as an economist was acknowledged by
Keynes as that of " an intellectual pioneer ". In the extracts in
No. 111 will be found his desire for international control of
Colonies; this he followed up in his work on the Bryce committee,
which prepared schemes for the League of Nations, and in his
Towards an International Government (1915).

THE economic root of Imperialism is the desire of strong
organised industrial and financial interests to secure and
develop at the public expense and by the public force
private markets for their surplus goods and their surplus
capital. War, militarism, and a " spirited foreign policy "
are the necessary means to this end. This policy involves
large increase of public expenditure. If they had to pay
the cost of this policy out of their own pockets in taxation upon incomes and property, the game would not be
worth the candle, at any rate so far as markets for commodities are concerned. They must find means of
putting the expense upon the general public. But in
countries where a popular franchise and representative
government exist this cannot be successfully done in an
open manner. Taxation must be indirect and must fall
upon such articles of consumption or general use as are

part of the general standard of consumption and will not shrink in demand or give way to substitutes under the process of taxation. This protection not only serves the purposes of imperial finance, taxing the impotent and ignorant consumer for the imperial gains of the influential economic interests, but it seems to furnish them a second gain by securing to them as producers their home market which is threatened by outside competition, and enabling them to raise their prices to the home consumers and so reap a rise of profits. To those who regard foreign trade in its normal condition as a fair interchange of goods and services, it may seem difficult to understand how these economic interests expect to exclude foreign goods from their market, while at the same time pushing their goods in foreign markets. But we must remind such economists that the prime motive force here is not trade but investment: a surplus of exports over imports is sought as the most profitable mode of investment, and when a nation, or more strictly its investing classes, is bent on becoming a creditor or parasitic nation to an indefinite extent, there is no reason why its imports and exports should balance even over a long term of years. The whole struggle of so-called Imperialism upon its economic side is towards a growing parasitism, and the classes engaged in this struggle require Protection as their most serviceable instrument.

The nature and object of Protection as a branch of imperialist finance is best illustrated in the case of Great Britain, because the necessity of subverting an accepted Free Trade policy lays bare the different methods of Protection and the forces upon which it relies. In other nations committed to or entering upon an imperialist career with the same ganglia of economic interests masquerading as patriotism, civilisation, and the like,

Protection has been the traditional finance, and it has only been necessary to extend it and direct it into the necessary channels.

J. A. Hobson, *Imperialism: a Study* (1902), pp. 113-4.

96: EARL OF ROSEBERY. Speech to the Liberal League

Hotel Cecil, London, 12 June 1903

It was considered necessary that Rosebery, as leader of the Liberal Imperialists, should clearly dissociate himself from Chamberlain's tariff reform policy. An earlier speech at Burnley had left some doubt about Rosebery's position—hence this statement.

THE burden of proof lies with those who would substitute the new arrangement for the present arrangements of the British Empire.

What is the present arrangement? The Empire is built up on Free Trade. And by Free Trade I do not mean, of course, that there are not multifarious tariffs throughout the Empire. That would show a very elementary ignorance of the situation—a situation which I have studied for many years. It does not mean that there are not tariffs throughout the Empire, but it does mean this—that your Empire is founded on the condition, and it could not have existed until now except on that condition, that every self-governing part of it shall have the right to work out its own prosperity by its own methods. I do not know why it should enter the heads of any statesmen to deny that liberty to the United Kingdom, which, after all, is not an insignificant part of the Empire. The system under which we have lived, that system of free option for every part of the Empire, has enabled us in these islands to bear the great but the grateful burden of Empire, and in that respect at any rate it is surely not to be passed on one side. It has made the heart of the Empire, which is this island, the mart of the world, and it has brought that united state of feeling which led to the remarkable outburst of loyalty during the late war of which we are never weary of boasting, and rightly boasting, but which, I think, in the course of a few weeks we shall be asked to believe was the result of some Protective tariff. Well, then I say that the burden of proof lies with those who would disturb the existing arrangements of the Empire which in different directions have had their fair development and under which it has grown to the present world-wide position which it occupies. If I may say a word to those who endeavour to force the pace with regard to the union of the Empire, I would say that I trust they may never have to write the epitaph of that Empire in the well-known words, 'I was well, I would be better, and here I am.' But I do not ask you to accept my view of the present relations of the Empire as being an authoritative one and as being weighty as against the idea of a Protective tariff. I would rather quote from the words of one who, I think, outside these islands, has the highest claim to be heard on the subject; and as he is the Prime Minister of the Canadian Dominion as well, I think his words may be entitled to some weight in view of what we hear of the relations of Great Britain and Canada. What did Sir Wilfrid Laurier say, I think five years ago? I think he has been continuously in office ever since, and I have not heard that he has ever revoked those words. ' There are parties,' he said, ' who hope to maintain the British Empire on lines of restricted trade. If the British Empire is to be maintained it can only be upon the most absolute freedom, politically and commercially. In building up this great enterprise, to deviate from the principles of freedom will be so much to weaken the ties and bonds which now‛hold it together.' I recommend that passage to the attention of the Colonial Office. I agree, I confess, with Sir Wilfrid Laurier; nor is it from any want of thought that I have come to that conclusion, because it is not one of the recent discoveries of the Colonial Office that the Empire might be united by a bond of trade. I was a member of the old Imperial Federation League—perhaps some of you, some of the hoary-headed ones among you, have been members, too —and we worked out this subject as well as we were able, and we were always met with the absolute and insuperable difficulties which I believe will confront any-body who attempts to deal with it. My view of the policy which is really adapted to raise the strength and prosperity of this Empire is that of Sir Wilfrid Laurier.

Well, then, I ask, will this policy have the effect of cementing the Empire? And my answer is that, if carried, it will not probably have that effect, because I may mention incidentally that I cannot conceive—I do not propose to enter at length into the Fiscal Question to-night—that I cannot conceive what are the Colonial markets which are to be offered to us in return for the markets we intend to resign or to forfeit, and that will produce some discontent in this country if not elsewhere. I say, if it is carried, I do not think it will have the effect of cementing the union of the Empire. If it is not carried, the ineffectual raising of this question will do, perhaps, irreparable damage. We shall have raised expectations which, under the hypothesis I am discuss-ing, are destined to be disappointed. We shall have set on foot discussions eminently detrimental, in my judg-ment, to what I may call the *moral* of the Empire. We shall have thrown the union of the Empire—a question so sacred that it has always been held aloft—into the base arena of party politics.

Printed in S. H. Jeyes, *Lord Rosebery* (London, 1906), pp. 109–112.

97: **W. B. HORNIDGE.** Presidential Address to the Trades Union Congress

8 September 1903

Here is 'official' working class reaction to Chamberlain's tariff reform proposals.

To those who have watched the Government of this country for the last four or five years, particularly the statesmanship of the right honourable member for West Birmingham, latest developments have not come as a surprise. The ideal of knitting the Imperial race together is a magnificent one, but I doubt very much whether it is likely to be achieved; and if the people of this country have to be taxed heavier than they are at the present time for our offspring in Canada and the Australian colonies, we require to know more of what we are likely to get in return. I cannot find that there is any great love shown on the part of the Canadians for the Mother Country. Certainly their best interests lie in a closer connection with their next-door neighbours, and that is generally being grasped by Canadians themselves. If we have to wait until the Canadians can provide us with all the cereals that are required for the sustenance of our people I am afraid we shall have to wait a long time. This question, to my mind, is one of the greatest moment, and I should doubt whether anything has so stirred the people during the last quarter of a century with the exception of the South African war.

Printed in the Official Report of the Thirty-sixth Trades Union Congress.

Part XIV

THE PROCONSULS

98: ALFRED, BARON MILNER. Despatch to Joseph Chamberlain

6 December 1901

Milner had served under Cromer in Egypt, 1889–92, producing in 1892 his *England in Egypt*. In 1897 Chamberlain sent him as High Commissioner to South Africa where he remained until 1905. For the reconstruction after the war Milner was responsible, refusing in 1903 the succession to Chamberlain at the Colonial Office as he considered he was of more value in South Africa. He gathered around him there a famous team, the 'Kindergarten', including Geoffrey Dawson, Lionel Curtis, Philip Kerr (later Lord Lothian) and John Buchan; it was this group which first publicized the word 'Commonwealth' which Smuts took up (cf. No. 115). For Milner's ideas and influence see V. Halpérin, *Lord Milner and the Empire* (1952).

WHILE sympathizing with the objects of the Anti-Slavery Society and the Aborigines' Protection Society, I cannot too earnestly protest against the tone of unjustified suspicion, and almost hostility towards their fellow-countrymen in South Africa, running through the letters of 9th November, 1900, and 11th January, 1901, a tone which vitiates and weakens their advocacy of the cause of the natives. Most especially would I raise a warning voice against the fatal doctrine that the Imperial Government is to deal with the native question regardless of colonial sentiment. That doctrine, absurdly enough, is often preached in the very quarters where there is the loudest demand for the immediate complete self-government of the new territories. I believe that such immediate self-government is absolutely impracticable, but for that very reason I am anxious that the

341

Imperial authorities, being obliged for a time to deal autocratically with the affairs of the colonists, should show, not less, but more regard for colonial sentiment. To run counter to it, will not only lead to the estrangement of the colonies, but it will react most injuriously upon the natives, whenever—and the time must come before many years—native and all other local affairs pass under local control. Moreover, it is a complete mistake to think that the Imperial authorities cannot do their duty by the natives without coming into conflict with colonial sentiment, always provided that they bear in mind that they have also a duty to the whites. The best colonial sentiment in this matter is not far removed from the best home sentiment, as represented for instance by temperate and reasonable advocates of native rights, such as the contributors to the collection of valuable and well-informed essays, recently published by the " Native Races Committee." And the two points of view tend more and more to approximate to one another. On the one hand, there is now a better appreciation at home of the difficulties confronting the colonists, and of the impracticability of governing natives, who, at best, are children, needing and appreciating a just paternal government, on the same principles as apply to the government of full-grown men. On the other hand, there is an increasing recognition on the part of the colonists of the heavy responsibility involved in the government of a vast native population, and of the duty and necessity of raising them in the scale of civilization. But this hopeful process of approximation would be utterly upset if the Imperial Government were to approach this delicate question in the prejudiced and ill-informed spirit which seems to animate many well-meaning people at home, but which would be justly resented by the whole of white South Africa, including those men who are most active in the defence of native rights.

The Milner Papers (ed. Headlam, 1931–3), Vol. II, pp. 311–2.

99: LORD MILNER. Address to the Municipal Congress

Johannesburg, 18 May 1903

WHAT is the good . . . of perpetually going on shouting that this is a white man's country? Does it mean that it is a country only inhabited by white men? That, of course, is an obvious absurdity, as the blacks outnumber us as five to one. Does it mean a country which ought only to be inhabited by white men? Well, as an ideal that would possibly be all very well, but as a practical statement it surely is perfectly useless. If it means anything, it means that we ought to try and expel the black population, thereby instantly ruining all the industries of the country. What it does mean, I suppose, if any sane meaning can be applied to it, is that the white man should rule. Well, if that is its meaning, there is nobody more absolutely agreed with it than I; but then let us say that plainly, and do not let us only say it, but let us justify it. There is only one ground on which we can justify it, and that is the ground of superior civilization.

The white man must rule, because he is elevated by many, many steps above the black man; steps which it will take the latter centuries to climb, and which it is quite possible that the vast bulk of the black population may never be able to climb at all. But then, if we justify, what I believe we all hold to, the necessity of the rule of the white man by his superior civilization, what does that involve? Does it involve an attempt to keep a black

343

man always at the very low level of civilization at which
he is to-day? I believe you will all reject such an idea.
One of the strongest arguments why the white man must
rule is because that is the only possible means of
gradually raising the black man, not to our level of
civilization—which it is doubtful whether he would ever
attain—but up to a much higher level than that which
he at present occupies. . . .

For all our sakes, it is of profound importance that
the general standard of native civilization should be
immensely raised. Even as a purely material question,
it is one of the greatest importance, for if there is one
thing that has come out in this discussion of this labour
question, it is that the mere mechanical value of the
native who has risen to some state of civilization is
enormously greater than that of the man still on bed-
rock. But if you are going to raise the mass of natives,
and mind you, it will take years and years to raise them
even so far as to the level of your waist, it stands to
reason that a certain number of them will rise to the
level of your shoulder. Are you going to put back the
whole progress of civilization by banging them on the
head the moment that they do so? . . . .

I feel even more strongly perhaps about the coloured
class. The vast majority of them are in a deplorably low
state of civilization. There is a small section, a very
small section, unfortunately, who have overcome the
enormous disadvantages of their origin, and who have
attained to a considerable degree of civilization. It is a
further consideration, which I do not wish to lay too
much stress upon, that throughout South Africa men of
that class, for whom personally I feel the deepest
sympathy, have stood most loyally in the great struggle
for enfranchisement by the side of those who have been

344

in favour of that wider extension of popular liberties, which is what the triumph of the British idea in this country means. They have been amongst its most ardent supporters; I should be sorry if one of the first fruits of our victory was to place an indelible stigma upon them. Speaking again my personal opinions, opinions perhaps not shared by the majority of those here, perhaps not shared by any of them, I shall think it an unhappy day when any large British community in South Africa completely and finally repudiates the doctrine of one of the greatest of South African statesmen—' equal rights for every civilized man.' [1]

Ibid, pp. 467–9.

100: GEORGE NATHANIEL, BARON CURZON OF KEDLESTON. Speech at Guildhall, London, on receiving the Freedom of the City

20 July 1904

After wide journeys in East Asia and the books that followed Curzon had been recognised as a leading authority on the East. He was Governor-General and Viceroy of India from 1899 to 1905, with a short break in 1904, making " efficiency " the motto of his powerful administration.

IF the nations of the earth were to stand up to be judged by some supreme tribunal I think that upon our European record, or upon our colonial record, we should survive the test. But if there were the slightest hesitation on the part of the judge or jury I would not hesitate to throw our Indian record into the scales. For where else in the world, my lords and gentlemen, has a race gone forth and subdued, not a country nor a kingdom, but a continent, and that continent not peopled by savage

[1] Cf. Sir L. Michell, *Life of Cecil Rhodes* (1910) vol. II, p. 275 (ed.).

tribes, but by races with traditions and a civilization older than our own; with a history not inferior to ours in dignity or romance, subduing them not to the law of the sword, but to the rule of justice, bringing peace and order and good government to nearly one-fifth of the entire human race, and ruling them with so mild a restraint that the rulers are the merest handful amongst the ruled, a tiny speck of white foam upon the dark and thunderous ocean? I hope I am no rhapsodist, but I will say that I would as soon be a citizen of the country that wrought this deed than I would be of the country that defeated the Armada, or produced Hampden or Pitt. But we all live in a severely practical age, and I can afford to be rather more concrete in my illustrations. I should like to convey to this audience some idea of the part India is capable of playing, nay, of the part that it has recently played in the Imperial burden. As I say, my illustrations shall be drawn from recent history and from my own experience... If you want to save your colony of Natal from being overrun by a formidable enemy, you ask India for help, and she gives it; if you want to rescue the white men's Legations from massacre at Peking, and the need is urgent, you ask the Government of India to despatch an expedition, and they despatch it; if you are fighting the Mad Mullah in Somaliland, you soon discover that Indian troops and Indian generals are best qualified for the task, and you ask the Government of India to send them; if you desire to defend any of your extreme outposts or coaling-stations of the Empire, in Mauritius, Singapore, Hong-kong, even Tien-tsin or Shan-hai-kwan, it is to the Indian Army that you turn; if you want to build a railway in Uganda or in the Sudan, you apply for Indian labour....

My Lord Mayor, it has been a work of reform and

346

reconstruction. Epochs arise in the history of every country when the administrative machinery requires to be taken to pieces and overhauled and readjusted to the altered necessities and growing demands of the hour. The engines are not working to their scheduled capacity, the engineers are perhaps slack. I agree with those who inscribe on their administrative banners the motto "Efficiency." But my conception of efficiency is to practice as well as to preach it. It is with this object that we have conducted an enquiry in India into every branch of the administration... It is impossible to satisfy all classes in India or elsewhere. There are some people who clamour for boons which it is impossible to give, but the administrator looks rather to the silent and inarticulate masses, and if he can raise even by a little the level of material comfort and well-being in their lives he has earned his reward. I am glad that our finances in India put us in the position to give the people the first reduction of taxation that they have enjoyed for 20 years. . . .

I have been talking to-day about the acts and symptoms of British rule in India. What is its basis? It is not military force, it is not civil authority, it is not prestige, though all these are part of it. If our rule is to last in India it must rest on a more solid basis. It must depend on the eternal moralities of righteousness and justice. This, I can assure you, is not a mere phrase of the conventicle. The matter is too serious on the lips of a Governor-General of India for cant. Unless we can persuade the millions of India that we will give to them absolute justice as between man and man, equality before the law, freedom from tyranny and injustice and oppression, then your Empire will not touch their hearts and will fade away. No one is more ready to admit than

347

I that if you put side by side the rulers of the European races and the rulers of the Asiatic races, and particularly the Indian and the English, where you have a small minority face to face with a vast alien conglomeration you cannot expect to have complete coalescence. On the one side you have pride of race, the duty of self-protection, consciousness of power; on the other you have struggling sentiments and stifled aspirations. But, my Lord Mayor, a bridge must be built between the two, and on that bridge justice must stand with unerring scales. Harshness, oppression, ill-usage, all these in India are offences, not only against the higher law, but against the honour and reputation of the ruling race. I am as strong a believer as any man in the prestige of my countrymen, but that prestige does not require artificial supports, it rests upon conduct and conduct alone. My precept in this respect does not differ from my practice. During the time I have been in India the Government have taken a strong stand for the fair treatment of our Indian fellow-subjects, who are equal with us in the eyes of God and the law. I rejoice to say that the conduct of Englishmen in general in India towards the Indians is exemplary, even in trying and provocative circumstances; but where exceptions occur I think the sentiment of the majority should be as quick to condemn them as is their conduct, and that the Government, which is above race or party, against whom any injustice is a reproach or a slur, should receive the unhesitating support of the entire community. That is the policy which the Government has pursued in my time, and by my conduct, my Lord Mayor and gentlemen, I am willing to be judged.

The Times, 21 July 1904.

101 : ALFRED, VISCOUNT MILNER. Farewell
Speech at Johannesburg

31 March 1905

THE question, as I see it—the future of the British
Empire—is a race, a close race, between the numerous
influences so manifestly making for disruption, and the
growth of a great, but still very imperfectly realised,
political conception. Shall we ever get ourselves understood in time? The word Empire, the word Imperial,
are, in some respects, unfortunate. They suggest domination, ascendancy, the rule of a superior state over
vassal states. But as they are the only words available,
all we can do is to make the best of them, and to raise
them in the scale of language by a new significance.
When we, who call ourselves Imperialists, talk of the
British Empire, we think of a group of states, independent of one another in their local affairs, but bound
together for the defence of their common interests, and
the development of a common civilisation, and so bound,
not in an alliance—for alliances can be made and un-
made, and are never more than nominally lasting,—but
in a permanent organic union. Of such a union, we
fully admit, the dominions of our sovereign, as they
exist to-day, are only the raw material. Our ideal is still
distant, but we are firmly convinced that it is not
visionary nor unattainable.

And see how such a consummation would solve, and,
indeed, can alone solve, the most difficult and most per-
sistent of the problems of South Africa, how it would
unite its white races as nothing else can. The Dutch can
never own a perfect allegiance merely to Great Britain.
The British can never, without moral injury, accept
allegiance to any body-politic which excludes their

349

motherland. But British and Dutch alike could, without
loss of dignity, without any sacrifice of their several
traditions unite in loyal devotion to an Empire-State, in
which Great Britain and South Africa would be partners,
and could work cordially together for the good of South
Africa as a member of that greater whole. And so you
see the true Imperialist is also the best South African.
The road is long, the obstacles are many. The goal may
not be reached in my lifetime, perhaps not in that of the
youngest man in this room. You cannot hasten the slow
growth of a great idea of that kind by any forcing process. But you can keep it steadily in view, lose no opportunity of working for it, resist, like grim death, any policy
which draws you away from it. I know that to be faithful
in this service requires the rarest of combinations, that
of ceaseless effort with infinite patience. But then think
of the greatness of the reward—the high privilege of
having in any way contributed to the fulfilment of one
of the noblest conceptions which have ever dawned on
the political imagination of mankind.

Milner, *The Nation and Empire,* pp. 90–1.

102: LORD CURZON OF KEDLESTON. Speech at Farewell Dinner

Byculla Club, Bombay, 16 November 1905

A hundred times in India I have said to myself, Oh that
to every Englishman in this country, as he ends his work,
might be truthfully applied the phrase " Thou has loved
righteousness and hated iniquity." No man has, I believe,
ever served India faithfully of whom that could not be
said. All other triumphs are tinsel and sham. Perhaps
there are few of us who make anything but a poor

approximation to that ideal. But let it be our ideal all the same. To fight for the right, to abhor the imperfect, the unjust, or the mean, to swerve neither to the right hand nor to the left, to care nothing for flattery or applause or odium or abuse—it is so easy to have any of them in India—never to let your enthusiasm be soured or your courage grow dim, but to remember that the Almighty has placed your hand on the greatest of His ploughs, in whose furrow the nations of the future are germinating and taking shape, to drive the blade a little forward in your time, and to feel that somewhere among these millions you have left a little justice or happiness or prosperity, a sense of manliness or moral dignity, a spring of patriotism, a dawn of intellectual enlighten- ment, or a stirring of duty, where it did not before exist —that is enough, that is the Englishman's justification in India. It is good enough for his watchword while he is here, for his epitaph when he is gone. I have worked for no other aim. Let India be my judge.

Printed in Sir T. Raleigh, *Lord Curzon in India* (1906), pp. 589– 90.

103: LORD MILNER. Speech to the Manchester Conservative Club

14 December 1906

WHAT is going to become of all your social well-being if the material prosperity which is essential to it, though not identical with it, is undermined? And you cannot have prosperity without power, you, of all peoples, dependent for your very life, not on the products of these islands alone, but on a world-wide enterprise and com- merce. This country must remain a great Power or she will become a poor country; and those who in seeking, as they are most right to seek, social improvement are tempted to neglect national strength, are simply building their house upon the sand. 'These ought ye to have done, and not to leave the other undone.' But greatness is relative. Physical limitations alone forbid that these islands by themselves should retain the same relative importance among the vast empires of the modern world which they held in the days of smaller states—before the growth of Russia and the United States, before united Germany made those giant strides in prosperity and commerce which have been the direct result of the development of her military and naval strength. These islands by themselves cannot always remain a Power of the very first rank. But Greater Britain may remain such a Power, humanly speaking, for ever, and by so remaining, will ensure the safety and the prosperity of all the states composing it, which, again humanly speaking, nothing else can equally ensure. That surely is an object which in its magnitude, in its direct importance to the welfare of many generations, millions upon millions of human beings, is out of all proportion to the ordinary objects of political endeavour. . . .

One throne, one flag, one citizenship. These are existing links of inestimable value. No friendship, no alliance even, with foreign countries, however strong, can give you anything to compare with them—any ties with roots so deep, with a vitality so enduring, or with results so precious.

Just think what it means, for at least every white man of British birth, that he can be at home in every state of the Empire from the moment he sets foot in it, though his whole previous life may have been passed at the other end of the earth. He hears men speaking his own language, he breathes a social and moral atmosphere which is familiar to him—not the same, no doubt, as that of his old home, but yet a kindred atmosphere. More than that, he is entitled to full rights of citizenship from the very outset. He is on absolute terms of equality in this respect with the native born . . . I doubt whether people in general at all realise the greatness of this birthright, the scope and range, the variety and wealth of opportunities, which it affords to us to-day, and may, if we have the wisdom to preserve it, afford to those who come after us for centuries. Our common citizenship is one of those great familiar blessings which men are apt to realise only when they have lost them. . . .

I know there are many who think—I wish I could agree with them—that the tie of sentiment alone is sufficient to hold our Empire together.

Milner, *The Nation and the Empire,* pp. 140–2.

104: J. RAMSAY MACDONALD. *Labour and the Empire*

1907

In wide travels before the first World War the future Labour Prime Minister produced *What I Saw in South Africa* (1903) and, after a world tour in 1906, this volume. For his ideas see also B. Sacks, *J. Ramsay Macdonald* (New Mexico, 1952) Part IV.

It has seemed fitting to include this and No. 106 in this section as immediate comment on the work of the 'proconsuls'.

THESE sons of the well-to-do are honest as a whole, and painstaking as a rule. They are the finest race in the world for keeping in old ruts, and that of itself is some qualification for the offices they hold. But they are also the least imaginative and sympathetic of men. Ninetenths of them return from their foreign appointments without having understood the mind of the natives they were ruling. One meets them in the Islands of the Seas, pining for home, surrounded by English influences. One asks them about native religion—that's not their subject; about native customs—that's not their subject; about native problems—that's not their subject. They come of a different race, they remain of a different race. Their work is mechanical. The failure of our Empire except to produce mechanical results, such as keeping warring tribes at peace, is largely owing to the fact that the Empire is governed by the most narrow-visioned of our social classes. National pride may be a valuable possession, but when it becomes a consciousness of racial superiority it ceases to be an Imperial virtue.

J. Ramsay MacDonald, *Labour and the Empire* (1907), pp. 26–7.

105: LORD CURZON OF KEDLESTON. Speech at Birmingham

11 December 1907

I would describe the Empire . . . as the result, not of an accident or a series of accidents, but of an instinct—that ineradicable and divinely implanted impulse, which has sent the Englishman forth into the uttermost parts of the earth, and made him there the parent of new societies and the architect of unpremeditated creations. . . .

I remember reading a few years ago a remark made by the present Prime Minister that the object of his party was the strengthening of the centre of the Empire, instead of wasting our force upon its outskirts. The first part of the sentence was sound enough. But there was a world of fallacy, and as I think of danger, in the second. It showed in a flash the difference between the Imperial and the anti-Imperial standpoint. To the Imperialist the outskirts of Empire—India, Canada, New Zealand, Natal—are not less important than London, Liverpool, or Birmingham. We ought not to think more of them, but we ought not to think less. If the Colonies had taken a similar line we should have had no Colonial contingents in South Africa. If they should henceforward begin to think mainly or exclusively of themselves as the inhabitants of these islands were invited in this passage to do, you would very soon have no Colonies to think about at all. If there were no outskirts there would be no Empire. . . .

The Empire is still only in a fluid and transitional formation; it has yet to be welded into a great world-state. The constituents are there; the spirit is there; but the problems are still unsolved and the plan has yet to be produced. We have so to work that the concentric rings shall continue to revolve round the central star, not merely because it has hitherto been the law of their being, but because it is their interest and their voluntary choice. In the economy of the imperial household we are dealing not with children but with grown men. At our table are seated not dependents or menials but partners as free as ourselves, and with aspirations not less ample or keen. That they are bound to us by sentiment is a priceless asset; to throw it away would be a criminal blunder. This is the Colonial problem. The Indian problem is much more difficult; for there we are dealing, not with young and eager democracies of our own blood, but with a society cast in a conservative and rigid mould, divorced from our own by religion, custom, and race; though here, too, a spirit of nationality is moving on the face of the waters, and unsuspected forces are dimly struggling to light. It is vain, however, to pretend that

355

India can be granted self-government on the Colonial lines. It would mean ruin to India and treason to our trust. The Empire cannot apply the same policy to the Colonies and to India; but it can be animated by the same spirit and it can pursue the same end, which is continued and contented incorporation in the Imperial union; albeit here again the limits of disruption would be very different. Were the Colonies to break away, they would survive and ultimately flourish, but the Empire would be weakened. Were India to be lost, she herself would reel back into chaos, and the British Empire, at any rate in Asia, would perish. . . .

Empire can only be achieved with satisfaction, or maintained with advantage, provided it has a moral basis. To the people of the mother State it must be a discipline, an inspiration, and a faith. To the people of the circumference, it must be more than a flag or a name, it must give them what they cannot otherwise or elsewhere enjoy; not merely justice or order, or material prosperity, but the sense of partnership in a great idea, the consecrating influence of a lofty purpose. I think it must be because in the heart of British endeavour there has burned this spark of heavenly flame that Providence has hitherto so richly blessed our undertakings. If it is extinguished or allowed to die our Empire will have no more life than a corpse from which the spirit has lately fled, and like a corpse will moulder.

As to the future, if I found any audience of my countrymen who were plunged in doubt as to what it might bring forth and who wondered whether the handwriting might not already be tracing its sentence on the wall of our Empire, as it has done upon those of Babylon, and Nineveh, and Rome, I would say to them: Have no such craven fears. From the sordid controversies and the sometimes depressing gloom of our insular existence look forth, and, if the summons comes to you, go forth, into the larger fields of Empire where duty still calls and an illimitable horizon opens. Preserve with faithful attachment the acquisitions of our forefathers, not tabulating them with vulgar pride, but accepting the legacy with reverence, and holding no sacrifice too great to maintain it. Be sure that in our national character, if we can keep it high and undefiled, still lies our national strength. Count it no shame to acknowledge our Imperial mission, but, on the contrary, the greatest disgrace to be untrue to it, and even if God no longer thunders from Sinai, and His oracles are sometimes reported dumb, cling humbly but fervently to the belief that so long as we are worthy we may still remain one of the instruments through whom He chooses to speak to mankind.

Printed in *The Nineteenth Century and After* (January, 1908), under the title, *The True Imperialism*, pp. 153, 156–7, 162–3, 165.

106: J. KEIR HARDIE. *India, Impressions and Suggestions*

1909

Keir Hardie (1856–1915), a coal miner, was first secretary of the Scottish Miners' Federation. He was Member of Parliament, 1892–5, being first Chairman of the I.L.P. He was Member again, 1900–15, and Chairman and Leader of the Parliamentary Labour Party in 1906 and 1907. In the cold weather of 1907–8 he visited India where his utterances, often seriously misrepresented, roused furious anger in Britain. There resulted this book published in 1909.

LET it not be forgotten that the Indian people are of the same Aryan stock as ourselves. Take a gathering of Indians. Remove their graceful, picturesque costumes, and clothe them in coat and trousers, wash the sun out of their skins, and then a stranger suddenly let down into the midst of them would have difficulty in saying whether he was in Manchester or Madras. This fact has a very important bearing upon the question of how far the Indian people can be trusted with the right of self-government.

For the moment the gulf between the British official and the Indian people is widening. I have fared sumptuously with princes, sat at the table and broken the bread of the educated middle-class, and munched grain with the ryots, and the uniform unvarying testimony has been the same in every case. The older generation of Anglo-Indian officials sorrowfully admit the fact, though they differ as to the explanation. Nor could I discern any signs of an immediate change for the better. The partition of Bengal not only alienated the Bengalees, but is regarded as an act of hostility by the Hindu population in every part of India. The treatment which is being meted out to Indians in British colonies, especially in Canada and South Africa, is also a running sore, particularly with the Mohammedans. Recent acts of the authorities, especially the deportation without trial of men of good social standing and position, against whom no charge could be formulated; the suppression of public meetings, the support given to corrupt and inefficient police officials, and the establishment of a secret police service, with its agents in every corner; the growing oppression of the ryots, and the supercilious way in which their claims for redress are met, are all tending to shake the belief which was formerly universal in the impartiality of British justice and the fairness of British administration.

J. Keir Hardie, *India, Impressions and Suggestions,* pp. 102–3.

107: LORD MILNER. Address to the Royal Colonial
Institute

16 June 1908

THERE is one general principle which seems to me to result clearly from the imminence of the problems which I have sought to adumbrate. It is the urgent need of a better organisation of the Empire, which shall enable the people of this country and those of the younger states to prepare in time to deal with the dependent Empire, as indeed with all their common interests, on the basis of partnership. It may be many years before the younger states are able or willing to share with us in the burden of the dependent Empire as a whole. But there are parts of it in which their interest is already great, and there is no part of it in which their interest is not increasing. Do not let us imagine that it is a matter of complete indifference to them even now. If we look at the influences which tend to keep them within the Empire, the strongest no doubt is affinity of race, but certainly the next strongest—and it is an influence of rapidly increasing importance as their relations with the outside world develop and their outlook widens—is pride in the vast extent and diversity of the British dominions. And observe that, while the tie of race is confined after all only to a portion—the majority, no doubt, but still only a portion—of their inhabitants, this other attraction, their sense of pride in belonging to so great a State, is not confined to those of them who are of British race. It is the common privilege of all British citizens, and it will be found to be a sentiment of great potency if we learn how to appeal to it.

But we must always bear in mind the saying of the Canadian statesman: 'If you want our help, you

359

must call us to your councils.' A real Council of Empire, be it in the first instance only a consultative body, is becoming every day a more urgent necessity. It is a necessity, because every year brings up fresh questions in which the new Dominions, though they have no representation in the British Parliament, are as much interested as the United Kingdom, and because it is our cue to welcome and encourage and not to repress that interest. It is a necessity, because there is no other means of preserving Imperial questions from the corroding influence of British party politics, and because with all its crudeness and inexperience there is a robustness and a sanity about the colonial attitude on these questions, which would be a wholesome corrective to certain tendencies among ourselves. It is a necessity above all because, however numerous and diverse the problems of our Empire are — indeed just because they are so numerous and diverse — we cannot hope to deal with them on any coherent plan, unless there is somewhere in our system a point from which these problems can at least be seen and considered as a whole. The great straggling body needs a central brain, and till that want is supplied, we shall not have taken even the first step to reshaping our political machinery and making it less hopelessly inadequate to the new conditions.

Milner, *The Nation and the Empire,* pp. 298–300.

108: EVELYN BARING, EARL OF CROMER.
Modern Egypt
1908

After service in India and Egypt Cromer was appointed, in 1883, British Agent and Consul-General in Egypt where he became that country's virtual ruler until 1907. His own account of his work there appeared in the volumes from which this and the succeeding extract are taken.

No one can fully realise the extent of the change which has come over Egypt since the British occupation took place unless he is in some degree familiar with the system under which the country was governed in the days of Ismail Pasha. The contrast between now and then is, indeed, remarkable. A new spirit has been instilled into the population of Egypt. Even the peasant has learnt to scan his rights. Even the Pasha has learnt that others besides himself have rights which must be respected. The courbash may hang on the walls of the Moudirieh, but the Moudir no longer dares to employ it on the backs of the fellaheen. For all practical purposes, it may be said that the hateful corvée system has disappeared. Slavery has virtually ceased to exist. The halcyon days of the adventurer and the usurer are past. Fiscal burthens have been greatly relieved. Everywhere law reigns supreme. Justice is no longer bought and sold. Nature, instead of being spurned and neglected, has been wooed to bestow her gifts on mankind. She has responded to the appeal. The waters of the Nile are now utilised in an intelligent manner. Means of locomotion have been improved and extended. The soldier has acquired some pride in the uniform which he wears. He has fought as he has never fought before. The sick man can be nursed in a well-managed hospital. The lunatic is no longer treated like a wild beast. The punishment awarded to the worst criminal is no longer barbarous. Lastly, the schoolmaster is abroad, with results which are as yet uncertain, but which cannot fail to be important.

All these things have been accomplished by the small body of Englishmen who, in various capacities, and with but little direct support or assistance from their Government or its representative, have of late years devoted their energies to the work of Egyptian regeneration. They have had many obstacles to encounter. Internationalism and Pashadom have stood in the path at every turn. But these forces, though they could retard, have failed to arrest the progress of the British reformer. The opposition which he has had to encounter, albeit very embarrassing, merely acted on his system as a healthy tonic. . . . Other nations might have equally well conceived the reforms which were necessary. It required the singular political adaptability of Englishmen to execute them. A country and a nation have been partially regenerated, in spite of a perverse system of government which might well have seemed to render regeneration almost impossible.

Yet, when it is said that all these things were accomplished by the Englishmen who have served the Egyptian government, one qualifying remark should in justice be made. It should never be forgotten that many Egyptians have themselves borne a very honourable and useful part in the work of Egyptian regeneration.

Is the skilled labour, the energy, the perseverance, and the patient toil of the English reformers and their Egyptian allies to be thrown away? Is Egypt again to relapse into a semi-barbarous condition? Will posterity declare that this noble effort to elevate a whole nation ended in ultimate failure?

Modern Egypt (London, 1908), Vol. II, pp. 556–8.

109: LORD CROMER. *Abbas II*

1915

THE corner-stone of Egyptian and Soudanese policy should be a full recognition of the fact that, in the absence of ties, such as community of race, language, religion and social customs, the only link between the governors and the governed is to be found in material interests, and amongst those interests by far the most important is the imposition of light fiscal burthens. I hold, therefore, that the political conditions with which we have to deal are such that all other considerations must yield to the necessity of keeping taxation low. Those who are really responsible for the administration of Egypt and the Soudan will have to rely almost wholly on themselves in the execution of a policy based on the principle indicated above. They will obtain but little support anywhere, for economy is always unpopular, whilst from many quarters they will of a surety be sharply criticised. They will not be able to rely to any great extent on the support of public opinion, whether local or British. Englishmen are, generally speaking, very prone to form their opinions on English precedents and English practices. In their own country they have recently experienced an expansion of State expenditure and an increase of public burdens which, but a few years ago, would have been scouted as impossible, with the result that public opinion on the subject of economy has become demoralised, and that the national conscience in dealing with the economical administration of its dependencies has probably become in some degree blunted. Then, again, many leading English politicians and influential newspapers are never tired of insisting on the political desirability of pushing on Egyptian education rapidly as a preliminary measure necessary to the speedy development of local autonomy. Personally, I do not believe that such education as can be imparted in the schools and colleges will ever render the Egyptians capable of complete self-government without some transformation of the national character, which must necessarily be a slow process. But that is not the point on which to insist at present. I merely wish to dwell on the costliness of education, and to indicate the political unwisdom of adopting an educational policy so advanced as to necessitate the imposition of burdensome taxation. Then, again, attacks are to be apprehended from another and very different quarter. The zealous administrator, conscious of the good he is capable of performing, will clamour for more roads, bridges, hospitals, and all the other paraphernalia of advanced civilisation, and will be apt to ignore the ultimate consequences which must result from any very heavy expenditure to secure these objects rapidly.

Responsible Egyptian and Soudanese statesmen, however much they may sympathise with proposals of this nature considered exclusively on their own merits, will do well to keep alike the political dreamer and the bureaucratic administrator at arm's length.

Abbas II (London, 1915), pp. xxii–iv.

PART XV

CRITICISM FROM THE LEFT

110: GEORGE BERNARD SHAW. *The Man of Destiny*

1896

Shaw's interest in the problems of the Empire was seen further in his editing in 1900 *Fabianism and the Empire,* though he maintained in the preface that he was " only the draughtsman " called in by the Fabian Society as " a literary expert " to make " its utterances readable ".

NAPOLEON: No Englishman is too low to have scruples: no Englishman is high enough to be free from their tyranny. But every Englishman is born with a certain miraculous power that makes him master of the world. When he wants a thing, he never tells himself that he wants it. He waits patiently until there comes into his mind, no one knows how, a burning conviction that it is his moral and religious duty to conquer those who have got the thing he wants. Then he becomes irresistible. Like the aristocrat, he does what pleases him and grabs what he covets: like the shopkeeper, he pursues his purpose with the industry and steadfastness that come from strong religious conviction and deep sense of moral responsibility. He is never at a loss for an effective moral attitude. As the great champion of freedom and national independence, he conquers and annexes half the world, and calls it Colonization. When he wants a new market for his adulterated Manchester goods, he sends a missionary to teach the natives the Gospel of Peace. The natives kill the missionary: he flies to arms in defence of Christianity; fights for it; conquers for it; and takes the market as a reward from heaven. In defence of his island shores, he puts a chaplain on board his ship; nails a flag with a cross on it to his top-gallant mast; and sails to the ends of the earth, sinking, burning and destroying all who dispute the empire of the seas with him. He boasts that a slave is free the moment his foot touches British soil; and he sells the children of his poor at six years of age to work under the lash in his factories for sixteen hours a day. He makes two revolutions, and then declares war on our one in the name of law and order. There is nothing so bad or so good that you will not find Englishmen doing it; but you will never find an Englishman in the wrong. He does everything on principle. He fights you on patriotic principles; he robs you on business principles; he enslaves you on imperial principles; he bullies you on manly principles; he supports his king on loyal principles and cuts off his king's head on republican principles. His watchword is always Duty; and he never forgets that the nation which lets its duty get on the opposite side to its interest is lost.

The Man of Destiny (1929 ed.), pp. 200–1.

III: J. A. HOBSON. *Imperialism: a Study*

1902

CAREFUL analysis of the existing relations between business and politics shows that the aggressive Imperialism which we seek to understand is not in the main the product of blind passions of races or of the mixed folly and ambitions of politicians. It is far more rational than at first sight appears. Irrational from the standpoint of the whole nation, it is rational enough from the standpoint of certain classes in the nation. . . .

In order to explain Imperialism on this hypothesis we have to answer two questions. Do we find in Great Britain to-day any well-organised group of special commercial and social interests which stand to gain by aggressive Imperialism and the militarism it involves? If such a combination of interests exists, has it the power to work its will in the arena of politics?

What is the direct economic outcome of Imperialism? A great expenditure of public money upon ships, guns, military and naval equipment and stores, growing and productive of enormous profits when a war, or an alarm of war, occurs; new public loans and important fluctuations in the home and foreign Bourses; more posts for soldiers and sailors and in the diplomatic and consular services; improvement of foreign investments by the substitution of the British flag for a foreign flag; acquisition of markets for certain classes of exports, and some protection and assistance for trades representing British houses in these manufactures; employment for engineers, missionaries, speculative miners, ranchers and other emigrants.

Certain definite business and professional interests feeding upon imperialistic expenditure, or upon the results of that expenditure, are thus set up in opposition to the common good, and, instinctively feeling their way to one another, are found united in strong sympathy to support every new imperialistic exploit.

If, contemplating the enormous expenditure on armaments, the ruinous wars, the diplomatic audacity of knavery by which modern Governments seek to extend their territorial power, we put the plain, practical question, *Cui bono?* the first and most obvious answer is, The investor. . . .

369

Investors who have put their money in foreign lands, upon terms which take full account of risks connected with the political conditions of the country, desire to use the resources·of their Government to minimise these risks, and so to enhance the capital value and the interest of their private investments. The investing and speculative classes in general also desire that Great Britain should take other foreign areas under her flag in order to secure new areas for profitable investment and speculation.

It is true that the motor-power of Imperialism is not chiefly financial: finance is rather the governor of the imperial engine, directing the energy and determining its work: it does not constitute the fuel of the engine, nor does it directly generate the power. Finance manipulates the patriotic forces which politicians, soldiers, philanthropists, and traders generate; the enthusiasm for expansion which issues from these sources, though strong and genuine, is irregular and blind; the financial interest has those qualities of concentration and clearsighted calculation which are needed to set Imperialism to work. An ambitious statesman, a frontier soldier, an over-zealous missionary, a pushing trader, may suggest or even initiate a step of imperial expansion, may assist in educating patriotic public opinion to the urgent need of some fresh advance, but the final determination rests with the financial power. The direct influence exercised by great financial houses in " high politics " is supported by the control which they exercise over the body of public opinion through the Press, which, in every " civilised " country, is becoming more and more their obedient instrument. While the specifically financial newspaper imposes " facts " and " opinions " on the business classes, the general body of the Press comes more and more under the conscious or unconscious domination of financiers. The case of the South African Press, whose agents and correspondents fanned the martial flames in this country, was one of open owner- ship on the part of South African financiers, and this policy of owning newspapers for the sake of manufac- turing public opinion is common in the great European cities. . . . Apart from the financial Press, and financial ownership of the general Press, the City notoriously exercises a subtle and abiding influence upon leading London newspapers, and through them upon the body of the Provincial Press, while the entire dependence of the Press for its business profits upon its advertising columns involves a peculiar reluctance to oppose the organised financial classes with whom rests the control of so much advertising business. Add to this the natural sympathy with a sensational policy which a cheap Press always manifests, and it becomes evident that the Press is strongly biassed towards Imperialism, and lends itself with great facility to the suggestion of financial or political Imperialists who desire to work up patriotism for some new piece of expansion. . . .

The play of these forces does not openly appear. They are essentially parasites upon patriotism, and they adapt themselves to its protecting colours. In the mouths of their representatives are noble phrases, expressive of their desire to extend the area of civilisation, to establish good government, promote Christianity, extirpate slavery, and elevate the lower races. Some of the business men who hold such language may entertain a genuine, though usually a vague, desire to accomplish these ends, but they are primarily engaged in business, and they are not unaware of the utility of the more unselfish forces in furthering their ends. Their true attitude of mind is expressed by Mr. Rhodes in his famous description of "Her Majesty's Flag" as "the greatest commercial asset in the world."

If the consuming public in this country raised its standard of consumption to keep pace with every rise of productive powers, there would be no excess of goods or capital clamorous to use Imperialism in order to find markets: foreign trade would indeed exist, but there would be no difficulty in exchanging a small surplus of our manufactures for the food and raw material we annually absorbed, and all the savings that we made could find employment, if we chose, in home industries.

An economy that assigns to the "possessing" classes an excess of consuming power which they cannot use, and cannot convert into really serviceable capital, is a dog-in-the-manger policy. The social reforms which deprive the possessing classes of their surplus will not, therefore, inflict upon them the real injury they dread; they can only use this surplus by forcing on their country a wrecking policy of Imperialism. The only safety of nations lies in removing the unearned increments of income from the possessing classes, and adding them to the wage-income of the working classes or to the public income, in order that they may be spent in raising the standard of consumption. . . .

Trade Unionism and Socialism are thus the natural enemies of Imperialism, for they take away from the "imperialist" classes the surplus incomes which form the economic stimulus of Imperialism.

The true political nature of Imperialism is best seen

by confronting it with the watchwards of progress accepted in the middle of the nineteenth century by moderate men of both great parties in the State, though with interpretations varying in degree—peace, economy, reform, and popular self-government. Even now we find no formal abandonment of the principles of government these terms express, and a large section of professed Liberals believe or assert that Imperialism is consistent with the maintenance of all these virtues.

This contention, however, is belied by facts. The decades of Imperialism have been prolific in wars; most of these wars have been directly motived by aggression of white races upon " lower races," and have issued in the forcible seizure of territory. Every one of the steps of expansion in Africa, Asia, and the Pacific has been accompanied by bloodshed; each imperialist Power keeps an increasing army available for foreign service; rectification of frontiers, punitive expeditions, and other euphemisms for war are in incessant progress. The *pax Britannica*, always an impudent falsehood, has become of recent years a grotesque monster of hypocrisy; along our Indian frontiers, in West Africa, in the Soudan, in Uganda, in Rhodesia fighting has been well-nigh incessant. Although the great imperialist Powers have kept their hands off one another, save where the rising empire of the United States has found its opportunity in the falling empire of Spain, the self-restraint has been costly and precarious. Peace as a national policy is antagonised not merely by war, but by militarism, an even graver injury. Apart from the enmity of France and Germany, the main cause of the vast armaments which are draining the resources of most European countries is their conflicting interests in territorial and commercial expansion. Where thirty years ago there existed one sensitive spot in our relations with France, or Germany, or Russia, there are a dozen now; diplomatic strains are of almost monthly occurrence between Powers with African or Chinese interests, and the chiefly business nature of the national antagonisms renders them more dangerous, inasmuch as the policy of Governments passes more under the influence of distinctively financial juntos.

Nothing short of the fear of an early invasion of these islands will induce the British people to undergo the onerous experience of a really effective system of compulsory military service; no statesman except under the shadow of a serious menace of invasion will dare to press such a plan. A regular provision for compulsory foreign service will never be adopted when the alternative of mercenary native armies remains. Let these " niggers " fight for the Empire in return for the services we render them by annexing and governing them and teaching them "the dignity of labour," will be the prevailing sentiment, and "imperialist" statesmen will be compelled to bow before it, diluting with British troops ever more thinly the native armies in Africa and Asia.

This mode of militarism, while cheaper and easier in the first instance, implies less and less control from Great Britain. Though reducing the strain of militarism upon the population at home, it enhances the risks of wars, which become more frequent and more barbarous in proportion as they involve to a less degree the lives of Englishmen. The expansion of our Empire under the new Imperialism has been compassed by setting the " lower races " at one another's throats, fostering tribal animosities, and utilising for our supposed benefit the savage propensities of the peoples to whom we have a mission to carry Christianity and civilisation.

The practices which are writ large in Rhodes, Beit, and their parliamentary confederates are widespread on a smaller scale; the South of England is full of men of local influence in politics and society whose character has been formed in our despotic Empire, and whose incomes are chiefly derived from the maintenance and furtherance of this despotic rule. Not a few enter our local councils, or take posts in our constabulary or our prisons: everywhere they stand for coercion and for resistance to reform. Could the incomes expended in the Home Counties and other large districts of Southern Britain be traced to their sources, it would be found that they were in large measure wrung from the enforced toil of vast multitudes of black, brown, or yellow natives, by arts not differing essentially from those which supported in idleness and luxury imperial Rome.

It is, indeed, a nemesis of Imperialism that the arts and crafts of tyranny, acquired and exercised in our unfree Empire, should be turned against our liberties at home. Those who have felt surprise at the total disregard or the open contempt displayed by the aristocracy and the plutocracy of this land for infringements of the liberties of the subject and for the abrogation of constitutional rights and usages have not taken sufficiently into account the steady reflux of this poison of irresponsible autocracy from our " unfree, intolerant, aggressive " Empire.

It is the great practical business of the century to explore and develop, by every method which science can devise, the hidden natural and human resources of the globe.

That the white Western nations will abandon a quest on which they have already gone so far is a view which

375

does not deserve consideration. That this process of development may be so conducted as to yield a gain to world-civilisation, instead of some terrible *débâcle* in which revolted slave races may trample down their parasitic and degenerate white masters, should be the supreme aim of far-sighted scientific statecraft.

To those who utter the single cry of warning, "*laissez faire*, hands off, let these people develop their resources themselves with such assistance as they ask or hire, undisturbed by the importunate and arrogant control of foreign nations," it is a sufficient answer to point out the impossibility of maintaining such an attitude.

If organised Governments of civilised Powers refused the task, they would let loose a horde of private adventurers, slavers, piratical traders, treasure hunters, concession mongers, who, animated by mere greed of gold or power, would set about the work of exploitation under no public control and with no regard to the future; playing havoc with the political, economic, and moral institutions of the peoples, instilling civilised vices and civilised diseases, importing spirits and firearms as the trade of readiest acceptance, fostering internecine strife for their own political and industrial purposes, and even setting up private despotisms sustained by organised armed forces. . . . The contact with white races cannot be avoided, and it is more perilous and more injurious in proportion as it lacks governmental sanction and control. The most gigantic modern experiment in private adventure is slowly yielding its full tale of horrors in the Congo Free State, while the handing over of large regions in Africa to the virtually unchecked government of Chartered Companies exposes everywhere the dangers of a contact based on private commercialism.

To abandon the backward races to these perils of

private exploitation, it is argued forcibly, is a barbarous dereliction of a public duty on behalf of humanity and the civilisation of the world. Not merely does it leave the tropics to be the helpless prey of the offscourings of civilised nations; it opens grave dangers in the future, from the political or military ambitions of native or imported rulers, who, playing upon the religious fanaticism or the combative instincts of great hordes of semi-savages, may impose upon them so effective a military discipline as to give terrible significance to some black or yellow " peril." Complete isolation is no longer possible even for the remotest island; absolute self-sufficiency is no more possible for a nation than for an individual: in each case society has the right and the need to safeguard its interests against an injurious assertion of individuality.

Again, though there is some force in the contention that the backward natives could and would protect themselves against the encroachments of private adventurers, if they had the assurance that the latter could not call upon their Government for assistance or for vengeance, history does not lead us to believe that these powers of self-protection, however adequate against forcible invasions, would suffice to meet the more insidious wiles by which traders, prospectors, and political adventurers insinuate their poisons into primitive societies like that of Samoa or Ashanti.

So far, we have established two tentative principles. First, that all interference on the part of civilised white races with " lower races " is not *prima facie* illegitimate. Second, that such interference cannot safely be left to private enterprise of individual whites. If these principles be admitted, it follows that civilised Governments *may* undertake the political and economic control of lower races—in a word, that the characteristic form of

377

modern Imperialism is not under all conditions illegitimate.

What, then, are the conditions which render it legitimate? They may be provisionally stated thus: Such interference with the government of a lower race must be directed primarily to secure the safety and progress of the civilisation of the world, and not the special interest of the interfering nation. Such interference must be attended by an improvement and elevation of the character of the people who are brought under this control. Lastly, the determination of the two preceding conditions must not be left to the arbitrary will or judgment of the interfering nation, but must proceed from some organised representation of civilised humanity.

The true "imperial" policy is best illustrated in the case of Basutoland, which was rescued in 1884 from the aggressive designs of Cape Colony, stimulated by industrial exploiters.

Here British imperial government is exercised by a Commissioner, with several British magistrates to deal with grave offences against order, and a small body of native police under British officers. For the rest, the old political and economic institutions are preserved— government by chiefs, under a paramount chief, subject to the informal control or influence of public opinion in a national assembly; ordinary administration, chiefly consisting in allotment of land, and ordinary jurisdiction are left to the chiefs. . . .

The widest and ultimately the most important of the struggles in South Africa is that between the policy of Basutoland and that of Johannesburg and Rhodesia; for there, if anywhere, we lay our finger on the difference between a "sane" Imperialism, devoted to the protec-

tion, education, and self-government of a " lower race,"
and an " insane " Imperialism, which hands over these
races to the economic exploitation of white colonists who
will use them as " live tools " and their lands as reposi-
tories of mining or other profitable treasure.

J. A. Hobson, *Imperialism: a Study* (1902), pp. 52–3, 62–3, 66–8,
86, 95–6, 132–3, 144–5, 159–60, 242–5, 258–60.

112: J. RAMSAY MACDONALD. *Labour and
The Empire*

1907

WHAT these Imperialists contemplate is a group of
independent States, each one irresponsible for the policy
and actions of the rest. But this is a negation of the idea
of any unity more vital than diplomatic and mechanical
alliance, whereas Empire presupposes a common racial
policy, or a uniform political purpose either imposed
by authority or agreed to by the allied States. The
Imperialist has not thought about his Empire. He has
not gone beyond the stage of wanting an Empire—that
is his principle, and of trusting the man on the spot—
that is his method; and he has not yet discovered that
his method is miserably inadequate in view of the nature
of his aspirations. He has only reached that primitive
state of thought in which whatever action his tribe or
tribesmen take is accepted as right irrespective of any
standard of qualitative worth, and in which the bigger
his tribe the more important does he appear to himself
to be. He has no sense of a " British " tradition, or a
" British " genius, or a " British " policy. He claims that
circumstances alter national and racial methods (which
is true), but from that deduces the corollary, so destruc-

379

tive to every Imperial idea, that practically no attempt
should be made by an Imperial authority to maintain
traditional and racial standards in the administration of
the several colonies. . . .

" The man on the spot " conception of Imperial
responsibility is a negation of the Imperial idea. It leads
to anarchy and chaos. No wonder that such Imperialists,
having in reality (however strongly they may protest to
the contrary) abandoned faith in the spiritual and
political bond of Empire, seek to cement it by trading
profits. . . .

I argue that no State within the Empire has the right
to adopt a policy of administration or a standard of civil
liberty contrary to, or lower than, the traditional policy
and standard of the Empire itself, and I base my argument mainly upon the consideration that if any such
departure is allowed, it involves the whole Empire.
State action becomes as a matter of fact Imperial action
and the Empire has to take the consequences.

J. Ramsay MacDonald, *Labour and the Empire* (1907), pp. 39–
41, 44.

113: EDMUND D. MOREL. *Africa and the Peace of Europe*

1917

E. D. Morel (1873–1924) founded in 1904 the Congo Reform
Association, taking a leading part in the attacks on Congo mis-
rule. He wrote much on West African affairs, continuing the work
of Mary Kingsley. He was Labour Member of Parliament from
1922 and would, but for his untimely death, probably have held
office as Under-Secretary for Foreign Affairs in the first Labour
Government.

THE whole tendency and evolution of British thought as
regards national responsibilities in relation to subject

races, since the days of the East India Company, have
been steadily gravitating towards the conviction that
oversea Dependencies must not be looked upon as preserves for a few favoured nationals, or as direct sources
of revenue to the Mother Country; but as territories
held in trust by the dominant Power for their indigenous
inhabitants. This conception of trusteeship, which is the
only moral justification of Empire over alien peoples,
necessarily involves an economic system untrammelled
by a differential treatment of economic agencies other
than those emanating from the Mother Country. For
only through the existence of such an untrammelled
economic system can the indigenous inhabitants of the
Dependencies dispose of their property and their labour
to the best advantage. To go back upon that conception
would be a sign of Imperial decadence.

E. D. Morel, *Africa and the Peace of Europe* (1917), p. 84.

114: LEONARD S. WOOLF. *Empire and Commerce in Africa*

1920

Woolf's period in the Ceylon Civil Service, 1904-11, is reflected
in his novel *The Village in the Jungle* (1913) and autobiography
Growing (1961). A vigorous critic, his works include *Economic
Imperialism* (1920) and *Imperialism and Civilization* (2nd. ed., 1933).

THE prophecies of the economic imperialist with regard
to the East Coast of Africa have proved completely false.
British possessions there are of negligible importance to
British industry, whether as sources of supply for raw
material or as markets for manufactures. The use of
the State's power in these regions has affected the
economic interests of very few of its citizens. A few

hundred Englishmen, capitalists and planters, who directly exploit the territories by the purchase of land and mining rights and the flotation of joint-stock companies, have made—and sometimes lost—money. But trade, industry, and labour, generally, have reaped no advantages. It is not difficult to discover the reasons for this. Economic imperialism in this part of Africa was founded upon two economic delusions. " By seizing this territory," said Sir William Mackinnon and Mr. Chamberlain, " we shall reserve it as a reservoir of raw materials for British industry." But this could only be accomplished in one way, namely, by preventing, through tariffs or other methods, the manufacturers of other European countries from purchasing the raw materials produced in East Africa, and so reserving them at low prices for British manufacturers. Now this is only possible where, as in the case of palm-kernels on the West Coast of Africa, the raw materials are produced by natives. Where, as in East Africa, the raw materials are produced by British capitalists, planters, and joint-stock companies, these European subjects of the European State take good care to see that they are not prevented from selling their products in the dearest market : if that market be Britain, they will sell to British industry ; but if it be Germany or France, they will sell to German or French industry. The Colonial Office is able to reserve the palm-kernels on the West Coast for British industry and to keep down the price paid for them to the West Coast native, because the native is powerless and inarticulate ; but it has never attempted—it knows it would be impossible—to apply the same system to the raw materials produced by the white man in East Africa. And what is true of British colonial policy in this respect, is true of the policy of the other European States. . . .

The other delusion of the economic imperialist has to do with the importance of these African territories as a market for European manufactures. " We must acquire Uganda and British East Africa for the British Empire," said *The Times* and Captain Lugard, " in order to preserve these rich and populous districts as a market for British exports, and so keep the wolf of unemployment from the door of the simple, British working-man." But these imperial economists forgot the law of economics that supply must depend upon demand. The rich and populous markets upon which they turned covetous eyes consist of a few hundred white men and several million Africans. The importance of these territories as a market for British industries depends therefore upon the demand of the Africans. Now the African is, according to European standards, wretchedly poor, and he is accustomed to invest such wealth as he has, not in the products of British industries, but in cattle.

You cannot combine the ideal of a League of Nations in Europe and America with the ideals of economic imperialism and *Machtpolitik* in Africa and Asia. If the power of the European State is to be used to promote the economic interests of its citizens and to damage the economic interests of those who are not its citizens, the final test of power or force will not be made in Africa and Asia, but upon the old graves in the battle-fields of Europe.

Such must be the inevitable international effects outside Africa of economic imperialism. Within the continent the policy must proceed to its logical conclusion. The millions of Africans, who belong to the black non-adult races, will remain subject to the autocratic government of alien white men. The belief that the economic development of the country should be the first duty of the administration in order that it may fit into and serve the economic—the industrial and financial —system of Europe will be the main principle of government. The acceptance of the principle that the power of the European State should be used in Africa to promote the economic interests of European citizens will subject the Colonial Offices and Colonial Governments to the irresistible pressure of the handful of white men who have economic interests in Africa. If those interests require that the native shall not be educated, he will not be educated; if they require that he shall be demoralized and poisoned by gin, gin will be sold to him; if they require that the native shall be forced to work on the white man's land for a penny a day, taxation or starvation will furnish the necessary inducement; if they require that land occupied by natives shall be sold to Europeans, the natives will be removed into Reserves, and the Reserves will then be cut down until the native is forced to return to work for a penny a day on the land from which the European expropriated him. In this process of what Mr. Chamberlain called " convincing the native of the necessity and dignity of labour," the whole tribal organization, and the bonds which bound together the fabric of native social life, will necessarily be destroyed. The Government will be powerless to substitute, whether by education or otherwise, anything in their place; for any real education will unfit the native to take his place as a docile labourer on a penny a day in the scheme of economic imperialism. Thus the natives will receive an ever larger measure of the blessings of law and order, and the European an ever increasing measure of cheap labour. The exploitation of Africa by Europe internally as well

as externally will be based upon force, the primitive
right of the stronger to enslave the weaker. At the
worst this right will be enforced with the cruelties and
atrocities which Europe associates with the Belgian
Congo and the German and Portuguese Colonies; at the
best the right will be enforced by the milder, more
respectable, and no less efficacious British method of
legislative enactment.

Such must inevitably be the future of Africa if it be
shaped, like the past and the present, by the desires,
beliefs, and policy of economic imperialism. The conditions necessary, if the evils are to be turned into blessings
and the professions of our civilization made good, are
not really so obscure or complicated as the economic
imperialist would have us believe. Africa is a continent
inhabited by a population which belongs almost entirely
to non-adult races. It is true that for Europe to withdraw
to-day from Africa and to leave these non-adult races to
manage their own affairs is impossible. For generations
Europe has exploited Africa for economic ends, at first
by the slave trade, and later by commerce, agriculture,
mining, and finance. No change for the better would be
brought about by the European State withdrawing its
control. Economic imperialism has itself created conditions in which that control must inevitably continue.
We are thus faced with a curious position in Africa.
Primitive peoples are suddenly confronted with a highly
complex alien civilization in which social policy is mainly
directed towards safeguarding its most cherished principles, the sacred rights of property and the even more
sacred right (and duty) of selling in the dearest and
buying in the cheapest market. In all the relations of
organized political, economic, and social life the primitive peoples are unable to hold their own with the

civilized. Only the sun, malaria, and sleeping sickness have saved and will continue to save the African from extermination at the hands of the white man. The white man is inferior to the native only in this inability to exist and propagate in the greater part of Africa. Thus millions of Africans must continue to co-exist with European civilization. But the ideals of Europe, the economic principles upon which our society is based, inevitably result in the political subjection and the economic exploitation of Africans by Europeans. The European State, if it remains in Africa, is necessarily an instrument of that exploitation; if it withdraws, it merely hands over the native to the more cruel exploitation of irresponsible white men.

L. S. Woolf, *Empire and Commerce in Africa* (n.d.), pp. 334–5, 356–8.

Part XVI

THE ACHIEVEMENT OF "PARTNERSHIP"

GENERAL JAN CHRISTIAN SMUTS.
Speech at Banquet given in his honour by members of
both Houses of Parliament

15 May 1917

I think we are inclined to make mistakes in thinking
about this group of nations to which we belong, because
too often we think of it merely as one State. The British
Empire is much more than a State. I think the very
expression " Empire " is misleading, because it makes
people think as if we are one single entity, one unity, to
which that term " Empire " can be applied. We are not
an Empire. Germany is an Empire, so was Rome, and
so is India, but we are a system of nations, a community
of states, and of nations far greater than any empire
which has ever existed ; and by using this ancient expression we really obscure the real fact that we are larger and
that our whole position is different, and that we are not
one nation, or state, or empire, but we are a whole world
by ourselves, consisting of many nations and states, and
all sorts of communities under one flag. We are a system
of states, not only a static system, a stationary system,
but a dynamic system, growing, evolving all the time
towards new destinies.

Here you have a kingdom with a number of Crown
colonies ; besides that you have large protectorates like
Egypt, which is an Empire in itself, which was one of the
greatest empires in the world. Besides that you have
great dependencies like India—an empire in itself, one
of the oldest civilisations in the world, and we are busy

there trying to see how East and West can work together, how the forces that has kept the East going can be worked in conjunction with the ideas we have evolved in Western civilisation for enormous problems within that State. But beyond that we come to the so-called Dominions, a number of nations and states almost sovereign, almost independent, who govern themselves, who have been evolved on the principles of your constitutional system, now almost independent states, and who all belong to this group, to this community of nations, which I prefer to call the British Commonwealth of nations. Now, you see that no political ideas that we evolved in the past, no nomenclature will apply to this world which is comprised in the British Empire; any expression, any name which we have found so far for this group has been insufficient, and I think the man who would discover the real appropriate name for this vast system of entities would be doing a great service not only to this country, but to constitutional theory.

I think that this is the fundamental fact which we have to bear in mind—that the British Empire, or this British Commonwealth of nations, does not stand for unity, standardisation, or assimilation, or denationalisation; but it stands for a fuller, a richer, and more various life among all the nations that compose it. And even nations who have fought against you, like my own, must feel that they and their interests, their language, their religions, and all their cultural interests are as safe and as secure under the British flag as those of the children of your household and your own blood. It is only in proportion as that is realised that you will fulfil the true mission which you have undertaken. Therefore, it seems, speaking my own individual opinion, that there is only one solution, that is the solution supplied by our past traditions of freedom, self-government, and the fullest development. We are not going to force common Governments, federal or otherwise, but we are going to extend liberty, freedom, and nationhood more and more in every part of the Empire.

The question arises, how are you going to keep this world together if there is going to be all this enormous development towards a more varied and richer life among all its parts? It seems to me that you have two potent factors that you must rely on for the future. The first is your hereditary kingship. I have seen some speculations recently in the papers of this country upon the position of the kingship of this country ; speculations by people who, I am sure, have never thought of the wider issues that are at stake. You cannot make a Republic in this country. You cannot make a Republic of the British Commonwealth of nations, because if you have to elect a President not only in these islands, but all over the British Empire, who will be the ruler and representative of all these peoples, you are facing an absolutely insoluble problem. Now, you know the theory of our Constitution is that the King is not merely your King, but he is the King of all of us. He represents every part of the whole Commonwealth of nations. If his place is to be taken by anybody else, then that somebody will have to be elected by a process which, I think, will pass the wit of man to devise. Therefore let us be thankful for the mercies we have. We have a kingship here which is really not very different from a hereditary Republic, and I am sure that more and more in the future the trend will be in that direction, and I shall not be surprised to see the time when our Royal princes, instead of getting their Consorts among the princelings of Central Europe, will go to the Dominions and the outlying portions of the Empire.

I think that in the theory of the future of this great Empire it is impossible to attach too much importance to this institution which we have existing, and which can be developed, in my opinion, to the greatest uses possible for its future preservation and development. It will, of course, be necessary to go further than that. It is not only the symbol of unity which you have in the Royal ruler, but you will have to develop further common institutions.

Everyone admits that it would be necessary to devise better machinery for common consultation than we have had hitherto. So far we have relied upon the Imperial Conference which meets every four years, and which, however useful for the work it has done hitherto, has not, in my opinion, been a complete success. It will be necessary to devise better means for achieving our ends. A certain precedent has been laid down of calling the Prime Ministers and representatives from the Empire of India to the Imperial Cabinet, and we have seen the statement made by Lord Curzon that it is the intention of the Government to perpetuate that practice in future. Although we have not yet the details of the scheme, and we have to wait for a complete exposition of the subject from his Majesty's Government, yet it is clear that in an institution like that you have a far better instrument of common consultation than you have in the old Imperial Conference, which was called only every four years, and which discussed a number of subjects which were not really of first-class importance. After all, what you want is to call together the most important statesmen in the Empire from time to time—say once a year, or as often as may be found necessary—to discuss matters which concern all parts of the Empire in common, and in order that causes of friction and misunderstanding may be removed. A common policy should be laid down to determine the true orientation of our Imperial policy.

Far too much stress is laid upon the instruments of government. People are inclined to forget that the world is getting more democratic, and that forces which find expression in public opinion are going to be far more powerful in the future than they have been in the past. You will find that you have built up a spirit of comradeship and a common feeling of patriotism, and that the instrument of government will not be the thing that matters so much as the spirit that actuates the whole system of all its parts. That seems to me to be your mission. You talk about an Imperial mission. It seems to me this British Empire has only one mission, and that is a mission for greater liberty and freedom and self-development. Yours is the only system that has ever worked in history where a large number of nations have been living in unity. Talk about the League of Nations —you are the only league of nations that has ever existed; and if the line that I am sketching here is correct you are going to be an even greater league of nations in the future; and if you are true to your old traditions of self-government and freedom, and to this vision of your future and your mission, who knows that you may not exercise far greater and more beneficent influence on the history of mankind than you have ever done before?

In the welter of confusion which is probably going to follow the war in Europe you will stand as the one system where liberty to work successfully has kept together divers communities. You may be sure the world such as will be surrounding you in the times that are coming will be very likely to follow your example. You may become the real nucleus for the world-government for the future. There is no doubt that is the way things will go in the future. You have made a successful start; and if you keep on the right track your Empire will be a solution of the whole problem.

Printed as a pamphlet, *The British Commonwealth of Nations*, (1917), pp. 5–11.

116: SIR FREDERICK DEALTRY LUGARD.
The Dual Mandate in British Tropical Africa

1922

After taking part in campaigns in Afghanistan, the Sudan and Burma, Lugard came to Africa to command an expedition against slave-traders near Lake Nyasa. He then served with the Chartered Companies in Uganda, West Africa and Bechuanaland, and raised the West Africa Frontier Force in 1897. Chamberlain appointed him High Commissioner in Northern Nigeria (1900–06). Then and in his subsequent service in Nigeria as Governor and Governor-General (1912–9) he put into effect his ideas of 'indirect rule'. These were developed in the book from which these extracts are taken, a book which has been compared with the Durham Report for its influence on British policy. From 1922 to 1936 Lugard was a member of the Permanent Mandates Commission of the League of Nations. He was raised to the peerage in 1928. See M. Perham, *Lugard* (1956 & 1960).

WITHOUT underrating the great work which France and Belgium are doing, it is to England that Beaulieu generously awards the palm in having led the way in the recognition of the responsibility which is inseparable from rule.[1] The moral obligations to the subject races include such matters as the training of native rulers; the delegation to them of such responsibility as they are fit to exercise; the constitution of Courts of Justice free

[1] Beaulieu, *Histoire de la Colonisation chez les peuples modernes*, I, p. 92, and II, p. 246. (Author's note).

394

from corruption and accessible to all; the adoption of a system of education which will assist progress without creating false ideals; the institution of free labour and of a just system of taxation; the protection of the peasantry from oppression, and the preservation of their rights in land, &c.

The material obligations, on the other hand, are concerned with development of natural resources for the mutual benefit of the people and of mankind in general. They involve the examination of such questions as "equal opportunity" and "Imperial Preference," and other problems of economic policy. . . .

Nor is the obligation which the controlling Powers owe to themselves and their race a lesser one. It has been well said that a nation, like an individual, must have some task higher than the pursuit of material gain, if it is to escape the benumbing influence of parochialism and to fulfil its higher destiny. If high standards are maintained, the control of subject races must have an effect on national character which is not measureable in terms of material profit and loss. And what is true for the nation is equally true for the individual officers employed. If lower standards are adopted—the arrogant display of power, or the selfish pursuit of profit—the result is equally fatal to the nation and to the individual. Misuse of opportunity carries with it a relentless Nemesis, deteriorating the moral fibre of the individual, and permeating the nation. . . .

But if the standard which the white man must set before him when dealing with uncivilised races must be a high one for the sake of his own moral and spiritual balance, it is not less imperative for the sake of the influence which he exercises upon those over whom he is set in authority. The white man's prestige must stand high when a few score are responsible for the control and guidance of millions. His courage must be undoubted, his word and pledge absolutely inviolate, his sincerity transparent. There is no room for "mean whites" in tropical Africa. Nor is there room for those who, however high their motives, are content to place themselves on the same level as the uncivilised races. They lower the prestige by which alone the white races can hope to govern and to guide. . . .

When Great Britain undertook the control of great regions in tropical Africa, she not only gave to her commercial rivals the same opportunities as were enjoyed by her own nationals, but she assisted in the development of these territories from Imperial revenues—not as loans to be repaid when they grew rich, but as free gifts—and later by the use of Imperial credit to float loans for development, while her Navy, and on occasion her troops, ensured their protection. She secured to their inhabitants an unrestricted market for their produce, and to all engaged in their development, of whatever nationality, equality of commercial opportunity and uniform laws.

She recognised that the custodians of the tropics are, in the words of Mr. Chamberlain, "trustees of civilisation for the commerce of the world"; that their raw materials and foodstuffs—without which civilisation cannot exist—must be developed alike in the interests of the natives and of the world at large, without any artificial restrictions. . . . The tropics are the heritage of mankind, and neither, on the one hand, has the suzerain Power a right to their exclusive exploitation, nor, on the other hand, have the races which inhabit them a right to deny their bounties to those who need them. The responsibility for adequate development rests on the custodian on behalf of civilisation—and not on behalf of civilisation alone, for much of these products is returned to the tropics converted into articles for the use and comfort of its peoples.

The democracies of to-day claim the right to work, and the satisfaction of that claim is impossible without the raw materials of the tropics on the one hand and their markets on the other. Increased production is more than ever necessary now, to enable England to pay the debts she incurred in preserving the liberties of the world. The merchant, the miner, and the manufacturer do not enter the tropics on sufferance, or employ their technical skill, their energy, and their capital as " interlopers," or as " greedy capitalists," but in fulfilment of the Mandate of civilisation. America, since she became a world Power, has adopted the same standards in the Philippines.

The policy of " the open door " has two distinct though mutually dependent aspects—viz., equal opportunity to the commerce of other countries, and an unrestricted market to the native producer. The tropics can only be successfully developed if the interests of the controlling Power are identical with those of the natives of the country, and it seeks no individual advantage, and imposes no restriction for its own benefit.

The acceptance of this policy of trusteeship involves, it may be said, some reciprocal obligation on the part of the natives. Their lands, which Germany coveted, and their liberties were at stake no less than our own in the recent war. They owe it to their inclusion in the Empire that they have escaped. Is, then, the native of the tropics to bear no share of the economic burden which the war has left, or in the cost of defence for the future? The

African is not by nature ungrateful, and would not shirk his share of the burden. I have no doubt as to the response he would make to such a suggestion if he understood. Would, then, a trustee be justified in demanding some reciprocity, or exacting some participation in the cost of defence, as an obligation properly due from his ward, after consulting the vocal minority and the more intelligent chiefs?

The Dual Mandate in British Tropical Africa (2 ed. 1923), pp. 58–9, 60–1, 62.

117: ARTHUR JAMES, EARL OF BALFOUR. Speech at Edinburgh

27 January 1927

The demand for the definition of Dominion status was met in the Report of the Inter-Imperial Relations Committee of the Imperial Conference of 1926. Balfour, who presided over the Committee, drew up the famous and skilfully worded declaration which was designed to satisfy Canada, the Irish Free State and South Africa, while not offending the more moderate and reserved views of Australia, New Zealand and Newfoundland.

Now the great technical importance, the formal importance of the Conference of 1926, is that all the representatives of these great Dominions—and our own Prime Minister is one of them—have met round a table, and have, in face of all the world, declared both the fundamental doctrine of equality of status, and the somewhat different, but not unimportant, corollary that, though there is equality in status, that must be associated with some differentiation of function. That is all I have to say about what I may call the formal side of this great development.

I should like to say something upon a side that is in

some respects far more important. Call it moral, emotional, sentimental, historical, or what you will, I mean that we should look at this problem from the standpoint of those who look behind and look in front, and who try to forecast the future of that great institution to which formal expression was given in December last.

You may ask me whether, having roughly explained what I conceive to be the Constitution of the self-governing portions of the Empire, I think it the best possible Constitution that could be contrived. The question is, in my opinion, an idle question, because the Constitution now formally declared is absolutely the only Constitution which is possible if the British Empire is to exist, and we need not argue whether it would not be better to have a central authority, whether some means of coercion in extreme cases ought not to be contrived.

All this constitution-mongering is utterly out of place when you are dealing with the natural growth of the British Empire, and when you remember that that Empire is scattered in fragments in every part of the habitable globe. It was possible for the framers of the American Constitution to give State rights and to combine with maintenance of State rights a central authoritative Government. But America, large as she is, is on one continent. We are scattered in every continent, and it would be quite impossible for us in any sense to copy or to imitate the great work that was done by the English-speaking inhabitants of North America after the separation from the Mother Country.

I myself, however, do not regard the absence of a central authority with the kind of fears that assail those who are brought up upon legal considerations, and who put emotional considerations on one side. I do not, of course, deny the importance of central authorities where you can have them. I should like to feel that every person of British blood could consult in some Chamber, through his immediate representatives, with regard to everything affecting the Empire, but that you cannot do and never will be able to do. I will not admit, however, that though we are deprived of that great advantage, we must inevitably describe ourselves as having to be content with the second best.

You may ask if I am not exaggerating the power of sentiment as a binding force. Remember, my imaginary critic might say, that some of the memories of some of our great Dominions are not entirely connected with matters in which there has been no controversy between this country and their predecessors. If memory is to be the foundation of your future greatness, are your memories always so satisfactory that they will supply a solid foundation for such a future? Well, I am a Scotsman addressing Scotsmen, and I feel, therefore, peculiarly qualified to speak on this subject. I maintain, and I appeal to the history of my country to show that I am right, that these different traditions can well be united in one whole; that although these different streams which have met together to make our kingdom and our Empire, may have flowed from different sources, none of them need feel that that difference destroys the unity of the stream which has resulted from their coalescence. I absolutely refuse to allow any man, be he English or be he Scottish, to rob me of my share in Magna Charta and Shakespeare because of Bannockburn and Flodden. What we have done, all can do. We can look back without shame, and we can look forward with unbroken hope.

Personally, I hazard what some may think the paradoxical opinion that this creation of the British Empire is the final crown of the endeavours, the half-unconscious endeavours, which we in these islands have made for centuries. All our greatest work has been, as it were, done unconsciously, done not in the spirit of system-makers, but in the spirit of dealing from moment to moment with the necessities of the moment. The English, without really knowing what they were doing, invented Parliaments. The Scottish, without really knowing what a lesson they were giving, were the first to show what democratic patriotism could do in the very height of the Middle Ages and the feudal system. The subjects of George III, when they had thrown off allegiance to the British Crown, set themselves to work, and on the basis of the liberties which they had inherited from our common forefathers, built up a Constitution which has shown itself equal to dealing with the unforeseen magnitude of the problems which must face so vast a territory, governed by so energetic a population.

We are the direct descendants and brothers of those who made this great and unique performance. No other nation has done anything like it at all. We, through the force of circumstances, without conscious premeditation, in no character of constitution-makers, find ourselves members of an Empire based on principles hitherto wholly unrecognised in the past, without any example, and yet, I think, in a spirit which looks forward to the future in hope and in belief.

I do not tell you that the task before us is an easy one. I do not tell you, or any of our brother-subjects of the King in other Dominions, that, though this has been laid down in black and white at a Conference in 1926, their labours are over. Their labours are just begun. I would not lay down the positive assurance that the future even of Parliamentary institutions, elsewhere or in this country, is absolutely safe. But I do say that the experiment we are trying is a result of a natural development, that it has that great security behind it ; and I am confident that the patriotism, common sense, the instinctive looking to the past, and working for the future which have been the characteristic of the English-speaking peoples, are going in the future to bring to a successful issue one of the noblest experiments mankind has ever tried.

Balfour, *Opinions and Argument*, (1927), pp. 196–200.

118: LEOPOLD S. AMERY. *The British Empire and the Pan-European Idea*

Paper to the Royal Institute of International Affairs, 3 December 1929

Amery, who was born in India, after organising in South Africa *The Times* reporting of the Boer war returned to become its colonial editor in 1900, and subsequently edit its *History of the War in South Africa*. He was Secretary of State for the Colonies, 1924–9, being also from the formation of the Dominions Office in 1925 its first Secretary of State; he was Secretary of State for India and Burma, 1940–5. See L. S. Amery, *My Political Life* (1953-5).

ONCE we went into a European league we should be accepting the principle that the new grouping of the world is to be entirely by geographical continents. There would be an inevitable tendency for the British Empire to break up, and for some of the Dominions to seek what would then be their natural affiliation with the United States in a North American Pacific group. The objections, overwhelming as they are from the political point of view, are equally reinforced by economic objections. The essence of any Pan-European scheme would be largely economic. If we entered any European scheme, such entry would be entirely incompatible with the development of any inter-Imperial system of trade. Between the two there is very little doubt as to where our choice should lie. Entry into a European system would probably mean for us somewhat lower tariffs in most of the European markets. But any advantage we might gain there would be very little as compared with the increasing advantage which Europe would enjoy in our market in view of its growing efficiency coupled with a lower wage standard and lower standard of living. Even if we tried to rectify that by cartel arrangements, those arrangements would be based on our present industrial position at best, and would afford very little scope for our expansion. The strongest objection of all is that it means, in fact, our tying ourselves up to an economic system which is already over-industrialised, and where the wage standard and general standard of conditions is much lower than our own.

From our point of view it is far better to link ourselves up with areas which, though becoming industrialised to some extent, are still in the main areas of primary production, where the standard of living is higher than ours, where by the forces of mutual trade and emigration we can hope to bring the standard of living in this country up to the Canadian and Australian level, rather than acquiesce in its gradually dropping down to meet an only slowly rising continental standard.

Therefore, greatly as I sympathise with the Pan-European movement, profoundly as I feel that it is a movement true in itself and calculated to meet the difficulties of the world situation to-day, I would fight to the last ditch against any suggestion that Great Britain should actually proclaim itself a European and not a World Power.

Printed in the Journal of the Royal Institute of International Affairs, IX (1930), pp. 8–9.

119: WINSTON S. CHURCHILL. Speech to the West Essex Conservative Association

23 February 1931

AT present the Government of India is responsible to the British Parliament, which is the oldest, the least unwise and the most democratic parliament in the world. To transfer that responsibility to this highly artificial and restricted oligarchy of Indian politicians would be a retrograde act. It would be a shameful act. It would be an act of cowardice, desertion and dishonour. It would bring grave material evils, both upon India and Great Britain; but it would bring upon Great Britain a moral shame which would challenge for ever the reputation of the British Empire as a valiant and benignant force in the history of mankind.

The faithful discharge of our duty in India is not only a cause, but a symbol. It is the touchstone of our fortunes in the present difficult time. If we cannot do our duty in India, be sure we shall have shown ourselves unworthy to preserve the vast Empire which still centres upon this small island. The same spirit of unimaginative incompetence and weak compromise and supine drift will paralyse trade and business and prevent either financial reorganisation or economic resurgence. What we require to do now is to stand erect and look the world in the face, and do our duty without fear or favour.

W. S. Churchill, *India Speeches* (1931), p. 97.

120: CLEMENT R. ATTLEE. *The Labour Party in Perspective*

1937

WHATEVER may have been the history of the acquisition

of the British Colonial Empire, the fact remains that Great Britain is responsible for the welfare of millions of coloured peoples. It is not possible simply to relinquish control, for the impact of European civilisation has been felt by all native communities, generally with a disintegrating effect upon the structure of native society. The task of adapting these communities to Western conceptions, while preserving all that is best in their own civilisations, is one that presents immense difficulties, but which must inevitably be tackled if the retention of these territories by Great Britain is to be justified. There are two dangers. One is that under the guise of introducing civilisation the native worker will merely be exploited by the European Capitalist; the other that under the pretence of preserving native institutions the natives may be kept ignorant and subordinate.

The Labour Party's objectives have been summed up in two words: "socialisation" and "self-government." The exact form which self-government will take must be decided in each case, for there is a grave objection to trying to transplant institutions which are indigenous to Britain into a soil in which they cannot flourish. There are colonies which are already ripe for a greater degree of autonomy than they now possess. A Labour Government would always prefer to err in being too soon rather than too late in the grant of self-government. There is an inevitable tendency, even in the best of colonial administrators, to lay too much stress on the deterioration in administrative standards which is almost certain to ensue, and not enough on the need for enabling backward peoples to learn to govern themselves.

There is a false demand for "self-government" which comes from ruling British minorities, which seek to escape from the impact of public opinion at home and to realise their ambition of governing the native population themselves. The Labour Party will always insist on the widest franchise being given, for exploitation by one set of oppressors may easily be exchanged only for that of another unless care is taken to see that the constitution is really democratic.

Over a large area the peoples are not ready yet for self-government, and in these territories the Labour Party considers that the British Government must act as trustee for the native races. In order to give full effect to the principle of trusteeship the British Government should accept the mandatory principle for all British colonial possessions. This will mean that it will accept regular examination by the League of Nations into its administration of all territories which are inhabited by backward races and are not self-governing, in the same way as Mandatory Powers accept it to-day for their mandated territories. It would necessarily follow from this that there would be an open door for all nations and an abandonment of the attempt to extend the principles of the Ottawa agreements. The extension of the mandatory principle would have other far-reaching effects. The defence of mandated territories concerns the League of Nations and not merely the Mandatory Power. The constant endeavour of the Conservative Party to draw a distinction between imperial defence and collective security would be defeated. The development of common standards in relation to the treatment of backward peoples by European nations would be immensely facilitated. In time there might develop an international civil service over all the world, drawn from the nationals of many countries but inspired by a common ideal: the raising of the standard of life and culture of the less advanced races. . . .

I have already stated that it is the intention of the Labour Party to reject altogether the conception of a Colonial Empire as an exclusive field of exploitation for the British Capitalist. The issue which this raises is of great importance in considering the causes of unrest which make for war. The demand of Germany and other countries for colonial possessions is being put forward with increasing vigour. The grounds of this demand will not stand examination. The point of prestige belongs to a conception of world politics which is foreign to the Labour conception of a world Commonwealth of Nations, and is indeed even antagonistic to the principles of the League of Nations. The demand for colonies on the ground that without them an advanced industrial country is denied access to raw materials, and is obliged to accept a low standard of life, is disproved by the facts. Germany's difficulty in obtaining raw materials is due to her own financial and economic policy. The standard of life in countries such as Sweden and Denmark, without colonies, is as high as, or higher than, that in France and Belgium, despite their great empires.

It is, however, difficult without an appearance of hypocrisy for Great Britain to make these replies sound convincing. The Labour Party does not believe in a reallocation of colonial territories between the various great Powers. That is no solution to the problem. The way to deal with these alleged grievances is by rejecting altogether the concepts of imperialism, and by establishing through the League of Nations international control of raw materials. It is obvious that the Labour Party will oppose the handing over of any native peoples to the tender mercies of a Government which is intoxicated with ideas of race superiority, and which has shown a complete inability to deal justly with minorities.

INDIA

There remain to be considered those countries which, possessing civilisations of their own, have yet been for many generations under the control of Great Britain. The outstanding example is India. The Labour Party has always fully accepted the right of the Indian peoples to govern themselves, but it has recognised that the problem involved in developing self-governing institutions in a great continent inhabited by peoples who differ in language, race, and creed is no easy one. The long period of British rule has created a situation in which there have been many rights acquired by particular sections of the Indian people. It is not right to abandon control without taking care to see that these rights will be respected. " India for the Indians " is a simple slogan, but it is necessary to see what it means in terms of human life. There is no particular gain in handing over the peasants and workers of India to be exploited by their own Capitalists and landlords. Nationalism is a creed that may be sustained with great self-sacrifice and idealism, but may shelter class domination and intolerance of minorities as well as economic exploitation.

Throughout all the enquiries into the constitutional position of India, and also of Burma, Labour members have always realised that nationalism was not enough. They have always sought to give to the Indian masses the potential power of bettering their economic conditions by political action. They have recognised frankly that it is unlikely that a poor and illiterate population will escape exploitation at the hands of the rich, the privileged, and the educated classes, but they have stood firm for giving them the possibility of advance. They have recognised also that it is impossible for an alien race to overcome the social and economic evils which are closely bound up with the whole conceptions of the Indian people. Only the Indian people themselves can work out their salvation. The sooner they have the full opportunity to do so the better. The same considerations apply to the much easier case of Burma and to some other parts of the British Empire.

To conclude, the Labour Party, having to deal with the actual existence of the British Empire and Commonwealth, will seek to apply in that sphere, as in all others, the principles of Socialism. The fact that over a huge area of the earth's surface there is a common sovereignty is advantageous, provided this unity is but a step in a greater unity. One of the vital questions for the future of world peace is the reconciliation of the interests of the white, the black, the brown, and the yellow races. The Labour Party fearlessly applies to this problem the principle of the brotherhood of man. It does not admit that the white race has any right of primogeniture in the world. It holds that the resources of the world must be developed in the interests of all people, and that the standard of life of the inhabitants of Asia and Africa must be raised, and not kept always below those of Europe, America and Australia.

C. R. Attlee, *The Labour Party in Perspective* (1937), pp. 239–42, 244–7.

121: DAVID LLOYD GEORGE. Broadcast Talk

4 June 1937

THERE is hardly anything which this great Empire could

not accomplish in the way of dragging the world out of its present condition of muddle and menace if it had a clear aim, a steadfast purpose and a readiness to take reasonable risks in the present in order to avoid certain catastrophe in the future. Its power and resources make it incomparably the greatest confederacy of nations on this globe. In area and in aggregate population there is none to equal it. In the number of its citizens it contains twice and three times as many as the next greatest. Amongst its peoples are some of the most virile races on earth. It possesses every kind and variety of riches—natural, developed and accumulated. The hundreds of nations within its vast territories display every form, stage and age of human civilization. Its lands are posted at some of the most vital strategic positions on sea and land. The Great War proved that as a confederation it was a reality and not a name. . . .

Is this powerful Commonwealth playing as decisive a part in world affairs during peace as it exerted during the War? The world has been made conscious of its inexhaustible strength when it is put forth, but peace-breakers and aggressors are relying today not on its impotence but on its apathy, on its lack of resolution, continuity and insistence in well doing. They are under the impression that if they resist its pressure long enough Britain will back out of enterprises which she herself has started. They are depending on its hesitancies, its vacillations, and its lack of full confidence in its mission. Largely, if not entirely, owing to these causes, the leadership of Britain in recent years at the League Councils in the cause of international peace, right and liberty has not been successful. The result is that these great human causes have sustained a disastrous setback, and the moral effect of the sacrifices made in the

Great War has been largely negatived and thrown away. . . .

It is essential that there should be a carefully pre-concerted policy between the constituent nations of the Empire.

The Listener (1937), pp. 1121–2.

122: WILLIAM MALCOLM, BARON HAILEY.
Romanes Lecture

Oxford, 14 May 1941

As a climax to a career in the Indian Civil Service (1895–1934) Hailey was Governor successively of the Punjab and the United Provinces. He then directed the African Research Survey (1935–8), producing the monumental *African Survey* (1938; *Revised 1956*, 1957). He was a member of the Permanent Mandates Commission (1935-9). His latest work is *Native Administration in the British African Territories* (1950-3).

THE objective of Colonial policy could no longer be viewed merely as the protection of the native peoples from exploitation; the emphasis now lay on the necessity for the active and systematic promotion of native welfare. The general recognition of this position was rendered easier by the growing influence on English political life of those classes which interpret the functions of the State as consisting primarily in the satisfaction of their own social needs. It would perhaps have been difficult without this influence to gain acceptance of the fact that a Colonial Power can no longer discharge its obligations by the management, however conscientious, of the resources of the estates which it administers. It must draw liberally on its own resources to supplement the provision which many of them are able to make. But the passing of the Colonial Development and Welfare

Act of 1940 is evidence that this principle is now an accepted axiom of British Colonial policy.

The principle [of extending self-government] has behind it all the force of sentiment which is deep-seated in the British character. The privileges which the Roman Empire held out to its subject peoples were the guarantee of peace, and participation in a system of law. The French philosophy of rule sees the fulfilment of the obligations of Colonial trusteeship is assisting its subject peoples to assimilate that measure of French culture and of legal and social institutions which will enable them to take rank as citizens of an overseas France. The instinct of the British people on the other hand is to attach to the grant of political rights the importance which others have given to the acquisition of social and cultural equality. In their view, we should fail to discharge the duty of a trustee did we not give to our dependent peoples the fullest opportunities for developing their own sense of national consciousness and for acquiring the control of their own affairs.

I suggested at an earlier stage in this address that if Colonies are to attain rank as members of the British Commonwealth of Nations, it will involve a double achievement on their part. It is not enough that they should acquire a status of responsible self-government; they must further gain from the existing members of the Commonwealth a recognition that they are, in other respects also, qualified for full association with them. The character of the British Commonwealth of Nations belongs perhaps to that class of things which are easy to comprehend, until we are asked to define them. But for my purpose it is sufficient to point to two features in the

412

character of the Commonwealth as it must appear to the outside world. It is, as at present constituted, an association of nations mainly of European origin. Their mode of living, their social relations, their system of law, their ideas about property—all the things, in fact, which make up the content of their lives and determine the nature of the political institutions which they employ—are those of European peoples. In particular, the Commonwealth draws its unity from a devotion to one special aspect of these conceptions, which is pre-eminently that which inspires the British people and those who feel themselves spiritually akin to them. A unity based on a community of sentiment of this description has been characterized as possessing only a metaphysical value. But the unity is nevertheless real, and it acquires a dynamic force in the face of any menace to the particular type of civilized life which it represents.

It has been necessary to refer to these aspects in the character of the Commonwealth, because the question must at some time arise whether its unity can be maintained if new elements, of the nature of those now existing in parts of the Colonial section of the Empire, are incorporated in it. That is, indeed, a question which has already been raised by some foreign observers. Let me put it in the form in which they have seen it. If the future envisaged for the Empire had a place for some form of central authority empowered to decide Imperial policy and to safeguard its execution, no difficulty would necessarily arise from the incorporation in the Commonwealth of new elements, mainly of non-European origin, whose character differs in so many respects from that of the existing members, and whose outlook on world affairs is not likely to be the same. But the surrender of any portion of their autonomy for this purpose forms no part of the conception which the Dominions have of their own future, and it would not be reasonable to expect the Colonies to accept a different procedure. Again, some of the difficulty might perhaps be removed if our Imperial policy were directed to securing a more complete assimilation by the Colonial peoples of the social and cultural ideas prevailing in Great Britain and the Dominions. But this is not to be looked for. The tendency is indeed all in the other direction, for the most marked feature of our Imperial philosophy is its opposition to what General Smuts has described as standardization. . . .

But perhaps the most crucial test of the unity of the Commonwealth will lie in evidence that its new members are ready to make the same sacrifices for the ideal which it represents as are those who are now associated in it.

Printed as a pamphlet (Oxford, 1941), pp. 10–11, 21–2, 34–6.

123: OLIVER FREDERICK GEORGE STANLEY. Speech at Oxford

5 March 1943

After holding a number of government appointments in the thirties and serving in the Royal Artillery, 1940–2, Colonel Stanley was Secretary of State for the Colonies, 1942–5, and was responsible for introducing the Colonial Development and Welfare Bill, 1945.

MANY years ago we declared that it was our intention to act as trustees for our Colonial Empire, and we have fully lived up to that promise. But in the very conception of trusteeship there are limitations with which I do not believe we can in future be content. I am myself trustee for a number of people. I set out to do for them on a small scale what we set out on a large scale to do for the Colonial Empire. I try and safeguard their estate from exploitation, to preserve it intact, to improve it as far as possible, and to see that the income of the estate is enjoyed by the recipient of the trust. But as trustee I feel no obligation to go further than that. I feel no call to make up out of my pocket any deficiency in the income of the beneficiary, to risk my money to improve the beneficiary's estate. Can we be satisfied in future with such a negative conception of trusteeship?

I am convinced that the first and fundamental principle is that the administration of the British Colonies must continue to be the sole responsibility of Great Britain. I myself give no support to a theory, which I think now gains few adherents, that it would be for the benefit of a particular Colony or for the benefit of the world as a whole, that the Colony should be administered by some international body. I can think of nothing which is more likely in practice to break down and less likely to lead to the steady development of the territory concerned. Administration, the right to administer—in other words, sovereignty—is not merely a right to power; it also carries with it many responsibilities. Responsibilities in the future in the Colonial Empire will not be confined to the making of laws or the keeping of order. They will entail . . . financial and economic aid on a large scale.

But if we alone are prepared to take that responsibility, are prepared to make those financial sacrifices which flow from our responsibility, then we alone are in a position to exercise the control and to have the power.

Printed in pamphlet, *In the Stirring Words . . .* (1944).

124: WINSTON S. CHURCHILL. Speech at
Guildhall, London, on receiving the Freedom of the
City

30 June 1943

IT is even more remarkable that the unity which has
existed and endured in this small, densely-populated
island should have extended with equal alacrity and
steadfastness to all parts of our world-wide Commonwealth and Empire. Some people like the word
Commonwealth; others, and I am one of them, are not
at all ashamed of the word Empire. But why should we
not have both?

Therefore I think the expression British Commonwealth and Empire may well be found the most convenient means of describing this unique association of
races and religions, which was built up partly by
conquest, largely by consent, but mainly unconsciously
and without design, within the all-embracing golden
circle of the Crown. . . .

Alone in history, the British people, taught by the
lessons they had learned in the past, have found the
means to attach to the Motherland vast self-governing
Dominions upon whom there rests no obligation, other
than that of sentiment and tradition, to plunge into war
at the side of the Motherland.

None of these Dominions, except Southern Ireland,
which does not under its present dispensation fully accept
Dominion status, has ever failed to respond, with all the
vigour of democratic institutions, to the trumpet-call of
a supreme crisis, to the overpowering influences and
impulses that make Canada, that make Australia—and
we have here in Dr. Evatt a distinguished Australian—
that make New Zealand, and South Africa send their
manhood across the ocean to fight and die.

In each one of these countries, with their long and varied history behind them, this extraordinary spectacle is an outstanding example of the triumph of mind over matter, of the human heart over fear and short-sighted self-interest.

In the vast sub-continent of India, which we trust will presently find full satisfaction within the British Commonwealth of Nations, the martial races and many others have thronged to the Imperial standards. . . . Many scores of thousands of troops have been drawn from the immense tropical spaces, or from lonely islands nursed by the waves of every sea. Many volunteers there were for whom we could not find arms. Many there are for whom even now we cannot find opportunities. But I say that the universal ardour of our Colonial Empire to join in this awful conflict, and to continue in that high temper through all its ups and downs, is the first answer that I would make to those ignorant and envious voices who call into question the greatness of the work we are doing throughout the world, and which we shall still continue to do.

The time came when this loosely and variously knit world-spread association, where so much was left unwritten and undefined, was confronted with the most searching test of all. The Mother Country, the home of the kingship, this famous island, seemed to enter the very jaws of death and destruction.

Three years ago, all over the world, friend and foe alike—everyone who had not the eye of faith—might well have deemed our speedy ruin was at hand. Against the triumphant might of Hitler, with the greedy Italians at his tail, we stood alone with resources so slender that one shudders to enumerate them even now.

Then, surely, was the moment for the Empire to break

up, for each of its widely-dispersed communities to seek safety on the winning side, for those who thought themselves oppressed to throw off their yoke and make better terms betimes with the all-conquering Nazi and Fascist power. Then was the time. But what happened?

It was proved that the bonds which unite us, though supple as elastic, are stronger than the tensest steel. Then it was proved that they were the bonds of the spirit and not of the flesh, and thus could rise superior alike to the most tempting allurements of surrender and the harshest threats of doom. In that dark, terrific and also glorious hour we received from all parts of His Majesty's Dominions, from the greatest and from the smallest, from the strongest and from the weakest, from the most modern to the most simple, the assurance that we would all go down or come through together. You will forgive me if on this occasion, to me so memorable, here in the heart of mighty London, I rejoice in the soundness of our institutions and proclaim my faith in our destiny.

W. S. Churchill, *War Speeches*, 1940–5 (1946), pp. 162–4.

125: ARTHUR CREECH JONES. Contributions to *Fabian Colonial Essays*
1945

Creech Jones was Under-Secretary of State for the Colonies (1945–6) and Secretary of State (1946–50). He had previously been Chairman of the Fabian Colonial Bureau and of the Labour Party Imperial Advisory Committee.

THE backward areas menace the rest of the world if they remain undeveloped with low standards of living, with disease rampant and the people weak and ignorant. In that condition they would be a continuing cause of friction among the imperial powers. Their development is necessary for the larger security of the world; their products and resources are wanted in the outside world; their low standards depress our higher levels; their disease threatens our health; their poverty prejudices our prosperity—in short, these distressed areas must be developed and integrated as progressing regions into the commonwealth of free nations. Already the outer world has shrunk as knowledge has expanded. The colonies to-morrow will be right in the midst of our normal life, and that fact must compel us to overhaul our methods of administration and the conventional assumptions of colonial policy so that rapid advances in welfare and development are secured and adjustments made to standards consistent with civilized living.

To-day, under the 1940 Act, it is not suggested that Britain should open her coffers and without restraint give great sums for creating and sustaining vast new services, and for welfare and economic development generally. The colonial people do not feel that way, and the most enlightened amongst them recognize that they should not be spoonfed, and that they should make contributions to costs within their capacity, and carry what burden they can in respect to any development and service they know to be necessary. Nevertheless, we should be generous. Western civilization needs sometimes to be reminded that it has a debt to meet in respect of some of the backward areas. Colonies have often been expoited as " possessions " for their wealth and resources; and both colonial wealth and the colonial people have contributed in a material way to Western progress. For many years there has also been a contribution from the profits of colonial enterprise to the national revenue of Britain. Dependencies also have their uses in any system of world security.

The fact is, of course, that the condition of vast colonial areas is utterly bad; the equipment is so poor, the ignorance and poverty are so great that without aid from outside no start can be made. The pump cannot be primed or any substantial advance achieved. In many colonies, the foundations of social policy are hardly as yet laid. It is therefore more than a sentimental gesture of the nation when it asserts that colonial policy in the social and economic fields should be made more positive and constructive. It is a mood that will cost a great deal of money.

Nevertheless, investment in good health and education and economic development is, on a long view, profitable not only in the human, but also in the material sense. By building up the quality and standard of living, new consumption is stimulated, new markets are opened, there are demands for products which cannot be made in the colony, and employment in Britain and the colonies is expanded.

Fabian Colonial Essays (ed. R. Hinden, 1945), pp. 10–11, 73–4.

126: CLEMENT R. ATTLEE. Speech in the House of Commons

15 March 1946

INDIA herself must choose what will be her future Constitution; what will be her position in the world. I hope that the Indian people may elect to remain within the British Commonwealth. I am certain that she will find great advantages in doing so. In these days that demand for complete, isolated nationhood apart from the rest of the world, is really outdated. Unity may come through the United Nations, or through the Commonwealth, but no great nation can stand alone without sharing in what is happening in the world. But if she does so elect, it must be by her own free will. The British Commonwealth and Empire is not bound together by chains of external compulsion. It is a free association of free peoples. If, on the other hand, she elects for independence, in our view she has a right to do so. It will be for us to help to make the transition as smooth and easy as possible.

We should be conscious that the British have done a great work in India. We have united India and given her that sense of nationality which she so very largely lacked over the previous centuries. She has learned from us principles of democracy and justice. When Indians attack our rule, they base their attack, not on Indian principles, but on the basis of standards derived from Britain. I was very struck the other day in the United States, at a dinner where I met a number of distinguished Americans, including a very distinguished Indian, where the talk was turning on the way in which principles worked out here have been applied on the continent of America. It was pointed out that America had a great heritage from Britain. My Indian friend said to me, "You know, the Americans sometimes forget there is another great nation that has also inherited these principles and traditions, and that is India. We feel that we have a duty, a right and a privilege because we also bring to the world and work those very principles that you evolved in Britain."

Hansard, Fifth Series, Vol. 420, cs. 1421–2.

127: Debate in the House of Commons

20 December 1946

CLEMENT ATTLEE: I would repeat, so far as Burma is concerned, what I have already said with regard to India. We do not desire to retain within the Commonwealth and Empire any unwilling peoples. It is for the people of Burma to decide their own future, but we are certain that it will be for their interest, as it will be to ours, if they decide to remain within the Commonwealth and we sincerely hope that they will arrive at such a decision. Likewise, we consider that the new Constitution for Burma should be settled by nationals of Burma and we believe that arrangements to this end can be made as a result of the forthcoming elections. . . .

It is the desire and intention of His Majesty's Government to hasten forward the time when Burma shall realise her independence, either within or without the Commonwealth, but for the sake of the Burmese people it is of the utmost importance that this should be an orderly—though rapid—progress. . . .

WINSTON S. CHURCHILL: It was said, in the days of the great Administration of Lord Chatham, that one had to get up very early in the morning in order not to miss some of the gains and accessions of territory which were then characteristic of our fortune. The no less memorable Administration of the right hon. Gentleman opposite is distinguished for the opposite set of experiences. The British Empire seems to be running off almost as fast as the American Loan. The steady and remorseless process of divesting ourselves of what has been gained by so many generations of toil, administration and sacrifice continues. In the case of Burma it is hardly a year since, by the superb exertions of the Fourteenth Army and enormous sacrifices in life and treasure—sacrifices in British blood and in Indian blood —the Japanese were forced to surrender, destroyed, or driven out, and the country was liberated. And yet, although barely a year has passed away, there is this extraordinary haste that we should take the necessary measures to get out of Burma finally and forever.[1]

Hansard, Fifth Series, Vol. 431, cs. 2342–3.

128: ARTHUR CREECH JONES. Speech in Committee on Supply

House of Commons, 29 July 1947

THE period since the war has been one of special difficulty, because of the troubled background in almost all regions of the world. We have had, in the Colonial Empire, to transform the territories back to normal peace-time conditions, to adjust their individual economies, to absorb their military forces, to restore the ravages of war, to review the colonial services, to cope with neglect and disturbances and grievances, to satisfy the claims of nationalism and expanding freedom, to discuss the highly controversial problems of international policy, to deal with planning in conditions of fluctuating economies and to make practical demonstrations, in spite of the shortages of manpower, materials and skills, of our desire to serve the colonial peoples in peace as in war.

It will be appreciated by the Committee that colonial

1 Churchill's feeling on this issue may have sprung from a recollection that his father, as Secretary of State for India, had arranged the proclamation of the annexation of Upper Burma as ' a New Year's present to the Queen ' for 1886. (W. S. Churchill, *Lord Randolph Churchill* (1906) vol. I p. 525.)

progress is not a matter merely of directives from the Colonial Office or the Government of the day. We have to get implemented in our territories our principles and policies, it is true, but, at the same time, in all our efforts, we have to remember that our territories are advancing to some degree of responsible self-government, and, accordingly, we cannot impose our will. We have to persuade them to build up their own institutions with the acceptance of the sound policies which we feel will make for the betterment of the colonial territories. If the Colonial Office is to perform its important services, it is essential that it should have the requisite knowledge for the work in hand, and our object is to transform the dependencies in the Colonial Empire to responsibility, and to exercise a trust so that each blossoms into a partnership of disinterested service and friendship.

My last word is that however comprehensive our planning may be in regard to colonial development, whatever enthusiasm and zeal we bring to the task, we cannot go far unless we have the co-operation and the understanding of the colonial peoples themselves. With the growth of responsibility in our overseas territories it becomes increasingly important that everything possible should be done to help the colonial peoples to an appreciation of our own disinterested service on their behalf. That is a problem of public relations as well as of the colonial service. We believe that we are not in our territories for our own limited material advantage. We are there in the general service of the colonial peoples. We hope that there will be a common appreciation and understanding of our efforts. With the recent development of our public relations department in the Colonial Office, it is our hope that our schemes and plans will be recognised as designed to that end and we shall secure greater understanding with the colonial peoples. It is not only that they themselves are demanding their place in the sun; it is that we have the privilege and the honour of helping them forward to that realisation. They are able by our service to make a contribution to the larger life of mankind.

Hansard, Fifth Series, Vol. 441, cs. 264 and 284.

R. KOEBNER: *Empire*. (Cambridge, 1961).

K. E. KNORR: *British Colonial Theories, 1570-1850*. (Toronto, 1944.)

MAX BELOFF: *The Debate on the American Revolution*. (London, 2nd ed., 1960.)

R. COUPLAND: *The American Revolution and the British Empire*. (London, 1930.)

R. L. SCHUYLER: *The Fall of the Old Colonial System: A Study in British Free Trade, 1770-1870*. (New York, 1945.)

W. P. MORRELL: *The Colonial Policy of Peel and Russell*. (Oxford, 1930.)

C. A. BODELSEN: *Studies in Mid-Victorian Imperialism*. (Copenhagen, 1924, London, 1960).

S. MACCOBY: *English Radicalism, 1832-1852*. Chap. 21. (London, 1935.)
English Radicalism, 1886-1914. passim (London, 1953).

H. L. HALL: *The Colonial Office*. (London, 1937).

C. P. STACEY: *Canada and the British Army, 1846-1871*. (London, 1936.)

J. E. TYLER: *The Struggle for Imperial Unity, 1868-1895*. (London, 1938.)

W. L. LANGER: *The Diplomacy of Imperialism*. Chap. 3. (New York, 2nd ed., 1951.)

B. SEMMEL: *Imperialism and Social Reform*. (London, 1960)

A. P. THORNTON: *The Imperial Idea and its Enemies*. (London, 1959.)

E. HALEVY: *Imperialism and the Rise of Labour*. (London, 1951.)

V. T. HARLOW: *The Character of British Imperialism*. (London, 1939.)

N. MANSERGH: *The Name and Nature of the British Commonwealth*. (Cambridge, 1954.)

E. STOKES: *The Political Ideas of English Imperialism*. (Oxford, 1960.)

E. BARKER: *Ideas and Ideals of the British Empire*. (Cambridge, 2nd ed., 1951.)

E. A. WALKER: *The British Empire: Its Structure and Spirit*. (Cambridge, 2nd ed., 1953.)

J. STRACHEY: *The End of Empire*. (London, 1959.)

RITA HINDEN: *Empire and After*. (London, 1949.)

Cambridge History of the British Empire. Vols. II & III. (Cambridge, 1940 & 1959.)

W. K. HANCOCK: *Survey of British Commonwealth Affairs*. (Oxford, 1937-42.)

C. E. CARRINGTON: *The British Overseas*. (Cambridge, 1950.)

INDEX

(Biographical or other notes are given in black figures, extracts in italics, and other references in roman type.)

INDEX

INDEX

— *see also* East India Company, charter renewal
India and Colonial Exhibition (1886), 296–7
India Office, 66, 204
Indian Civil Service, 16, 411
Indian Mutiny (1857), 279
Indian National Congress, 16, 18
India, Star of, 238
Indies, East, 46, 66–7
Ionian Islands, 236
Ireland, 49, 104, 127, 201, 229, 246, 248, 263, 291, 398, 416
Irish, the, 91, 259
Irwin, Lord, *see* Halifax, Lord
Islam, 15, 17
Ismail, Pasha, 361
Italy, 18, 417

JAMAICA, 22
Jameson raid, 12
Japan, 232, 423
Java, 25, 66–7
Johannesburg, 343, 349, 378

KAFFIRS, 12, 13, 159, 182, 210
Keith, A. Berriedale, *Select Speeches and Documents on British Colonial Policy*, 8n
Kenya, 23–4
Keynes, John Maynard, 332
Khartoum, 25, 294
Kimberley, John Wodehouse, Earl of, 312
Kimberley, South Africa, 12
Kingsley, Mary, 380
Kingston, Ont., 259
Kipling, Rudyard, 27
Knaplund, P., 150, 199

LABOUR PARTY, 5–6, 28, 404–9, 418
Lambton, John George, *see* Durham, Earl of
Laurier, Sir Wilfrid, references to speeches of, 323, 329, 335–6, 359–60
Lawrence, Henry and John, 15
League of Nations, 9, 21, 332, 383, 393–4, 406–7, 410
Leeds, 302
Lenin, 19
Leopold II of Belgium, 21, 325
Leverhulme, Lord, 22
Lewis, George Cornewall, 8n, 166, 166–9, 200

Liberals, 16, 24, 28, 257, 281, 291, 309, 373
Liberal Imperialists, 28, 281, 334
Liberal League, 334
' Little Englanders ', 28, 309, 314
Liverpool, 7, 12, 13, 81, 200, 355
Livingstone, David, 13
Lloyd George, David, Earl, *409–11*
Lobengula, 318
London, 4, 5, 12, 26, 35, 52, 81, 140, 157, 293, 355, 418
Lothian, Philip Kerr, Lord, 341
Lowe, Robert, later Viscount Sherbrooke, 227, *227–8*
Lugard, Frederick Dealtry, Lord, 17, 19, 21, 383, 394, *394–8*

MACAULAY, THOMAS BABINGTON, LORD, 15, 19, 54, 71, *71–5*
McDermott, P. L., *I.B.E.A.*, 26n
MacDonald, J. Ramsay, 353, *353–4*, *379–80*
Mackinnon, Sir William, 382
Madras, 15, 68, 358
Magna Charta, 50–4, 400
Mahrattas, 64
Malacca, 65–6
Malaya, 12, 23, 66–7
Malcolm, Sir John, 68
Malta, 166, 195
Malthus, Rev. T. R., 91
' Malthusianism ', 4, 91
Manchester, 169, 263, 351, 358, 367
' Manchester School ', 11, 166, 172, 217
Mandate system, 21
Mandates, Permanent Commission of League of Nations, 394, 411
Maoris, 9, 106–11, 182, 186, 210, 233–4, 240
Marlborough, John Churchill, Duke of, 123
Marx, Karl, 5, 20
Mauritius, 25, 183, 224, 346
Mediterranean, 81, 124, 224
Melbourne, Australia, 234, 300
Melbourne, William Lamb, Viscount, 115, *119–20*
Merivale, Herman, 204, *204–11*
' Merv-ousness ', 25
Metcalfe, Sir Charles, 68, as Governor-General of Canada, 143, 181

431

INDEX

433